AUTHORING

CW01511775

Kate McLoughlin's *Authoring War* is an ambitious and pioneering study of war writing across all literary genres from earliest times to the present day. Examining a range of cultures, she brings wide reading and close rhetorical analysis to illuminate how writers have met the challenge of representing violence, chaos and loss. War gives rise to problems of epistemology, scale, space, time, language and logic. McLoughlin argues that certain literary devices have been mobilised again and again in literary history as a response: the autopsy tropes, synecdoche, pastoral, 'superposition', avoidance tactics and the evocation of laughter. She emphasises the importance of form to an understanding of war literature and establishes connections across periods and cultures from Homer to the 'War on Terror'. Exciting new critical groupings arise in consequence, as Byron's *Don Juan* is read alongside Heller's *Catch-22* and English Civil War poetry alongside Second World War letters. Innovative in its approach and inventive in its encyclopedic range, *Authoring War* will be indispensable to any discussion of war representation.

KATE McLOUGHLIN is Reader in Modern Literature at Birkbeck College, University of London. She has edited *The Cambridge Companion to War Writing* (2009).

Praise for *Authoring War*

'At once a fine piece of writing and a wonderful exercise in scholarly bravura.'
— Robert Douglas-Fairhurst, *The Times Literary Supplement*

'Its scope is astonishing: McLoughlin writes authoritatively about Homer and Heller, Virgil and Vonnegut . . . impeccably scholarly and well written . . . an extraordinarily impressive book.'
— Tim Kendall, http://war-poets.blogspot.co.uk

'[A] remarkable and compelling monograph that incisively and originally engages with a great number of war texts and a vast body of research on war literature.'
— Holly Faith Nelson, *War, Literature and the Arts*

'The range of references is just stunning . . . theoretically astute and beautifully written.'
— Santanu Das, Reader in English Literature, King's College London

AUTHORING WAR

The Literary Representation of War from the Iliad *to Iraq*

KATE McLOUGHLIN

CAMBRIDGE
UNIVERSITY PRESS

CAMBRIDGE
UNIVERSITY PRESS

32 Avenue of the Americas, New York, NY 10013, USA

Cambridge University Press is part of the University of Cambridge.

It furthers the University's mission by disseminating knowledge in the pursuit of education, learning and research at the highest international levels of excellence.

www.cambridge.org
Information on this title: www.cambridge.org/9781107623637

© Kate McLoughlin 2011

First published 2011
4th printing 2012
First paperback edition 2014

Printed in the United States of America

A catalogue record for this publication is available from the British Library.

Library of Congress Cataloguing in Publication data
McLoughlin, Catherine Mary, 1970–
Authoring war : the literary representation of war from the Iliad to Iraq / Kate McLoughlin.
p.   cm.
Includes bibliographical references and index.
ISBN 978-1-107-00390-3 (hardback)
1. War in literature.   2. War and literature.   I. Title.
PN56.W3M43   2011
809'.933581 – dc22   2010043701

ISBN 978-1-107-00390-3 Hardback
ISBN 978-1-107-62363-7 Paperback

For Nick

If at the end of a war story you feel uplifted, or if you feel that some small bit of rectitude has been salvaged from the larger waste, then you have been made the victim of a very old and terrible lie.

Tim O'Brien, *The Things They Carried*

Contents

Acknowledgements

It is a pleasure to thank the following people, who provided advice, support and expert assistance: Katherine Duncan-Jones, Stuart Gillespie, Nigel Leask, Hermione Lee, Donald MacKenzie, Robert Parker, Karen Peña, Luke Pitcher, Darya Protopopova, Bryony Randall, Jon Stallworthy, Maja Starcevic and Corin Throsby. Gill Plain and Jay Winter read and provided invaluable comments on the first two chapters, as did Elena Baraban, Stephan Jaeger and Adam Muller on Chapter 5 (an earlier version of part of which appears in their *Fighting Words and Images: Representing War Across the Disciplines* (2011)). Willy Maley deserves special thanks for reading and commenting on the entire manuscript: I am fortunate to have such a mentor. (None of these people are responsible for the final text.) I am also grateful to Natasha Alden at Aberystwyth, Ron Bush at Oxford, Renee Lee at Wolfson and Emma Sutton at St Andrews for the opportunity to present material from the book in their seminar series: the feedback I received was enormously helpful. Similarly, the work-in-progress seminars at the University of Glasgow's Department of English Literature provided a friendly and critically constructive forum in which to develop ideas. I am extremely grateful to the Faculty of Arts and Department of English Literature at Glasgow for granting me a semester's leave to complete the book, and to my colleagues for covering my duties while I was away. Wolfson College, Oxford, was a congenial and intellectually stimulating place to spend that leave, and I thank the President and Fellows for electing me a Visiting Scholar. Ray Ryan and the team at Cambridge University Press have been extraordinarily patient and supportive of the project, and I am also grateful to the readers of the drafts.

The bulk of this book was written in three places – Oxford, Podere il Pino and Berlin – and, for me, their atmospheres suffuse its pages. With me in all of them was Nick Trefethen. As surely as it is mine, this book is his.

Note on translations

Translations are my own unless otherwise stated. Foreign language originals are given in the footnotes when particular words or phrases are the subject of commentary.

Introduction
Authoring war

In *War and Peace* (1865–9), Nikolai Rostov responds enthusiastically to a request from Boris Drubetskoy to describe how and where he got his wound:

> He described the Schön Graben affair exactly as men who have taken part in battles always do describe them – that is, as they would like them to have been, as they have heard them described by others, and as sounds well, but not in the least as they really had been. Rostov was a truthful young man and would never have told a deliberate lie. He began his story with the intention of telling everything exactly as it happened, but imperceptibly, unconsciously and inevitably he passed into falsehood. If he had told the truth to his listeners who, like himself, had heard numerous descriptions of cavalry charges and had formed a definite idea of what a charge was like and were expecting a precisely similar account from him, either they would not have believed him or, worse still, would have thought Rostov himself to blame if what generally happens to those who describe cavalry charges had not happened to him. He could not tell them simply that they had all set out at a trot, that he had fallen off his horse, sprained his arm and then run from the Frenchman into the woods as fast as his legs would carry him. Besides, to tell everything exactly as it had been would have meant the exercise of considerable self-control to confine himself to the facts. It is very difficult to tell the truth and young people are rarely capable of it. His listeners expected to hear how, forgetful of himself and all on fire with excitement, he had rushed down like a hurricane on the enemy's square, hacked his way in, slashing the French right and left; how his sabre had tasted flesh, and he had fallen exhausted, and so on. And that is what he told them.[1]

There is no doubt that Rostov has participated in the 'Schön Graben affair',[2] no doubt that he is eager and willing to speak of his actual experiences there – indeed, that for a number of reasons he *needs* to speak of them – and no doubt that his intention is to do so. But as he talks, he begins to tell a

[1] L. N. Tolstoy, *War and Peace*, trans. Rosemary Edmonds (London: Penguin, 1957, 1982), 279.
[2] Also known as the Battle of Schöngrabern and the Battle of Hollabrunn. The nomenclature reveals further variations in the telling of the matter.

war story he has heard before. His tale 'imperceptibly' and 'unconsciously'[3] metamorphoses from a description of what has happened to him into a handed-down account of war, a depiction of conflict as it is generally believed and imagined to be, but not as he has actually found it to be in his experience. Unable, for various reasons, to convey his own truth about war, Rostov yields to a 'stronger', more established version of belligerent events.

This is curious. And yet, Tolstoy dryly insists, there is nothing unusual about the way in which Rostov's story develops. He describes the engagement 'exactly as men who have taken part in battles always do describe them'. The transition into falsehood is '*inevitable*'.[4] Developing the scene, Tolstoy even arranges for Rostov to confirm his tale, as Prince Andrei Bolkonsky, overhearing it, comments, 'Ah, there are a great number of stories now about that affair!' Under this contrived provocation, Rostov, instead of taking the opportunity to resile from his account, actually endorses it by invoking the authority of first-hand combat experience:

The stories we tell are the accounts of men who have been under the enemy's fire. *Our* stories carry some weight, they're not the tales of little staff upstarts who get decorations for doing nothing.[5]

The 'false' version is now thoroughly entrenched. So, the reader may wonder, what about those who previously told the tale that Rostov is now relating? Did they accurately recount what happened to them or did they also yield to prior versions (receding to an *ur*-war story?) imagined and believed but not actually experienced? If so, why? What about Tolstoy's own account of his fictional character's rendition of the battle? Why, instead of describing the Schön Graben affair as he, Tolstoy, understood it to be (drawing on his own combat experience as a second lieutenant in the Crimean War), does he present his reader with a description of a failed attempt to recount it?

Such questions persist as variations on the phenomenon occur throughout representations of war, and throughout representations of such representations. (War itself, as this book tries to show, is often left in the distance.) In September 1919, the *Women's Home Companion* carried a short story by Edith Wharton with the self-reflexive title 'Writing a War

---

[3] The Russian adverbs are 'nezametno' (imperceptibly, with the sense of being unnoticeable) and 'nevol'no' (involuntarily, unintentionally) (L. N. Tolstoy, *Voina i mir* [*War and Peace*] (Moscow: Zakharov, 2000), 288): Rostov cannot control the deviation.

[4] In Russian 'neizbezhno' (inevitably) (Tolstoy, *Voina i mir*, 288).

[5] Tolstoy, *War and Peace*, 280, 227–8.

Story'. The example of a depiction of war contained in the piece is again generated by a request, and value is again placed on first-hand experience of conflict as means of authentication. Miss Ivy Spang of Cornwall-on-Hudson, USA, who 'had published a little volume of verse before the war', is asked by a (male) patient in the big Anglo-American hospital in France where she pours tea to contribute a 'war story' to a forthcoming anthology, the significantly titled 'Men-at-Arms'. The request is couched as follows:

A good rousing story, Miss Spang . . . We want the first number to be an 'actuality', as the French say; all the articles are written by people who've done the thing themselves, or seen it done. You've been at the front, I suppose? As far as Rheims, once? That's capital!

Initially 'dizzy with triumph' at this commission, Miss Spang then struggles to find an opening and a plot. The more she thinks about the matter, the less she seems to understand how a war story is written. All that is apparent is that 'in a war story the flowers must be at the end and not at the beginning'. Ultimately, she is saved only by her old French governess who has a copybook full of stories she took down from soldiers in a military hospital during 1914. 'Mademoiselle' supplies Miss Spang's rendition of one of these tales with 'certain consecutiveness' but polishes the rustic speech in which she originally transcribed the story so that it issues forth 'in the language that a young lady writing a composition on the Battle of Hastings would have used in Mademoiselle's school day'. To the 'purely military' anecdote, Miss Spang adds 'a touch of sentiment'. When the anthology comes out, she is upset that her soldier patients pay exclusive attention to the photograph of her in her nurse's uniform accompanying the piece.[6]

This story highlights a number of the challenges confronting all war writers while making clear that the problems faced by women war writers are particularly egregious. The two women war writers in the story, Ivy Spang and Mademoiselle, both face the primary difficulty of gaining first-hand experience of their subject matter: the story eventually published is at least third-hand. Even to obtain this material, they must perform parapolemical[7] work in hospitals. The interest taken in the photo is monitory: femininity can be a way of gaining access to material (and hence readers) during conflict, but it can also be a bar. The lowly pourer of tea

---

[6] Edith Wharton, *Collected Stories 1911–1937*, sel. Maureen Howard (New York: Library of America, 2001), 247, 248, 250, 253.

[7] See Kate McLoughlin, *Martha Gellhorn: The War Writer in the Field and in the Text* (Manchester: Manchester University Press, 2007), 105: parapolemics are the temporal and spatial borders of war, its adjectival phenomena.

finds it impossible to be taken seriously as a writer of war. But beyond this, Mademoiselle and Miss Spang encounter generic difficulty: not specifically a gender issue, it faces all those who seek to convey the complex, massive phenomenon that is war. How indeed to begin, to end, to find appropriate words? Like Rostov, the two women turn, in their helplessness, to established narratives. For Mademoiselle, these are the historical compositions she remembers from school. For Miss Spang, they are sentimental stories with a romantic twist. In each case, as for Nikolai Rostov, inchoate attempts are discarded in favour of a 'strong' version already available. And Wharton herself, who had personally witnessed the Front on a number of visits, does not write about battle but about the difficulties of representing it.

The phenomenon recurs in another intensely self-reflexive war story with a title very similar to Wharton's: Tim O'Brien's 'How to Tell a True War Story' (1990). The title can be understood in two ways: how to distinguish a true war story and how to relate one. In the course of the piece, O'Brien, adopting a narrative persona also called 'Tim O'Brien', suggests that the truest account of war may actually be fictional: 'a thing may happen and be a total lie; another thing may not happen and be truer than the truth'.[8] A 'true war story', in his terms, is, accordingly, often unbelievable, unreal, embarrassing and pointless. It makes no sense, except in the gut. It goes on and on forever and there can be no meaningful response to it – except, perhaps, more questions.

These observations are made in a story which itself is knowingly misleading, kaleidoscopic and self-contradictory. Opening with what seems to be a tale about a GI, Rat Kiley, writing to the sister of his dead friend Curt Lemon, it shifts into an unfinished account of Lemon's death; then into a completely unrelated story told by another GI; then into an amendment of that story; then into a description of Kiley torturing a baby water buffalo; then into a return to the account of Lemon's death, differently angled this time; then into a brief reference to an apocryphal tale; then into an admission that the story is about something else entirely. These divagations make 'How to Tell a True War Story' impossible to grasp: like Rostov's original account or Miss Spang's fumblings, each section is abandoned for a further apparently futile attempt to convey the actuality.

The phenomenon reaches a culmination in another piece of Vietnam War literature – *The Sorrow of War* (1991) – by the Vietnamese writer Bao Ninh, who, like Tim O'Brien, personally served in the conflict. In a novel which is as much about war representation as it is about war, Ninh

---

[8] Tim O'Brien, *The Things They Carried* (London: Flamingo, 1991), 79.

presents a writer-combatant protagonist, Kien, whose struggles with the challenges of recording his experiences are never less than excruciating. This is a 'war author [who] cannot even bear to enter a cinema where people may be shooting each other on the screen', an author 'who avoids reading anything about any war, the Vietnam war or any other great wars', an author, indeed, 'who is frightened by war stories'. Nonetheless, as one who has 'perhaps watched more killings and seen more corpses than any contemporary writer', Kien endows the act of authorship with the status of a mission: 'he has to finish his novel and life cannot be ended until the writing is done'.[9]

His writing project synonymous with crisis, Kien reaches a point where 'the novel seem[s] to be in charge'. It has 'its own logic, its own flow' and even seems 'to structure itself, to take its own time, to make its own detours'. The novel, not the writer, is the active agent, 'unfold[ing] on the cluttered desk' in front of him. Kien 'meekly accept[s]' this take-over, 'passively letting the stream of his novel flow as it [will]'.[10] No more than a conduit, the authorial figure in this moment has abdicated all responsibility. It is as though the war has ambushed the writing, assuming the task of expressing itself.

All four writers, then, depict a *surrender* in the face of representing war. In each of the key scenes, an attempt to convey conflict is aborted as a less troublesome option is embraced: in Rostov's and Miss Spang's cases, a popular, stereotypical version; in 'O'Brien's' case, another in the series of discarded vignettes; in Kien's case, a trance-like, automatic state. Now, these examples, at first glance, function in ways similar to those in which literary influence in general is thought to operate. The most influential influence theorist, Harold Bloom, proposed over thirty years ago that 'strong poets make [poetic] history by misreading one another' through such means as 'completion', 'correction' and 'antithesis'.[11] The implication is that the poets who fail to overcome their powerful precursors are somehow wanting: in Bloom's terms, Rostov, Miss Spang, 'Tim O'Brien' and Kien would be characterised as weak war writers, too feeble to deploy the tropes of resistance. Critics of Bloom who reject his 'anxiety of influence' theory as a male-oriented, Oedipal model, nonetheless continue to locate debility in the writer. The 'anxiety of authorship' theory proposed by Sandra Gilbert and Susan Gubar suggests that, far from experiencing anxiety

---

[9] Bao Ninh, *The Sorrow of War*, trans. Frank Palmos (London: Minerva, 1994), 51, 82, 180.
[10] *Ibid.*, 81, 81, 91, 81.
[11] Harold Bloom, *The Anxiety of Influence* (Oxford: Oxford University Press, 1997), 5, 14.

of influence, writers outside the dominant male canon feel anxiety about writing at all. Imbued with 'a radical fear that she cannot create' and 'culturally conditioned timidity', the woman writer struggles with 'isolation that [feels] like illness, alienation that [feels] like madness, [and] obscurity that [feels] like paralysis': unsurprisingly, most lack the 'extraordinary strength' required to produce literature.[12] Other theories of influence – the ideas of intertextuality promulgated by Julia Kristeva and Roland Barthes, for example – depend upon an understanding of text as boundaryless, receptive, subjectile. 'Any text is constructed as a mosaic of quotations; any text is the absorption and transformation of another,' writes Kristeva, drawing on Bakhtin's theory of dialogism,[13] while Barthes, using a battle metaphor for discourse itself, insists that 'a text is . . . a multi-dimensional space in which a variety of writings, none of them original, blend and clash'.[14] Though radically opposed to the humanistic ideas of agency on which the approaches of Bloom, Gilbert and Gubar are founded, these theorists also offer concepts which are paradigms of lack of resistance. But, arguably, something else is at work in the 'capitulations' depicted by the four writers under consideration.

Strikingly, these are meta-capitulations. Rostov, Miss Spang, 'Tim O'Brien' and Kien falter in the fiction, but Tolstoy, Wharton, O'Brien and Ninh also fail, in these instances, to write about war, writing instead about the difficulties of its representation. That all four depict authorial anxiety is instructive (and their personal combat experience – in Wharton's case, experience of visiting the Front – has been cited to make the point that none lacked first-hand knowledge of armed conflict). The argument of this book is that the representation of war is inherently anxiogenic – but the anxiety is not primarily related to the problems of influence or authorship characterised by Bloom or Gilbert and Gubar, nor is it primarily a symptom of textual porousness, nor is it primarily a matter of what, after post-modernism, might be termed the ontological indeterminacy of reality. When war writers 'swerve' (the word is a loaded one in influence theory), the moment is an acknowledgement of a complex set of problematics relating now to authorial powers, now to the nature of the subject matter, now to the medium of representation, now to the reader's response – and now to other intangible variables. War, in other words, resists depiction, and

---

[12] Sandra Gilbert and Susan Gubar, *The Madwoman in the Attic: The Woman Writer and the Nineteenth-Century Imagination* (New Haven: Yale Nota Bene Press, 2000), 49, 50, 51, 51.

[13] Julia Kristeva, 'Word, Dialogue and Novel', *The Kristeva Reader*, ed. Toril Moi (Oxford: Blackwell, 1986), 37.

[14] Roland Barthes, *Image, Music, Text*, trans. Stephen Heath (London: Fontana, 1977), 146.

does so in multifarious ways. *Agon,* or the contest for aesthetic supremacy,[15] is transformed in war writing from a wrestling match solely between poet and powerful predecessor into a struggle between writer and Hydra-like adversary with inexhaustible means of defence and attack.

Yet, even as it resists representation, conflict demands it. The reasons that make war's representation imperative are as multitudinous as those which make it impossible: to impose discursive order on the chaos of conflict and so to render it more comprehensible; to keep the record for the self and others (those who were there and can no longer speak for themselves and those who were not there and need to be told); to give some meaning to mass death; to memorialise; to inform civilians of the nature of battle so as to facilitate the reintegration of veterans into peacetime society; to provide cathartic relief; to warn; and even, through the warning, to promote peace. And despite – perhaps because of – the difficulties, depiction of conflict is ubiquitous and of ancient standing. War representation is 12,000 years old, dating from at least the Mesolithic period (10,000–5,000 BCE) in the form of rock-paintings of battle scenes found in the Spanish Levant.[16] The modes by and media in which armed conflict has been recorded over the thousands of years since are multifarious: an inexhaustive list would include all the literary, musical and fine art genres; film, television, radio and the internet; games of every description, battle re-enactments and anti-war demonstrations; advertisements, photographs and posters; dance and movement; post-cards, coinage and papier-mâché models; mugs, cereal bowls, tea towels, thimbles, bow-ties, pencil sharpeners and key-rings;[17] and, unlikeliest of all, the spun sugar from which the Viennese court confectioner wove a model of the Battle of Esztergom for the Empress Maria Theresia.[18] Representations of war can be as long as *War and Peace* or as short as a bloodcurdling battle cry containing all the fury of previous encounters and present intentions (in the *Iliad,* Ares and Poseidon both have war cries as loud as nine or ten thousand warriors (5.860, 14.148)). Analytic and aesthetic discourses have also been imposed *onto* armed conflict, the subject treated by, *inter alia,* anthropological, legal, economic and psychological – as well as literary – analyses and taxonomies. Written war representation itself is thickly textual: depictions of conflict typically contain and comment upon other depictions of conflict and even, in the case of Byron's *Don Juan* (1819–24), petition

---

[15] Bloom, *The Anxiety of Influence,* xxiv.
[16] Azar Gat, *War in Human Civilisation* (Oxford: Oxford University Press, 2006), 27.
[17] Gifts available from the Imperial War Museum, London.
[18] W. G. Sebald, *The Rings of Saturn,* trans. Michael Hulse (London: Harvill, 1999), 194.

them as aids to inventiveness: 'Oh, ye great bulletins of Bonaparte! /
Oh, ye less grand long lists of killed and wounded!'[19] Simultaneously
impossible and necessary to convey, war gives rise to representations that
are palimpsestic, self-reflexive, hypertextual.

Authoring War sets out to understand this complex set of imperatives:
firstly, to identify what makes war impossible or very difficult to write
about and, secondly, to explore the means by which it has, nevertheless,
been written about with some success. It also offers thoughts on why,
despite the obstacles, attempts to write about war are myriad and ongoing
and what is achieved when such attempts are made. As is described in
more detail later in this Introduction, the subject is approached in terms
of specific challenges and responses. *Authoring War* does not seek to give
a normative account of war writing – there is no suggestion that one, true
version exists or should be striven for, either of war in general or wars in
particular – but rather to show *what writing can do* with the ineffable and
intractable.

What makes armed conflict such a slippery opponent is its *extremity* as
an experience. 'Extremity' is not here defined in any absolute or relative
sense. It is conceived in the same terms as Maurice Blanchot's characterisation of 'the disaster' as that which 'couldn't possibly belong to the order of
things which come to pass, or which are important, but is rather among the
things which export or deport'.[20] 'Export or deport': the extremeness that
is war carries the individual who experiences it away from the familiar and
the ordinary. In exploring the representation of the extreme, the abnormal,
the intractable, *Authoring War* participates in lines of thought about how
'difficult' subjects might be conveyed – thought that takes in concepts of
the sublime developed over millennia as well as recent work in Holocaust
representation[21] and the depiction of trauma, pain and memory. In the
field of 'war studies', it both benefits from and builds upon the movement, originating with Angus Calder's *The People's War: Britain 1939–45*
(1969) and Paul Fussell's *The Great War and Modern Memory* (1975) and
ongoing in, for example, the *Journal of War & Culture Studies* (founded

---

[19] Lord Byron, *Don Juan*, ed. T. G. Steffan, E. Steffan and W.W. Pratt (London: Penguin, 2004),
canto 7, stanza 82, lines 1–2.
[20] Maurice Blanchot, *The Writing of the Disaster*, trans. Anne Smock (Lincoln: University of Nebraska
Press, 1986), 9.
[21] On the idea of the 'extreme' in Holocaust theory, see, for example, Dominick LaCapra, *History
and Memory After Auschwitz* (Ithaca: Cornell University Press, 1998), 48, and Michael Rothberg,
Traumatic Realism: The Demands of Holocaust Representation (Minneapolis: University of Minnesota
Press, 2000), 106, 109, 129.

2008), to understand armed conflict in terms of its cultural delivery and consumption[22] – here, specifically, in its written mediation.

In a broader context still, its concern with the nuts and bolts of written expression situates *Authoring War* within the (renewed) formalist tendency in literary analysis. One of the book's premises is the belief that war, as a subject, is the greatest test of a writer's skills of evocation, a belief shared by Ernest Hemingway,[23] who commented in a letter to F. Scott Fitzgerald that 'it [war] groups the maximum of material and speeds up the action and brings out all sorts of stuff that normally you have to wait a lifetime to get'.[24] Other areas of human experience – love and grief spring to mind – have their own representational challenges, but war is specially charged because huge in scale, devastating in impact and encompassing of human behaviour in its greatest trials and intimacies. In its formalist approach, *Authoring War* bucks the prevailing conflict-specific trend in war studies, even as it keeps in view the local and particular factors shaping each attempt to convey war's extremeness.

The formalist approach involves the dismantling of some traditional categories, the most significant of which is 'war' itself. Rather than confine itself to a dictionary[25] or legal[26] definition,[27] *Authoring War* embraces all aspects of what Walt Whitman called 'the red business',[28] whose product

---

[22] See Martin Evans, 'Opening Up the Battlefield: War Studies and the Cultural Turn', *Journal of War and Culture Studies* 1.1 (2008), 47–51. Most recently, this turn has been pursued in Mary A. Favret's *War at a Distance: Romanticism and the Making of Modern Wartime* (Princeton: Princeton University Press, 2009).

[23] Though not by Yeats, who notoriously omitted 'certain poems written in the midst of the great war' from his 1936 edition of *The Oxford Book of Modern Verse* on the questionable grounds that 'passive suffering is not a theme for poetry' ('Introduction', *The Oxford Book of Modern Verse, 1892–1935*, ed. W. B. Yeats (Oxford: Clarendon, 1936), xiv).

[24] Ernest Hemingway, *Selected Letters 1917–1961*, ed. Carlos Baker (London: Granada, 1981), 176.

[25] 'Any kind of active hostility or contention between living beings' (*Oxford English Dictionary* (*OED*) I.1.b).

[26] 'In accordance with international treaty law, for an armed conflict to result in a state of affairs governed by international law and constituting a war in the legal sense of that term, the hostilities should be preceded by a reasoned declaration or an ultimatum with a fixed time limit, indicating that a formal declaration would issue if the conditions laid down in the ultimatum were not met' (Leslie C. Green, *The Contemporary Law of Armed Conflict*, 2nd edn (Manchester and New York: Manchester University Press / Juris Publishing, 2000), 72). The requirement for war to be declared goes back to Grotius and seems tantamount to saying that war is what war is announced to be.

[27] For extended discussion of the definition of war, see Nick Mansfield, *Theorizing War: From Hobbes to Badiou* (Basingstoke: Palgrave Macmillan, 2008) and Hew Strachan, 'The Idea of War', in *The Cambridge Companion to War Writing*, ed. Kate McLoughlin (Cambridge: Cambridge University Press, 2009), 7–14.

[28] Walt Whitman, 'First O Songs for a Prelude' (1861, 1867), *Complete Poetry and Selected Prose*, sel. Justin Kaplan (New York: Library of America, 1982), 417.

is what Ivor Gurney called the 'red wet / Thing'.[29] There is no attempt,
therefore, to identify 'war writing' as that written by a combatant, produced
contemporaneously or related to events on the battlefield (though these
distinctions must be recognised in certain contexts, particularly when the
issue of credentials is explored in Chapter 1). Rather, the concern is with
the extreme experiences (dying, killing, injury, pain, loss, displacement,
familial and national upheaval, etc) to which the red business and the red
wet thing give rise. These parameters are sufficiently wide to permit the
inclusion of 'all strike, / All quarells / contecks, and all cruell iarres':[30]
writing about revolutions and counter-revolutions, colonial and civil wars,
skirmishes and sieges (though not 'cold' hostilities). Reference is also made
to representations of genocide and terrorism, but these phenomena involve
special considerations and have accrued their own bodies of theoretical
writing (from which *Authoring War* benefits): their *sui generis* status is
therefore respected.

The question immediately raised by this scope is whether it is legitimate
to take a common approach to 'war writing' when the wars being written
about took place in different periods and cultures and varied enormously
in kind. That each war differs from every other is beyond question. Indeed,
each individual's experience of a war is different: 'When a war is ended it is as
if there have been a million wars, or as many wars as there were soldiers.'[31]
In particular, it has been noted that twentieth-century wars (especially
the world wars) are 'phenomenologically and ontologically discontinuous'
with previous conflicts, whether due to their industrial scale or to the
fact that 'modern weapons technology has fundamentally altered the locus
of agency'.[32] Such differences may account for the impression that each
war has its own poesis, its 'natural' way (or ways) of being represented.
Sometimes, this is a question of genre: in ancient Rome, warfare was such
an entrenched part of epic that *bella* ('wars') became a shorthand for the
genre,[33] while it now seems evident that the First World War's natural form
was the lyric poem, that the Second World War's was the epic novel, that
the Vietnam War's was the movie, that the Iraq Wars' may well turn out
to be the blog. Beyond this, how a war may be represented is determined

---

[29] Ivor Gurney, 'To His Love' (1919), *Collected Poems of Ivor Gurney*, ed. P. J. Kavanagh (Oxford:
    Oxford University Press, 1984), 41.
[30] George Gascoigne, *The Fruites of Warre* (1575), *The Complete Works of George Gascoigne*, ed. John
    W. Cunliffe, 2 vols. (Cambridge: Cambridge University Press, 1907), vol. I, lines 225–6.
[31] Tim O'Brien, *Going After Cacciato* (London: Flamingo, 1988), 189.
[32] Margot Norris, *Writing War in the Twentieth Century* (Charlottesville: University Press of Virginia,
    2000), 16.
[33] See Virgil, *Eclogues* 6.3; Horace, *Ars Poetica* 73; Ovid, *Amores* 1.1 (L. V. Pitcher, 'Classical War
    Literature', in *The Cambridge Companion to War Writing*, ed. McLoughlin, 73).

by a number of factors. The *casus belli* affects how a particular conflict is perceived and may be characterised, as do the political dispositions of the states involved. Weapons technology also plays a part: plunging a sword into the chest of someone a foot away involves very different notions of honour and bravery than does, for example, pressing a button on a computer that produces an explosion at a distance of hundreds of miles.[34] De Quincey encapsulated this point when inviting his readers to consider Roman warfare in which troopers were 'forced to plough sabres into faces' and then to

> pass to a modern field of battle, where all is finished by musquetry and artillery amidst clouds of smoke, no soldier recognising his own desolations, or the ghastly ruin of his own right arm; so that war by losing all its brutality is losing half of its demoralization.[35]

The inability to see the 'ghastly ruin' perpetrated by one's own right arm reconfigures the experience of conflict and must necessarily inform its representation.[36] The same idea occurs in R. N. Currey's poem 'Disintegration of Spring Time' (*c*.1944) in the two sections headed 'Unseen fire':

> This is a damned inhuman sort of war.
> I have been fighting in a dressing-gown
> Most of the night; I cannot see the guns,
> The sweating gun-detachments or the planes;
> I sweat down here before a symbol thrown
> Upon a screen, sift facts, initiate
> Swift calculations and swift orders; wait
> For the precise split-second to order fire.[37]

---

[34] Weapons technology also affects terminology and hence literary diction, as Byron observes in *Don Juan*: 'now instead of slaying Priam's son, / We only can but talk of escalade, / Bombs, drums, guns, bastions, batteries, bayonets, bullets – / Hard words, which stick in the soft Muses' gullets' (7.78.5–8).

[35] Thomas de Quincey, *The Works of Thomas De Quincey*, ed. Robert Morrison, 21 vols. (London: Pickering and Chatto, 2003), vol. XVI, 279. Cf. David Jones's concern, in the introduction to *In Parenthesis* (1937), that 'a rubicon has been passed between striking with a hand weapon as men used to do and loosing poison from the sky as we do ourselves. We doubt the decency of our own inventions, and are certainly in terror of their possibilities' (*In Parenthesis: Seinnyessit E Gledyf Ym Penn Mameu* (London: Faber, 1963), xiv).

[36] James Dickey's poem 'The Firebombing' (1967) disputes this point: 'cool and enthralled in the cockpit, / Turned blue by the power of beauty', the bomber-pilot can, nonetheless, evoke (if not, by his own admission, imagine) 'ears crackling off / Like powdery leaves', 'children of ashes' (*Poems 1957–1967* (London: Rapp and Carroll, 1967), 186, 188) as he muses on his own American suburban home and the Japanese suburbs he is about to annihilate. Nonetheless, much of the poem's impact depends upon the remoteness of the pilot from the horrifying injuries he causes.

[37] R. N. Currey, *Collected Poems* (Oxford and Cape Town: James Currey / David Philip Publishers, 2001), 94.

This is technological warfare removed from conventional battle in a number of ways: dressing-gowns instead of uniforms, screens instead of arms. 'Beyond the phones', ghosts give orders to other ghosts and 'guns roar / Abruptly'. Currey uses the word 'inhuman' twice in his three stanzas and though the speaker 'sweats' at his screen, a human response is noticeably absent. 'To us he is no more than a machine / Shown on an instrument,' Currey writes of the pilot carrying out the phantasmagorical commands: 'what can he mean / In human terms?'[38] In contrast, one-to-one combat is rarely depicted without an account of the personal qualities that a preparedness to kill and be killed at close quarters entails:

> Also in the vanguard stood Eadweard the tall;
> ready and eager, he spoke determined words
> that he would not flee one foot of ground,
> retreat back, while his better man lay dead.
> He broke the shield-wall and fought against the warriors,
> until, among those Vikings, he avenged his treasure-giver
> honourably, before he himself lay among the dead.[39]

How, then, can 'Disintegration of Spring Time' (*c.*1944) and 'The Battle of Maldon' (late tenth / early eleventh century) benefit from, or even justify, a common analytical approach? The answer is that, while it is indisputable that all wars are different, it is simultaneously also the case that all wars have certain elements in common: violent death, adverse conditions, the requirement to kill and risk one's own life. Conveying these elements comprises a shared set of challenges, the responses to which emerge as similarities in written representations across periods and cultures. In part, these similarities testify to the irresistible influence of the 'strong' war stories identified at the beginning of this Introduction, but in part they also reflect the force of like experience. Homer refers to Nestor using 'experience he had gained in battles long ago' to inspire his troops;[40] twenty-eight centuries later, C. S. Lewis, hearing his first bullet in action in the First World War, thought 'This is War. This is what Homer wrote about.'[41] 'The men who fought at Verdun, at Waterloo, at Flodden, at Senlac, at Thermopylae – every one of them had lice crawling over his testicles', observed George

---

[38] *Ibid.*, 94, 94, 95.

[39] 'The Battle of Maldon', lines 273–9, quoted in Elaine Treharne, ed., *Old and Middle English c.890–c.1400: An Anthology*, 2nd edn (Oxford: Blackwell, 2004), 153.

[40] Homer, *Iliad* 4.310–11. It is appreciated that 'Homer' does not reflect an author as conventionally understood and that the *Iliad* is a composite, orally-transmitted text. Nonetheless, the usage is adopted here for ease of explication.

[41] C. S. Lewis, *Surprised By Joy* (London: Geoffrey Bles, 1955), 185.

Orwell, testifying in Catalonia to a sense of combat experience having remained unchanged over millennia.[42] In Charles Hamilton Sorley's poem, 'I have not brought my Odyssey' (1915), the speaker, after apologising for not having brought his copy of the *Odyssey* to the Western Front, remarks that 'now the fight begins again, / The old war-joy, the old war-pain'.[43] But are the old war-joy and the old war-pain really recurring features of combat or are they ongoing constructions in war writing, in these instances imbibed from their classical representations by public-school-educated British officers?[44] Sorley suggests the latter possibility in his poem. Alluding to Odysseus' sojourn with Alcinous in Book 8 of the *Odyssey* when he and his fellow-veterans are entertained with songs of Troy sung by the minstrel Demodocus, the poem conveys the inflationary nature of 'tales of great war'. Listening to them, Odysseus and his comrades feel:

> that they were unreal then,
> Visions and shadow-forms, not men.
> But those the Bard did sing and say
> (Some were their comrades, some were they)
> Took shape and loomed and strengthened more
> Greatly than they had guessed of yore.[45]

The speaker of the poem, it is implied, looks forward to similar magnification on his Odysseus-like return to 'warmth and welcome and wassail' at his alma mater.[46]

The responses of Lewis, Orwell and Sorley to armed conflict confirm Paul Fussell's suggestion that 'literature leak[s] in':[47] perceptions (as well as representations) of warfare are shaped by previous representations. But alongside the effect of 'strong' war stories, there can be sensed real affinities as individuals experience war and recognise what they have read. The character Doc Peret in Tim O'Brien's *Going After Cacciato* (1978) insists on the point in his determination to avoid war being politicised, notably claiming commonality between eleventh- and twentieth-century combat experiences to posit an archetypal 'feel' of war:

---

[42] George Orwell, *Homage to Catalonia*, ed. Peter Davison, *The Complete Works of George Orwell*, 20 vols. (London: Secker and Warburg, 1986), vol. VI, 51.

[43] Charles Hamilton Sorley, *The Collected Poems of Charles Hamilton Sorley*, ed. Jean Moorcroft Wilson (London: Cecil Woolf, 1985), 130.

[44] Sorley's reference to not bringing his Odyssey, for example, may allude to the fact that Alexander the Great, as reported by Plutarch, always carried the *Iliad* on military expeditions and commended the *Odyssey* (Plutarch, *Alexander* 8.2, 26.1–2, 26.4).

[45] Sorley, *Collected Poems*, 130.   [46] *Ibid.*, 132.

[47] Paul Fussell, *The Great War and Modern Memory* (Oxford: Oxford University Press, 1975), 173.

[W]ar is war no matter how it's perceived. War has its own reality. War kills and maims and rips up land and makes orphans and widows. These are the things of war. Any war. So when I say that there's nothing new to tell about Nam, I'm saying it was just a war like every war . . . I'm saying that the *feel* of war is the same in Nam or Okinawa – the emotions are the same, the same fundamental stuff is seen and remembered . . . I'll wager that troops at Hastings or the Bulge had the same problem.[48]

Accordingly, when Nick Mansfield describes it as a 'truism' that 'each war redefines the nature of war itself, due to changes in arms technology, military organisation or geo-strategic history',[49] it may be the case that such 'redefinition', rather than rendering conflicts distinct, creates a kind of bellicose canon in which each war exerts an influence on its successor, insofar as it represents the current culmination of weapons design and military strategy (hence the notion that military forces prepare to fight the last war instead of the present war) – and also on its *predecessor*, insofar as it confers new understanding of the successes and limitations of previous encounters. Wars, then, may work in the same way as the literary tradition as described by T. S. Eliot in 'Tradition and the Individual Talent' (1919): 'the past [is] altered by the present as much as the present is directed by the past'.[50]

As these examples suggest, likeness of experience has itself become a trope: a complex meeting of representation and reality capable of further exploitation. The result is that representations of wars – like the wars themselves – are often heavily intertextual (or interbellical). In 'The Foreign Gate' (1942), for example, Sidney Keyes petitions voices from the battles of Künersdorf, Naseby and Tannenberg, from Dunkirk and the Spanish Civil War, and from other, unnamed, conflicts, to create a sense of soldierly solidarity across centuries (simultaneously creating, via allusions to Dante, Rilke and T. S. Eliot, a sense of literary community).[51] In 'Embarcation' (1899), remarking the departure of British soldiers for the Boer War, Hardy deploys the affinity trope to suggest and regret a lost opportunity for progress:

> Here, where Vespasian's legions struck the sands,
> And Cerdic with his Saxons entered in,
> And Henry's army leapt afloat to win

---

[48] O'Brien, *Going After Cacciato*, 190–1.
[49] Nick Mansfield, 'War and Its Other: Between Bataille and Derrida', *Theory & Event* 9.4 (2006), unpaginated.
[50] T. S. Eliot, *The Sacred Wood* (London: Faber, 1997), 41.
[51] Sidney Keyes, *Collected Poems*, ed. Michael Meyer (Manchester: Carcanet, 2002), 57–66.

Convincing triumphs over neighbour lands,
Vaster battalions press for further strands,
To argue in the selfsame bloody mode
Which this late age of thought, and pact, and code,
Still fails to mend.[52]

Modern constitutional thought and diplomacy still resort to 'the self-same bloody mode' of settling territorial disputes: by linking the scene at Southampton docks to other invasions and departures taking place on Wessex shores, Hardy invests the 'tragical To-be' with a nostalgic heaviness that accepts the inevitability of the impending conflict even as it laments it. The simple evocation of the campaigns of Vespasian, Cerdic and Henry V therefore allows nuanced meaning to be given to the distant war in South Africa: there is common ground between conflicts separated by thousands of years.

Commonality between armed conflicts is assumed in a number of theories about warfare (those, for example, of Hobbes, Kant, Clausewitz, Carl Schmitt, Lévinas, Bataille, Deleuze and Guattari and Derrida,[53] all of whom treat 'war' as a monolithic concept) and forms the basis of certain psychoanalytic approaches to trauma. 'All wars are the same in theory', writes Nick Mansfield, explaining Freud's conception of warfare, 'and specific wars should not be mistaken for themselves. They are, in fact, an expression or realisation of collective human subjectivity.'[54] War's sameness has also become an established anthological principle. In 1945, the Greenwood Press of Connecticut published *War and the Poet: An Anthology of Poetry Expressing Man's Attitudes to War from Ancient Times to the Present*, edited by Richard Eberhart and Selden Rodman. The collection, wrote Eberhart in the Preface, 'may give the reader a sense of the continuity of man's varying reactions to war through the centuries'.[55] Ranging from 'Hymn of Victory: Thutmose III' by Amon-Re, Lord of Thebes (*c.*1800 BCE) to Second World War poems, *War and the Poet* juxtaposes Hebrew, Greek (ancient and modern), Chinese, Roman, Arabic, Hindu, Old Norse, Anglo-Saxon, English, Irish, Breton, Provençal, French, Italian, German, Russian, Czech, Venezuelan, Chilean, Australian, Japanese and American texts of war. In a similar vein, Jon Stallworthy, editor of *The Oxford Book*

---

[52] Thomas Hardy, *The Complete Poetical Works of Thomas Hardy*, ed. Samuel Hynes, 5 vols. (Oxford: Clarendon, 1982), vol. I, 116.
[53] See Mansfield, *Theorizing War*. [54] *Ibid.*, 41.
[55] Richard Eberhart, 'Preface: Attitudes to War', in *War and the Poet: An Anthology of Poetry Expressing Man's Attitudes to War from Ancient Times to the Present*, ed. Richard Eberhart and Selden Rodman (Westport: Greenwood Press, 1945), v.

of War Poetry (1984), which stretches from the book of Exodus (eleventh or twelfth century BCE) to Peter Porter's 'Your Attention Please' (1962), writes, in another work subtitled 'From Maldon to the Somme', of 'the hypnotic power of a long cultural tradition',[56] while Lorrie Goldensohn introduces *American War Poetry: An Anthology* (2006) with the remark, 'the poetry . . . gives a sense of how nearly four centuries of warfare continue to affect the human beings of a multiethnic society . . . as they find themselves in the age-old grip of collective violence'.[57]

In the case of *Authoring War*, 'the age-old grip of collective violence' permits a structural tropological methodology extending from the *Iliad* to poetry about the wars in Iraq. With the difficulty of conveying war's extremeness its starting point, the book identifies certain specific challenges inherent in representing conflict and explores the common rhetorical strategies which, in different times and places, have been used to meet them. In taking a (neo-)rhetorical approach, *Authoring War* resonates with a theoretical tendency, begun in the twentieth century by I. A. Richards in *Philosophy of Rhetoric* (1936) and developed by Roland Barthes ('The Old Rhetoric: An Aide-Mémoire' (1965)), Gérard Genette ('Rhetoric Restrained' (1970)), Jacques Derrida ('Plato's Pharmacy' (1972)) and Paul de Man (essays in *Allegories of Reading* (1979)), whose broad premise is the 'rhetoricality'[58] of all language use and hence the dual nature of rhetoric as both creative and critical practice. More specifically, *Authoring War* draws on and contributes to a strand of thinking beginning with the dialectical tradition inaugurated by Petrus Ramus and variously refined in the twentieth century by, among others, Chaïm Perelman and Lucie Olbrechts-Tyteca (*The New Rhetoric* (1958)), Clifford Geertz ('Blurred Genres: The Reconfiguration of Social Thought' (1980) and 'The Way We Think Now: Toward An Ethnography of Modern Thought' (1982)), George A. Kennedy (*Comparative Rhetoric* (1997)) and Wayne C. Booth (*The Rhetoric of Rhetoric* (2004)). This strand of thinking finds rhetoric to be not only formal 'decoration' but vehicle and producer of meaning; indeed, in the last-mentioned work, Booth proposes a 'listening-rhetoric' that functions at the 'deepest possible level', not just to distinguish 'defensible and indefensible forms of rhetoric' but actually

---

[56] Jon Stallworthy, *Survivors' Songs: From Maldon to the Somme* (Cambridge: Cambridge University Press, 2008); 63.

[57] Lorrie Goldensohn, 'Preface', in *American War Poetry: An Anthology*, ed. Lorrie Goldensohn (New York: Columbia University Press, 2006), xxi.

[58] John Bender and David E. Welberry, 'Rhetoricality: On the Modernist Return to Rhetoric', in *The Ends of Rhetoric: History, Theory, Practice*, ed. John Bender and David E. Welberry (Stanford: Stanford University Press, 1990), 25.

to find common ground.[59] Booth's belief that '[e]ven our survival, now that mass destruction threatens, depends upon the rhetoric of our leaders and our responses to them' underpins *Authoring War* as a discursive-ethical project – a point returned to later in this Introduction.

In literary critical, as opposed to ethical, terms, the appositeness of (new) rhetoric as a methodology in the present context derives from the extremeness that texts of war have as their subject matter. If, as John Bender and David E. Wellbery remark, transparency of communication vitiates rhetoric as a critical approach, texts of war manifest 'the groundless, infinitely ramifying character of discourse' that renders it indispensable.[60] Critics have already begun the work of identifying the tropes of war which *Authoring War* continues across a wider range. To give two recent examples: James Dawes has isolated image-streams traversing literature from the American Civil War to the Second World War (*The Language of War* (2002)) and Vincent Sherry has described how the contradictory topoi and tricks of the Liberal discourse selling the First World War to the British public were appropriated in parodic fashion by modernism (*The Great War and the Language of Modernism* (2003)).

The approach of isolating difficulties and formal responses provides the book's structure as well as its methodology. There are myriad reasons why war is impossible to represent: logistical difficulties; censorship and self-censorship; squeamishness (on the part of writer, publisher and reader); the particular difficulties involved in conveying physical pain; the inhibiting psycho-physiological effects of trauma; moral considerations ranging from exploitation of others' suffering to voyeurism to sadism; an absence of sympathetic response; ethical-aesthetic factors such as taste, sensibility and responsibility. Each of these might be explored in detail, but there is simply insufficient space. Instead, *Authoring War* concentrates on the specific challenges of epistemology, scale, space, time, language and logic. Not only are these fundamental categories, but they also range across the logistical, political, psycho-physiological and ethical-aesthetic considerations just cited.

The challenge addressed in Chapter 1, 'Credentials', is that of believability. Given the complexity, the hugeness, the unfamiliarity of war, how do its recorders gain audience for their accounts and, having done so, render those accounts plausible? Use of tropes of singularity and autopsy to achieve hearing and acceptance is explored with reference to George

---

[59] Wayne C. Booth, *The Rhetoric of Rhetoric* (Oxford: Blackwell, 2004), 10.
[60] Bender and Wellbery, *Rhetoricality*, 25.

Gascoigne's *The Fruites of Warre* (1575), war reporters appearing in Shakespeare's history plays, Defoe's *Memoirs of a Cavalier* (1720), Mary Seacole's *Wonderful Adventures of Mrs Seacole in Many Lands* (1857), messenger-poems by Longfellow and Browning, and W. H. Auden and Christopher Isherwood's *Journey to a War* (1939). Chapter 2, 'Details', considers the problem of war's scale, considering how a phenomenon both massive and chronic is framed for human comprehension. The name-tallying approach (exemplified by the Vietnam Veterans' Memorial) is compared with the synecdochic approach (exemplified by the Unknown Warrior). The texts discussed include speeches from *1 Henry VI* (*c.*1588–90) and *Henry V* (*c.*1599); Milton's *Paradise Lost* (1667, 1674); Byron's *Don Juan* (1819–24) and naming-poems by Robert Southey, Cecil Day Lewis and George Orwell; Siegfried Sassoon's 'The Effect' (1918); Dalton Trumbo's *Johnny Got His Gun* (1939) and Keith Douglas's '*Vergissmeinnicht*' (1943). The representational challenge of Chapter 3, 'Zones', comprises war's alienness and the difficulties involved in conveying something outside the range of most normal experience; the 'solution' that it identifies is a radical use of pastoral. Here, the main texts for discussion are Virgil's *Eclogues* (42–37 BCE), Joseph Addison's 'The Campaign' (1705), Ambrose Bierce's 'What I Saw at Shiloh' (1881), Rupert Brooke's 'The Soldier' (1914), Edward Thomas's 'As the team's head-brass' (1916) and Henry Reed's 'Lessons of the War' (1946–91). In Chapter 4, 'Duration', the representational difficulty is the fact that, when a war is in progress, it is not known when, how or even if it is going to end: its 'meaning' is therefore indeterminate. The chapter explores the narratological implications of this phenomenon in Henry Vaughan's 'An Elegie on the Death of Mr. R. W. slain in the Late Unfortunate Differences at Routon Heath, near Chester, 1645' (1646); Henri Barbusse's First World War autobiographical novel *Under Fire* (*Le Feu*) (1916); Antoine de Saint-Exupéry's Second World War pilot narrative, *Flight to Arras* (*Pilote de guerre*) (1942); Kurt Vonnegut's *Slaughterhouse-Five* (1969) and Ian McEwan's *Atonement* (2001). Chapter 5, 'Diversions', considers the challenge of finding adequate words to represent conflict, looking at the phenomenon of 'not writing about war' in Charles Wolfe's 'The Burial of Sir John Moore after Corunna' (1816), Wilfred Owen's 'Anthem for Doomed Youth' (1917), Dylan Thomas's 'A Refusal to Mourn the Death, By Fire, of a Child in London' (1944) and Ernest Hemingway's 'On the Quai at Smyrna' (*c.*1926–7). The link between literary diversion tactics and the sublime is explored, a concept also crucial to the final chapter. Chapter 6, 'Laughter', noting the fact that warfare often makes no sense to the individual caught up in it since its prosecution appears inimical to human needs, considers what the depiction and evocation of laughter achieves in war texts, with particular reference to Byron's *Don Juan*, Jaroslav Hašek's *The Good Soldier Schweik*[61] (1923), Virginia Graham's undated Second World War poem 'It's All Very Well Now', Joseph Heller's *Catch-22* (1961) and the collected war memoirs of Spike Milligan (1971–86).

Performing both close analysis of the rhetorical devices that have been deployed in response to the various challenges and structural comparison of them, *Authoring War* offers a transhistorical and cross-cultural study of war writing. In the process, it produces new critical groupings, reading, for example, Byron's *Don Juan* alongside Heller's *Catch-22*, English Civil War poetry alongside post-modern novels. But the potentially massive range of the work requires a caveat. The aim is not to account for *every* piece of war writing ever produced, nor to provide an historical survey,[62] nor to propose a historiography (though overlapping in some respects with rhetorical analysis, the historiography of war writing has its own debate).[63] It is, rather, to identify how writers from different periods and countries have found common solutions to common difficulties and to emphasise what a purely historicist approach does not: the importance of formal techniques in debates about war writing. No doubt, it will be possible to point to omissions. 'In nearly every conversation about this project, someone suggested yet another literary text I have not read', commented Margot Norris in her introduction to the richly informative and pioneering *Writing War in the Twentieth Century* (2000).[64] The same has been true of *Authoring War*, but the hope is that absent examples will be treated not as unfortunate oversights but as opportunities to apply the analysis in question. No doubt, it will also be possible to point to counter-examples. The objective is not to propose fixed templates which all war writing must match but to reveal patterns of challenges and responses that recur to an extent significant enough to make their remarking a useful exercise, in the belief that it is possible to be illuminating without being exhaustive. So, while the earliest text to be discussed is the *Iliad* and the most recent a poem written in 2009 about the First World War,[65] and while an attempt has been made in each chapter to mix well-known texts with those possibly less

---

[61] *Švejk* in the original.

[62] This is wording adapted from another formalist project: Barbara Herrnstein Smith, *Poetic Closure: A Study of How Poems End* (Chicago: University of Chicago Press, 1968), viii–ix.

[63] See Saul Friedlander, 'Introduction', in *Probing the Limits of Representation. Nazism and the 'Final Solution'*, ed. Saul Friedlander (Cambridge, MA: Harvard University Press, 1992), 1–21.

[64] Norris, *Writing War*, 5.

[65] Carol-Ann Duffy's 'Last Post', published in *The Guardian* on 31 July 2009.

well-known, the bias of *Authoring War* is towards the war representation the author knows best: that of twentieth-century Britain and America.

The premise of *Authoring War* is that accounts of war are *always* authored, in the sense that the gap between the experience and the representation of conflict can be narrowed but never completely eliminated. This is *not* the same as claiming that war is somehow not real or actually happening,[66] nor does it necessarily imply fault on the part of those telling the stories. Of course, the authoring of war can involve distortion, exploitation and even plain lying, and one of the two motivations for this book is the conviction that understanding how the obfuscations, misrepresentations and deliberate decoys are put together is an act of good citizenship, potentially on a global scale. The other motivation is the belief that the authoring of war can also be a beneficent democratic act in itself: conflict *must* be conveyed and all the tricks and tropes of language employed to do it. These two motivations correspond to what James Dawes calls the 'disciplinary' and 'emancipatory' models of the relationship between language and violence. In the disciplinary model, language and violence are 'mutually constitutive':[67] indeed, violence is done to language. In the emancipatory model, language and violence are 'mutually exclusive':[68] discourse is the alternative to, and means of escape from, force (mirroring the Hobbesian and Kantian view that war is what civil society and sovereign authority are instituted to avoid).[69]

The four examples given at the outset of this Introduction reveal that the language of war can be *simultaneously* emancipatory and disciplinary, that it obfuscates even as it aims to illuminate, and vice versa. The critic who aims to disentangle its complexity must be vigilant. Tim O'Brien's great warning about war writing that is taken as the epigraph to this book informs all its readings. While war literature may dazzle with its technique and resourcefulness, its subject matter can – should – sadden and horrify. *Authoring War* springs from the belief that the two elements of this proposition are bound in an ethical-aesthetical nexus. The dazzlement's *raison d'être* is to keep the horror in view.

---

[66] This has been a criticism of Baudrillard's *The Gulf War Did Not Take Place* (1994). Baudrillard's case was in fact that the 'Gulf War' (as opposed to the Gulf War) was a contrived series of pseudo-events and sound- and action-bites. See further Richard Keeble, 'Information Warfare in an Age of Hyper-Militarism', in *Reporting War. Journalism in Wartime*, ed. Stuart Allan and Barbie Zelizer (London and New York: Routledge, 2004), 43–58.

[67] James Dawes, *The Language of War: Literature and Culture in the US from the Civil War through World War II* (Cambridge, MA: Harvard University Press, 2002), 1.

[68] *Ibid.*, 1.   [69] Mansfield, *Theorizing War*, 4.

CHAPTER I

Credentials

As a 'mark of especial favour', Prince Andrei Bolkonsky is entrusted with the task of taking news of the Russian victory at Krems to the Austrian Court.[1] The battle has recorded itself on the Prince in the form of a slight graze on his hand: now, as he journeys on his errand, he formulates his own record of events, imagining himself stating each detail to the Emperor Francis 'in due sequence, word for word'.[2] As well as picturing his delivery of the news, he also pleasurably anticipates its reception: 'vividly he imagined the casual questions that might be put to him and the answers he would give'.[3] Driving in his post-chaise, he cuts an impressive figure, stopping to distribute gold pieces to wounded soldiers. The errand will not only ensure him a decoration but also constitutes an important step towards promotion.

But Prince Andrei's reception at Brünn is deflating. Greeted by an adjutant, he is kept waiting for five minutes before being ushered in to see the minister of war. The minister's reaction to the dispatch is dismay at the death of the Austrian general Schmidt: he virtually ignores the Russian victory. Bolkonsky's 'exultant feelings' are 'considerably impaired'; he feels 'affronted', about as 'welcome as a dog in a game of skittles'.[4] A 'sense of wounded pride' changes into disdain for his audience on the grounds of their lack of experience: '"Gaining victories probably seems easy to them, when they don't know the smell of gunpowder!" he said to himself.'[5] His audience with Francis, which eventually takes place the following day, is farcical: the Emperor speaks 'as though his sole aim were to put a given number of questions – the answers to which, as was only too evident, could have no interest for him'.[6] The situation is saved only by the general reception of the news at court. Prince Andrei is at last overwhelmed with invitations and has 'to spend the whole morning calling on the principal dignitaries of Austria'.[7]

---

[1] Tolstoy, *War and Peace*, 171.   [2] *Ibid.*, 173.   [3] *Ibid.*   [4] *Ibid.*, 173, 176.   [5] *Ibid.*, 173.
[6] *Ibid.*, 183.   [7] *Ibid.*, 184.

Tolstoy extends this account of news-giving over two chapters. More accurately, it is a sequence of accounts of news-giving. Bolkonsky delivers his message to the wounded soldiers he encounters en route; to the adjutant; to the minister of war; to Bilibin; to the Emperor and to the rest of the court – and, indeed, he is given news himself. The reception of his tidings both changes his view of them – the battle of which he had such a proud and pleasant recollection becomes 'a remote, far-away memory'[8] – and also impairs his ability to absorb new information. Obliged to discharge the roles of both performer and audience, he is initially unable to 'take in the full significance' of the information he is given about Vrbna's visit to Bonaparte; he cannot understand that the Russians have failed to blow up a key bridge; and he believes Bilibin to be 'jesting' about the French generals who have taken the bridge.[9] The tidings carried by the ironically termed 'messenger of victory'[10] are quickly rendered old news.

These scenes dramatise the representational challenge explored in this chapter: how successfully to deliver an account of war. The stakes are high, for all the reasons given in the Introduction. It quickly becomes apparent that the chances of success are greatest if the account in question is *salient* and, crucially, *credible*. But how are salience and credibility to be achieved? Attempting to answer this question raises further questions. Who tells of war? What factors enhance the telling (opportunity and authority seem to be basic requirements) and how are they acquired and conveyed? Why is the telling of war itself so frequently depicted (such depictions can come to resemble a hall of mirrors as war reporters observe and describe other war reporters, who in turn observe and describe them: 360° reporting)?[11] Why is the figure of the war reporter given such close attention? What is the recipient's role in the communication of information about war?

In exploring literary responses to these questions, this chapter analyses the representation (including self-representation) of those who, like Prince Andrei, tell others about war. Though the term 'reporter' is used, the carriers/couriers in question are not necessarily official messengers nor professional (journalistic) correspondents, but all those who, by some means, inform others about conflict. War does not discriminate in whom it overtakes: hence the war reporter is potentially everywhere and everyone. Evidencing this, the figures discussed in this chapter are combatants

---

[8] *Ibid.*, 174.   [9] *Ibid.*, 178, 184, 185.   [10] *Ibid.*, 175.
[11] See, for example, Mary Seacole on William Howard Russell and Russell on Seacole (Mary Seacole, *Wonderful Adventures of Mrs Seacole in Many Lands*, ed. Sara Salih (London: Penguin, 2005), 147–8).

and non-combatants, professionals and amateurs, men and women: they include an Elizabethan mercenary (the narrator of George Gascoigne's *The Fruites of Warre* (1575)); some of Shakespeare's war reporters; a seventeenth-century gentleman volunteer (the narrator of Daniel Defoe's *Memoirs of a Cavalier* (1720)); the protagonists of messenger-poems by Longfellow and Browning; a nineteenth-century nurse (Mary Seacole as she appears in her memoirs, *Wonderful Adventures of Mrs Seacole in Many Lands* (1857)) and two twentieth-century *literati* (W. H. Auden and Christopher Isherwood in their guises in *Journey to a War* (1939)).

The first reporter of war is war itself, a phenomenon that illuminates the qualities required in human reporters. Conflict announces or expresses itself through noise and commotion, incidentally providing metonyms for battle, as in Emerson's 'shot heard round the world'.[12] War's 'acoustic imprint' is 'the horrible sounds of death and destruction'; its 'gruesome polyphony'[13] includes alarums (the etymology of which is the call *all' arme*); the boom and crackle and whine and thud of weaponry; human cries, screams and shouts; the sounds of vehicles and armies moving; the crash of falling buildings; and weird aural hallucinations like those described by Tim O'Brien: 'gook opera and a glee club and the Haiphong Boys Choir and a barbershop quartet and all kinds of weird chanting and Buddha-Buddha stuff'.[14] War insists on drowning all other noise, deafening peacetime discourses, demanding complete attention. Noise, though, is not armed conflict's sole means of self-expression. Prince Andrei's grazed hand is an example, albeit minor, of war's self-inscription on the bodies (and minds) of its participants. Potentially the loudest war reporter of all is the dead body – 'the limp, mangled work of a gun'[15] – but this is a species of reporter most often denied the chance to deliver its message. Conflict might be global, but those who have personally witnessed the body of a person killed in war are in the minority and even television does not afford numerous opportunities for western non-combatants to view war-dead directly. But the surviving body tells a story, too. Wounds report war. Some are endowed with voice, like those of the Sergeant in *Macbeth* whose

---

[12] Ralph Waldo Emerson, 'Hymn: Sung at the Completion of the Concord Monument, April 19, 1836' ('Concord Hymn') (1836), *Collected Poems and Translations*, ed. Harold Bloom and Paul Kane (New York: Library of America, 1994), 125.

[13] Carolin Emcke, *Echoes of Violence: Letters from a War Reporter* (Princeton: Princeton University Press, 2007), 40.

[14] O'Brien, *The Things They Carried*, 72.

[15] Edgar Wallace, 'War', in *The Oxford Book of War Poetry*, ed. Jon Stallworthy (Oxford: Oxford University Press, 1984), 155.

'gashes cry for help' (1.2.43). Most obviously, they register presence. En route with his own tidings, Prince Andrei is stopped by the sight of '[s]ix or more white-faced, bandaged, dirty men . . . being jolted over the stony road';[16] as much as he, they tell the story of the action just concluded. Bodily symptoms other than physical injuries also convey that war has been experienced. According to Eric J. Leed, battle is 'learned' through 'physical immersion': knowledge of war is, like sexual knowledge (or, more mundanely, the ability to ride a bicycle), 'acquired in the body'.[17] Those who have experienced war carry its news despite themselves, inescapably and for life: de facto war reporters, living bulletins.

The reporting of war, then, need not be articulate. In addition to physical symptoms, it emerges in 'the sounds . . . humans make before language is learned':[18] cries and screams, or, in Emily Dickinson's phrase, 'Piles of solid Moan'.[19] As noted in the Introduction, Homer judges the battle cries of Ares and Poseidon to be as loud as nine or ten thousand warriors.[20] Such cries are the harbingers of terror or (as in the case of the paeanismus) registrations of triumph,[21] while screams are real-time registrations of what has been done – is being done – to the body. Beyond these primal sounds, war is expressed in language that is disturbed and uncontrollable: phenomena such as somniloquy and logorrhoea. In *1 Henry IV*, Lady Percy reproaches her husband, Hotspur, for sleep-talking:

> In thy faint slumbers I by thee have watched,
> And heard thee murmur tales of iron wars,
> [. . .]
> And thou hast talked
> Of sallies and retires, of trenches, tents,
> Of palisadoes, frontiers, parapets,
> Of basilisks, of cannon, culverin,
> Of prisoners' ransom, and of soldiers slain,
> And all the currents of a heady fight.
> Thy spirit within thee hath been so at war,
> And thus hath so bestirred thee in thy sleep.

---

[16] Tolstoy, *War and Peace*, 172.

[17] Eric J. Leed, *No Man's Land: Combat and Identity in World War I* (Cambridge: Cambridge University Press, 1979), 74.

[18] Elaine Scarry, *The Body in Pain: The Making and Unmaking of the World* (Oxford: Oxford University Press, 1985), 4.

[19] Emily Dickinson, 'My portion is defeat – today –', *The Complete Poems of Emily Dickinson*, ed. Thomas H. Johnson (Boston: Little, Brown, 1960), 316.

[20] *Iliad* 5.860, 14.148.

[21] Philippa Sheppard, 'Tongues of War: Studies in the Military Rhetoric of Shakespeare's History Plays', unpublished D.Phil. thesis, University of Oxford, 1994, 61.

> That beads of sweat have stood upon thy brow
> Like bubbles in a late-disturbéd stream,
> And in thy face strange motions have appeared,
> Such as we see when men restrain their breath
> On some great sudden hest.   (2.3.49–50, 51–65)

It is the fact, as much as the content, of Hotspur's somniloquy which records the effect that war has had on his mind and body. This symptom is accompanied by other physical reporters: the beads of sweat, the 'strange motions' in his face. The discharged soldier encountered at the end of Book 4 of Wordsworth's *The Prelude* (1799–1850) has similar symptoms, seemingly unable to control what comes from his mouth: 'From his lips, ere long, / Issued low muttered sounds, as if of pain / Or some uneasy thought'.[22] Examples of 'non-semantic' language, these *ur*-war reports are cited to make the point that the representation of conflict begins before 'jaw-jaw' or what is verbal, conscious and deliberate.

War's means of self-reporting – noise, wounds and other imprints left on and in the body – evince certain qualities. Indexical,[23] they are traces of battle, sensible proof that conflict has taken place and been seen to have taken place. Striking, even shocking, they insistently attract attention and their effects on the recipient range from distraction to permanent physical or mental change. To these elements of effective war reporting can be added those evident in the military's own means of in-battle communication. From the Torch Telegraph used in ancient Greece to the present-day Royal Signals Corps' digital, satellite, computer and tactical communications systems (the Falcon Secure Trunk Communication System, BOWMAN, Personal Role Radio and others),[24] the military has depended upon technologies that are capable of interpreting war even as it unfolds, and of constantly revising and updating those interpretations. Animals, too have been used to carry data through and from battle,[25] since they are able to evade the restrictions placed on humans and move unnoticed within the war zone, qualities noted by Isaac Rosenberg in the 'droll rat' which has 'cosmopolitan sympathies' (or a war reporter's desired neutrality) because it

---

[22] William Wordsworth, *The Fourteen-Book Prelude*, ed. W. J. B. Owen, 21 vols. (Ithaca: Cornell University Press, 1985), vol. XIV, 90 (lines 404–6).

[23] See Charles S. Peirce, 'From "On the Algebra of Logic: A Contribution to the Philosophy of Notation"', *The Essential Peirce: Selected Philosophical Writings*, vol. I: *1867–1893*, ed. Nathan Hauser and Christian Kloesel (Bloomington: Indiana University Press, 1992), 226–8.

[24] Information derived from The Royal Signals Museum, Blandford Camp, Blandford Forum, Dorset DT11 8RH.

[25] See Juliet Gardiner, *The Animals' War: Animals in Wartime from the First World War to the Present Day* (London: Portrait in association with the Imperial War Museum, 2006).

can cross no-man's-land at 'pleasure'.[26] Whether technological or animal, means of communication must be quick, difficult for the enemy to detect, capable of covering significant distances, function reliably and keep data secure.

A cluster of desiderata in war reporting therefore emerges. Some of the qualities mentioned – attributes such as swiftness and reliability – relate primarily to the efficient carriage of the information. Others – attributes such as noticeability, authoritativeness, accountability and credibility – relate primarily to its smooth reception. There is, though, a good deal of overlap: efficient carriage can itself contribute to an impression of authoritativeness and accountability which renders data more palatable. As already stated, the 'war reporter' considered in this chapter does not necessarily personally carry news directly from the battlefield for delivery in real time;[27] the term is intended to cover all those who represent conflict. Nonetheless, the traits of the courier provide tropes which are used to characterise all kinds of representation. There follows an exploration of the motifs of efficient carriage followed by those of smooth reception.

As the scenes with Bolkonsky demonstrate, the war reporter's trajectory typically involves a commission; an arduous journey; an arrival; and a set of interactions incorporating a delivery. Each of these stages offers opportunities to endow the figure with attributes such as courage, resourcefulness, stamina and persistence. This not only underscores the importance and freshness of the data to be delivered but also elevates the courier's moral standing in the text, conferring on him or her a special aura. The phenomenon can be observed in several messenger-poems by Longfellow and Browning: the former's 'Paul Revere's Ride' (1860)[28] and the latter's 'Incident of the French Camp' (1842), 'How They Brought the Good News from Ghent to Aix' (1845) and 'Pheidippides' (1879).

'Paul Revere's Ride' is a messenger-poem which created, on the eve of the American Civil War, a national legend of endeavour and patriotism. The ballad's famous opening, taking as a reference point the first day of the American Revolution, simultaneously demands the recipients' attention ('*Listen*, my children') and, by raising a concern as to what may happen to

---

[26] Isaac Rosenberg, 'Break of Day in the Trenches' (1916), *The Poems and Plays of Isaac Rosenberg*, ed. Vivien Noakes (Oxford: Oxford University Press, 2004), 128.

[27] The figure nonetheless haunts meta-representations of war representation. As Jon Stallworthy writes, '[c]entral to the British mythology of the First World War is the figure of the poet who descends like Orpheus into the Underworld, like Dante into the Inferno, and comes back singing of what he has seen' (*Survivors' Songs*, 128).

[28] The Landlord's Tale from *Tales of a Wayside Inn* (1863).

the information when no one with first-hand experience of it remains alive to remember it, underlines the importance of onward transmission:

> Listen, my children, and you shall hear
> Of the midnight ride of Paul Revere,
> Of the eighteenth of April, in Seventy-five;
> Hardly a man is now alive
> Who remembers that famous day and year.[29]

The poem as a whole could not place greater emphasis on the importance of the messenger's task. A sequence of signals – given and received – interlaces the text: the 'lantern aloft in the belfry arch' which will indicate how the British are coming ('one, if by land, and two, if by sea'); Revere on the opposite shore 'ready to ride and spread the alarm'; the friend who 'wanders and watches with eager ears'; 'a glimmer, and then a gleam of light!'; 'a voice in the darkness, a knock at the door'.[30] Packed with aural and visual stimuli, this is a poem which insists upon constant sensory alertness from its reader. Revere's ride takes place when eyes and ears have been primed to watch and listen out for him; those waiting are apprised of the fact that the delivery of his message has required personal risk-taking and uncommon skill.

In building the legend of the ride, Longfellow strayed considerably from strict historical truth. Revere, a prominent Boston silversmith who had previously ridden to New York with news of the Boston Tea Party, was not the sole rider that night, but one of a number; the lantern signal in the Old North Church was from, not to, him; he did not ride into 'Concord town' but was captured by the British soon after passing through Lexington.[31] The thrust of these historical inaccuracies is to focus the spotlight on the single messenger, who is courageous ('a cry of defiance and not of fear'), thorough (he rides '[t]hrough every Middlesex village and farm'), 'impatient', 'impetuous' and 'eager'.[32] Barely alluding to the American victory in the Revolution – 'you know the rest' – Longfellow renders daring communications, with their combined ingredients of collaboration and individual heroism, an indispensable element in the republic's founding: 'the fate of a nation was riding that night'.[33] Having achieved maximum publicity for the perilousness of its delivery, the poem can claim

---

[29] Henry Wadsworth Longfellow, *Poems and Other Writings*, ed. J. D. McClatchy (New York: Library of America, 2000), 362.
[30] *Ibid.*, 364, 362, 363, 364, 365.
[31] See David Hackett Fischer, *Paul Revere's Ride* (Oxford: Oxford University Press, 1994), 331–2.
[32] Longfellow, *Poems*, 365, 362, 364.   [33] *Ibid.*, 365, 364.

with confidence an afterlife for Revere's message: his 'word . . . shall echo forevermore'.[34]

Browning's messenger-poems have similar focus on the demands of carriage and delivery. 'How They Brought the Good News from Ghent to Aix' features the 'stout galloper'[35] Roland, who outstays two other horses to enable his rider safely to relay the (unrevealed) good news. By accumulating, stanza by stanza, references to the qualities of endurance displayed by the 'horse without peer'[36] and by withholding the nature of the good tidings, Browning underscores the equine messenger's special status. This is a character of noteworthy courage and fortitude (not for nothing does the horse bear the name of a legendary hero) – attributes transferred by association to his rider. The final stanza does not disclose whether horse and rider will actually survive the journey: their ultimate fates are less important than their errand. In 'Incident of the French Camp' (1842) and 'Pheidippides' (1879), the expiry of the envoys immediately after delivering their messages removes any doubt about where the centre of interest lies. 'Incident of the French Camp' features another galloping figure – a boy who rides to tell Napoleon that the French have taken Ratisbon. It is notable that the young envoy has been shot in the chest, and also that, as he conveys word of the victory, 'so tight he kept his lips compressed, / Scarce any blood came through':[37] that his lips are clamped together paradoxically says more than any words he manages to enunciate. Able to exhibit first-hand experience of battle and great endurance, both in the ride and in the communication of his message, the boy dies 'smiling'.[38] That his mouth is more communicative when closed than open again focuses attention on his errand of carriage, the successful completion of which contrasts his courage with that of the passively waiting Napoleon.

In 'Pheidippides', three great messenger journeys – runs by a hemerodromes or professional runner – are featured.[39] Having returned to the Greek forces from Sparta, Pheidippides, 'the best runner of Greece',

[34] *Ibid.*, 365.
[35] Robert Browning, *The Poems*, ed. John Pettigrew, 2 vols. (New Haven: Yale University Press, 1981), vol. I, 395.
[36] *Ibid.*, 396.
[37] Robert Browning, *The Poems*, ed. John Pettigrew, 2 vols. (New Haven and London: Yale University Press, 1981), vol. II, 355.
[38] *Ibid.*, 356.
[39] Browning was 'the first to combine the Herodotus tradition of the race before Marathon and the vision of Pan, with the later story, told by Plutarch and Lucian, of the race after Marathon, and the dramatic death of the runner in delivering his message' (John W. Cunliffe, 'Browning and the Marathon Race', *PMLA* 24.1 (1909), 155, 157–8, 157–8); see Herodotus, *Histories* 6.105–6; Plutarch, *De Gloria Atheniensium* 347 (in *Moralia*); Lucian, *Pro Lapsu Inter Salutandum* 3.727–8.

rehearses the scene of his commission: 'Crowned with the myrtle, did you command me, Athens and you, / "Run Pheidippides, run and race, reach Sparta for aid!"'.[40] The great physical – superhuman, even (he runs like wildfire) – effort of his running is made clear:

> Ran and raced: like stubble, some field which a fire runs through,
> Was the space between city and city: two days, two nights did I burn
> Over the hills, under the dales, down pits and up peaks.[41]

The return run with the Spartans' prevaricatory reply involves an encounter with the god Pan, who advises the Greeks to 'laugh Persia to scorn', thereby inspiring Pheidippides to even greater swiftness: 'if I ran hitherto – / Be sure that, the rest of my journey, I ran no longer, but flew'.[42] With Pheidippides' extraordinary qualities of velocity, patriotism and eagerness established, the final run takes place. The character relates that Pan has promised him 'release / From the racer's toil'[43] as a reward for his efforts, and he looks forward, after fighting again in the Greek ranks, to a domestic life with wife and children. But having participated in the Battle of Marathon, he is urged to 'one race more', to take 'to Akropolis' the message '"Athens is saved, thank Pan"'.[44] He flings down his shield, a detail that draws attention to his combatant status,[45] then runs 'like fire once more' and, at Athens, manages to shout '"Rejoice, we conquer!"' before collapsing: 'Like wine through clay, / Joy in his blood bursting his heart, he died – the bliss!'.[46] The poem is not strictly specific as to the motive of this 'joy', leaving open the possibility that it is the opportunity to deliver the great tidings as much as the fact of victory or having participated in it which causes Pheidippides his 'bliss':

> He saw the land saved he had helped to save, and was suffered to tell
> Such tidings, yet never decline, but, gloriously as he began,
> So to end gloriously – once to shout, thereafter be mute.[47]

---

[40] Browning, *The Poems*, vol. II, 588, 585.   [41] *Ibid.*, 585.
[42] *Ibid.*, 587.   [43] *Ibid.*, 588.   [44] *Ibid.*, 588.
[45] Plutarch, one of Browning's sources for 'Pheidippides', would have approved of this detail: 'This man came as a self-sent messenger regarding a battle in which he himself had fought; but suppose that some goatherd or shepherd upon a hill or a height had been a distant spectator of the contest and had looked down upon that great event, too great for any tongue to tell, and had come to the city as a messenger, a man who had not felt a wound nor shed a drop of blood, and yet have insisted that he have such honours as Cynegeirus received, or Callimachus, or Polyzelus, because, forsooth, he had reported their deeds of valour, their wounds and death; would he not have been thought of surpassing impudence?' (Plutarch, *De Gloria Atheniensium* 347). The significance of first-hand experience is discussed in detail later in this chapter.
[46] Browning, *The Poems*, vol. II, 588.   [47] *Ibid.*, 588.

Pheidippides' glory appears to reside in the act of shouting the good news. The poem as a whole renders the messenger's role – not the commandant's – synonymous with extraordinary human qualities and achievement.

Focusing on the practical risks and difficulties involved in bringing news of war, Longfellow's and Browning's poems not only communicate that the information carried is important, up to date and securely transmitted but also render the reporter a cynosure. Paul Revere, Roland and his rider, the boy envoy and Pheidippides all possess the ability to make head-turning interventions, and this enhances the salience of their information, which in turn improves the chances of its acceptance. The special charge and status of the messenger/war reporter, who is both welcomed and warded off, feted and feared, is therefore a key element in successful data delivery. The motifs of smooth reception – examined next – suggest how *noticeability* can be achieved.

According to Jean Seaton, the modern television war correspondent is expected to be sombre, calm, clean, tidy and orderly – and to stand still.[48] Such qualities set the reporter apart: he or she is at once involved in war yet aloof from it, moving within an ambiguous space on its outskirts. Journalists in battle zones are now protected by the Geneva Conventions (and hence explicitly distinguished from combatants),[49] but the reporter has always enjoyed special status, as is evident in the sixth-century Welsh poem by Aneirin, 'The Gododdin', in which the singer notes his fate:

> Of all those who charged, after too much drink,
> But three won free through courage in strife,
> Aeron's two war-hounds and tough Cynon,
> And myself, soaked in blood, for my song's sake.[50]

Spared 'for his song's sake': while the reporter deserves safe passage to deliver his information, he or she is also likely to be blamed if the bearer of bad news. (This is especially true of the *parrhesiastes*: the figure who speaks candidly (discussed further below).) For this reason, in addition to the others, he or she must establish and maintain an aura of *singularity* that

---

[48] Seaton, *Carnage and the Media: The Making and Breaking of News About Violence* (London: Allen Lane, 2005), 188, 217.

[49] Protocols adopted in 1977 to the 1949 Geneva Conventions explicitly recognise journalists to be civilians and therefore due all the civilian (as opposed to military) protections. They therefore have an obligation to differentiate themselves from combatants by not wearing uniforms or openly carrying firearms. See Ingrid Detter Delupis, *The Law of War*, 2nd edn (Cambridge: Cambridge University Press, 2000), 323f.

[50] Aneirin, 'From "The Gododin"', trans. Joseph P. Clancy, in *The Oxford Book of War Poetry*, ed. Stallworthy, 17.

in turn confers untouchability, keeping the reporter intact. But by what means is singularity to be established?

As already noted, in concentrating upon the demands of commission and journey (to the extent of straying considerably from the historical facts), Longfellow and Browning invest their war reporters with exceptional qualities. Together with the manner of data delivery, these qualities render the imparted information noticeable, and the instant death of the messenger is the ultimate attention-drawing event. In other versions of the reporting figure, singularity is signalled not so much by the heroic performance of perilous missions as by the construction of unorthodox personae. George Gascoigne (1534/5?–77), lawyer, courtier and Member of Parliament, was jailed for debt in 1570 and joined Sir Humphrey Gilbert's military expedition to the Netherlands in order to escape his creditors and repair his fortunes.[51] Those who opposed his parliamentary candidacy described him as a 'notorious Ruffiaune and especiallie noted to be bothe a Spie, an Atheist and a Godlesse personne', 'a common Rymer and a deviser of slaunderous Pasquelles against divers personnes of greate callinge'.[52] Hard to ignore in real life, in his verse miscellany *The Posies* (1575) Gascoigne created a gamut of guises, including the persona of the Greene Knight, possessor of the suggestive 'peerlesse firelock peece'[53] and simultaneous prodigal penitent.[54] The point of these disguises and disappearances is that the reader must actively seek out the protean war reporter, a task likely to increase receptiveness to the information to be imparted. To similar effect, the eponymous hero of Defoe's *Memoirs of a Cavalier* advises the reader on a number of occasions that he is a remarkable individual. 'Some extraordinary Influence' affected his Birth; his father saw something 'in [his] Genius . . . which particularly pleased him'; indeed, his father 'loved . . . him above all the rest of his Children'.[55] His auspiciousness entitles the Cavalier at least to a hearing; his implicit claim is that his tale will be as noteworthy as his beginnings.

[51] G. W. Pigman III, 'George Gascoigne', in *The Oxford Dictionary of National Biography*, eds. H. C. G. Matthew and Brian Harrison, 60 vols. (Oxford: Oxford University Press, 2004), vol. XXI, 582, 583; C. T. Prouty, *George Gascoigne: Elizabethan Courtier, Soldier and Poet* (New York: Columbia University Press, 1942), 49.

[52] Quoted in William Hazlitt, 'Preface', in *The Complete Poems of George Gascoigne*, ed. William Hazlitt, 2 vols. (London: The Roxburghe Library, 1869), vol. I, xxi.

[53] George Gascoigne, 'The Complaint of the Greene Knight', *The Complete Works*, line 15.

[54] See Gillian Austen, 'The Literary Career of George Gascoigne: Studies in Self-Presentation', unpublished D.Phil. thesis, University of Oxford, 1997.

[55] Daniel Defoe, *Memoirs of a Cavalier, or A Military Journal of the Wars in Germany and the Wars in England from the Year 1632, to the Year 1648* (Oxford: Blackwell, 1974), 1, 2, 3.

Women are immediately singular when they enter the male-dominated war zone but, as carriers of information about conflict, they cannot count on an easy reception. The particular challenges faced by women seeking to represent war constitute a complex subject beyond the scope of this chapter and, indeed, this book as a whole, but some strands can be drawn out. There are few war reporters – male or female – as outstanding, in field and text, as Mary Seacole. Seacole, born in Jamaica in 1805, combined wanderlust, a fascination with war and a medical vocation. Her memoir, *Wonderful Adventures of Mrs Seacole in Many Lands*,[56] itself clamoured for attention: launched at an 'outrageous party' funded by Seacole's supporters, it was bound in 'bright boards of scarlet and yellow, with a swashbuckling sketch of Mary on the front'.[57] Its first pages record Seacole's 'longing to travel which will never leave me while I have health and vigour', her 'sympathy with what I have heard my friends call "the pomp, pride and circumstance of glorious war"' and her 'yearning for medical knowledge and practice which has never deserted me'.[58] Following her mother into the 'doctress' profession,[59] Seacole attended the Crimean War in the capacity of freelance nurse and sutler. To do so, she had to surmount various obstacles, including racial prejudice and the coolness of Florence Nightingale, who declared that recruiting her to her nursing service was 'absolutely out of the question'.[60] Rejected, insulted, but all the more determined, Seacole made her way to the Crimea 'upon my own responsibility and at my own cost'.[61]

Seacole's anxiety about her presence in the war zone rarely left her and throughout her memoirs she evinces a compulsion to justify her being there. Downplaying her own accomplishments through the use of litotes, she compensates by citing extensively the approbation expressed by those she nursed or impressed in the field.[62] The effect is twofold: to imply her closeness to the centre of the military (a factor discussed further below) and to claim attention for her account by revealing her own remarkableness. Believing her 'one and only claim to interest the public' to be her 'services to the brave British army in the Crimea', she makes constant reference to her medical expertise in order to establish both her right to be present in the field and her story's deservingness of an audience: 'I . . . longed to carry my busy (and the reader will not hesitate to add experienced) fingers

---

[56] Jane Robinson's theory is that Seacole dictated *Wonderful Adventures* to an editor, most likely W. J. Stewart (*Mary Seacole: The Charismatic Black Nurse Who Became a Heroine of the Crimea* (London: Constable & Robinson, 2005), 168).

[57] *Ibid.*, 176.   [58] Seacole, *Wonderful Adventures*, 13, 11, 12.   [59] *Ibid.*, 12.
[60] *Ibid.*, 180.   [61] *Ibid.*, 74.   [62] *Ibid.*, see particularly ch. 13.

where the sword or bullet had been busiest'; 'the grateful words and smile which rewarded me for binding up a wound or giving a cooling drink was a pleasure worth risking life for at any time'.[63]

Seacole's gender and ethnicity could have been disadvantages in the war zone, exposing her to charges that her presence was inappropriate or simply functioning as a convenient basis on which to ignore her. Instead, she turned them to her advantage through associating her femininity and race with an unthreatening concern for soldiers and an ability to comfort and heal. Throughout *Wonderful Adventures*, there are numerous allusions to both her gender and her ethnicity. The second sentence defines its author as 'a female, and a widow'; as the book progresses, she terms herself 'an unprotected female', 'the yellow woman whom no excuses could get rid of'.[64] Wounded soldiers call her 'mother'.[65] Seacole redeploys her femininity as a source of strength: a maternal, and hence reassuring, figure to the injured men, her prosopon of 'unprotected female' emphasises her independence and resourcefulness, rather than any vulnerability.[66] The fact of being a 'motherly yellow woman'[67] becomes a claim for special notice.

This, then, is a figure of remarkable strength of character and an avowed affinity for attending war: courageous, indefatigable, resourceful, sanguine, self-reliant and strong-minded ('the best term I can think of to express it being "judicious decisiveness"');[68] a born fighter. In a number of other ways, Seacole renders 'Mrs Seacole' a phenomenon. She refers to herself in the third person; she announces her arrival; she records the 'astonishment' that her physique and presence elicit.[69] She also quotes others' opinions, to the effect that they find her 'an amusing specimen', 'a highly intelligent woman', an 'excellent woman'.[70]

But having built a larger-than-life character, Seacole proceeds to send it up. *Wonderful Adventures* makes it quite clear that its author is fully aware of her own comic potential. This emerges in the account she gives of ascending the clayey bank at Gatun 'in a light blue dress, a white bonnet prettily trimmed, and an equally chaste shawl'; in her description of her 'well-filled-out, portly form'; in her confessed inability to load a pistol; in her having to 'embrace the earth' with 'very undignified and unladylike haste' whenever a shell falls.[71] Unconcerned with standing on her dignity, Seacole records

[63] *Ibid.*, 110, 70, 136.   [64] *Ibid.*, 11, 16, 40, 73.   [65] *Ibid.*, 112.

[66] Seacole's ungoverned peregrinations, combined with her resourcefulness, render her representative of the war reporter as a tactical consumer of the kind described by Michel de Certeau (see McLoughlin, *Martha Gellhorn*, 112 for further discussion).

[67] Seacole, *Wonderful Adventures*, 72.   [68] *Ibid.*, 71.   [69] *Ibid.*, 38, 74, 78.

[70] *Ibid.*, 173, 117.   [71] *Ibid.*, 20, 78, 100, 136.

the laughter that such exploits induce.[72] In painting a humorous picture of 'Mrs Seacole', Seacole partakes in a tradition of rendering the representation of war (or the one who represents it) comic, a tradition stretching from the *miles gloriosus* or braggart-soldier of Plautine comedy and later the *commedia dell'arte*[73] to Garry Trudeau's Roland Hedley in the comic strip *Doonesbury*, by way of *Tristram Shandy*'s running joke about Uncle Toby's unmentionable injury, sustained at the Siege of Namur, and the character's numerous abortive attempts to describe what happened;[74] the obstacles and lack of interest that turn Prince Andrei's mission into a farce; Mr Jingle and his bomphiologic assertions in *The Pickwick Papers* (1836–7);[75] Richard Harding Davis's claims of taking whole towns single-handedly during the Spanish-American War;[76] Evelyn Waugh's William Boot (*Scoop* (1948));[77] Ernest Hemingway's slyly self-sabotaging accounts of his actions as a war correspondent, including his liberation of the Paris Ritz;[78] and Private Cheeseman, the Welsh war correspondent with protruding teeth in the BBC's *Dad's Army*.

What this tradition demonstrates is that singularity and its attendant claim on being noticed need not be a matter of high seriousness. The

[72] *Ibid.*, 147.
[73] See Sheppard, 'Tongues of War', 199–202; Nick de Somogyi, *Shakespeare's Theatre of War* (Aldershot: Ashgate, 1998), 146; John Hale, 'Shakespeare and Warfare', in *William Shakespeare: His World, His Work, His Influence*, ed. John F. Andrews, 3 vols. (New York: Scribner's, 1985), vol. I, 87.
[74] 'As this was the principal attack of which my uncle Toby was an eye-witness at Namur . . . [he] was generally more eloquent and particular in his account of it; and the many perplexities he was in, arose out of the almost insurmountable difficulties he found in telling his story intelligibly, and giving such clear ideas of the differences and distinctions between the scarp and the counterscarp, – the glacis and the covered way, – the half-moon and ravelin, – as to make his company fully comprehend where and what he was about' (Laurence Sterne, *The Life and Opinions of Tristram Shandy* (London: Penguin, 1967), 103).
[75] Mr Jingle is immediately noticeable, being a shabbily attired individual with 'an indescribable air of jaunty impudence and perfect self-possession' (Charles Dickens, *The Pickwick Papers*, ed. James Kinsley (Oxford: Clarendon, 1986), 13). On being informed that Mr Snodgrass has a 'strong poetic turn', he claims to have composed an epic 'on the spot' at the July Revolution:

"You were present at that glorious scene, sir?" said Mr. Snodgrass.
"Present! I think I was; fired a musket, – fired with an idea – rushed into wine shop – wrote it down – back again – whiz, bang – another idea – wine shop again – pen and ink – back again – cut and slash – noble time, Sir." (*Ibid.*, 17)

A footnote alerts the reader that this is 'a remarkable instance of the prophetic force of Mr Jingle's imagination; this dialogue occurring in the year 1827, and the Revolution in 1830' (*ibid.*).
[76] Richard Harding Davis, *Notes of a War Correspondent* (New York: Scribner's, 1911), 10.
[77] Boot notably queries whether his assignment as war correspondent to Ismaelia 'Mightn't be rather dangerous?' and is informed: 'You'll be surprised to find how far the war correspondents keep from the fighting. Why Hitchcock reported the whole Abyssinia campaign from Asmara and gave us some of the most colourful, eye-witness stuff we ever printed' (Evelyn Waugh, *Scoop: A Novel About Journalists* (London: Chapman and Hall, 1948), 32).
[78] See Hemingway, *Selected Letters*, 634. For a discussion of Hemingway as war correspondent, see McLoughlin, *Martha Gellhorn*, 138–45.

satirising of the war reporter figure may reflect weakening public confidence in the possibility of conveying significant information about conflict, whether due to its hugeness, to the problems inherent in the notions of accuracy or to the limitations of a single individual. One technique of successfully delivering data about war might therefore be to *down*play the skills of the reporter. While incompetence potentially attracts as much attention as mastery, it has the happy side-effect of lowering expectations to a more realistic level.

This approach to war reporting is adopted in W. H. Auden and Christopher Isherwood's *Journey to a War* (1939).[79] The Foreword explains that the pair became correspondents accidentally: having been commissioned to write 'a travel book about the East', they decided to go to China because of the outbreak of the Sino-Japanese War.[80] This casual beginning sets a tone of dilettantish amateurism, perpetuated by the two carrying on like a comedic double-act. After a 'dream-like, unreal' arrival,[81] they exhibit bumbling ineptness as war journalists. Isherwood feels an 'irresponsible, school-boyish' excitement as the adventure is about to start but soon experiences anxiety under fire and has to be reassured like a 'slightly nervous child about a thunderstorm'.[82] They witness only one air-raid. Scenes in a hospital make Isherwood vomit.[83] The pair are unfortunately conspicuous (indeed, at one point they are naïve enough to walk on a ridge 'like brilliantly illuminated targets') and have an ambivalent relationship with the 'field', always returning to 'Number One House' for lunch.[84] Indeed, since their high profile makes them 'tiresomely notorious foreigners'[85] to the military, their actual contribution is to increase the danger to which the Chinese are exposed and add to their responsibilities. Of this, Isherwood feels 'rather ashamed'.[86] The analogies they draw are within comfortably familiar parameters: Canton is like the 'Severn Valley'; Paak Hok Tang like 'one of the pleasanter London suburbs'; the countryside around Kiukiang 'as green as Devonshire'.[87] Only able to comprehend China in terms of England, the pair are, as Auden put it in sonnet XIV, 'as remote as plants'.[88] When their progress is stymied at Kiukiang through lack of trains, Isherwood comments that, 'if we had been true poets . . . we should, no doubt, have laughed gaily and wandered off, hand in hand, into the fields to make

---

[79] *Journey to a War* comprises prefatory poems by Auden; a 'travel-diary' by Isherwood titled 'In Time of War'; a sonnet sequence by Auden (later published as 'Sonnets from China' in *Collected Shorter Poems 1927–1957* (1966)); and a verse 'Commentary' by Auden. 'Second Thoughts', a paragraph by each of the writers, was added in the 1973 edition.

[80] W. H. Auden and Christopher Isherwood, *Journey to a War* (London: Faber, 1973), 6.

[81] *Ibid.*, 18.   [82] *Ibid.*, 19, 23.   [83] *Ibid.*, 83.   [84] *Ibid.*, 103, 242.

[85] *Ibid.*, 212.   [86] *Ibid.*, 182, 212.   [87] *Ibid.*, 20, 21, 175.   [88] *Ibid.*, 254.

each other crowns of wild flowers'.[89] The image of the garlanded bards never quite leaves the account, potentially undermining any claims the pair may have had to being serious correspondents.

Auden and Isherwood certainly emerge as singular, but does the general picture of their ineptitude vitiate their claims on the reader's attention? This depends on what their representation of slapstick amateurism purports to convey. In parodying the professional correspondents they encounter, they are exposing the limitations of the uninformed, temporary observer. The pair regard an unnamed young American journalist 'thrilled and goggling... from a respectful distance, with awe'.[90] To the assembled hacks, Isherwood hastens to clarify his and Auden's status:

> The old hands viewed us with inquisitively hostile eyes. We hastened to explain that we were not real journalists, but mere trippers, who had come to China to write a book.[91]

But this raises the awkward question of what the 'real journalists' might be able to achieve. Insisting on their status as 'ignorant English civilian[s]'[92] and their inability properly to appreciate the military significance of what they see, the two poets question the assumptions that correspondents can gain a meaningful understanding of the conflict or the country or, indeed, that bringing news of war is ever reliable or informative. 'Here war is harmless as a monument', wrote Auden in Sonnet XII of 'In Time of War':

> A telephone is talking to a man;
> Flags on a map declare that troops were sent;
> A boy brings milk in bowls.[93]

The remark encapsulates the outlook of the whole of *Journey to a War*: an understanding, and a comic rendering, of the difficulties of conveying so vast a subject. What the two saw in China was too huge, too incomprehensible, too *foreign* to afford a platform from which to preach. The moment when this is at its clearest is when the pair receive news of the Austrian Anschluss: 'all the guns and bombs of the Japanese seem suddenly as harmless as gnats', wrote Isherwood.[94]

But the Japanese guns and bombs were not harmless and Auden and Isherwood's account is thrown into relief by comparison with that of another observer and correspondent, Agnes Smedley. Auden and Isherwood visited Smedley in Hankow,[95] finding her to be 'really not unlike Bismarck'.[96] But

---

[89] *Ibid.*, 174.   [90] *Ibid.*, 20.   [91] *Ibid.*, 42.   [92] *Ibid.*, 106.   [93] *Ibid.*, 253.   [94] *Ibid.*, 49.
[95] See Ruth Price, *The Lives of Agnes Smedley* (Oxford: Oxford University Press, 2005), 326.
[96] Auden and Isherwood, *Journey to a War*, 50.

their sending up the august figure falls flat, if what is intended is to suggest the impossibility of acquiring and transmitting a meaningful understanding of the Sino-Japanese War. Smedley herself was fully conversant with the difficulties involved in war correspondence:

Over this problem of the Chinese wounded I used to torture myself through endless nights. Should I write the truth, or should I throw a romantic veil over China's heroism? Sometimes I would say to myself: 'Listen! If you write the facts, the neat little souls of Americans and Englishmen will be so shocked that they will give no money at all for relief; they will just go to another movie in which Love solves everything.'

Then I would answer myself: 'Think of the wounded soldiers. Did any government in history ever take one step forward unless under the lash of public criticism?'[97]

China Correspondent (1943) follows her second instinct, providing detailed, graphic and harrowing depictions of war and its casualties, including those in the hospital wards that made Isherwood vomit. To singularity, Smedley could add credentials based on extensive first-hand experience and corresponding depth of insight. Auden and Isherwood's incompetence and ignorance confirm the importance of these attributes, if only by functioning as disclaimers regarding the quality of their data. That the tropes of singularity convey so much about the nature of information about war requires caution in their deployment. While singularity is indispensable to the reporting figure, therefore, it must be sensitively judged. To stand out to the point of seeming unreliable no longer ensures smooth communication of the message about war but obscures and distorts that message, aborting its delivery.[98]

If singularity, properly judged, secures an audience, what qualities increase the likelihood of the data, once heard, being accepted (acceptance might comprise retention and/or onward transmission of the information, a change in the recipient's outlook as a result of learning it, taking action consequent upon it)? The key elements are *authoritativeness* and *credibility*.

---

[97] Agnes Smedley, *China Correspondent* (London: Pandora Press, 1984), 153.

[98] In consequence, the war reporter can become a pariah figure, unwelcome both as gatherer and imparter of information about conflict. The character of the 'Writer' in Gregory Burke's 2007 play *Black Watch* occupies this position. In a play in which the demarcation between insiders (members of the regiment) and outsiders is crucial, the Writer is certainly singular – but by virtue of being a pathetic, diffident and linguistically differentiated figure. Indeed, the troops whom he tries to interview bully him, questioning his masculinity ('He looks like a poof' (*Black Watch* (London: Faber and Faber, 2007), 5)), commenting explicitly on his lack of war experience ('Go tay fucking Baghdad if you want tay ken what it's like' (*ibid.*, 7)) and, when he tries to express understanding, simply refuting him ('You dinnay' (*ibid.*, 60, 61)). Standing out does not help this war reporter.

The former guarantees the recipient that the information can be trusted, the latter ensures that it is believed, but the two overlap as reliability itself contributes to believability.

One source of authoritativeness is the data itself, in a complex interplay with the manner of its delivery. The unadorned truth (complex though that is as a concept) delivered frankly and with attention drawn to the frankness conveys a kind of auto-reliability. The trope of candid speaking – and asking forgiveness for so speaking – is parrhesia,[99] about which Foucault writes:

[P]arrhesia is a kind of verbal activity where the speaker has a specific relation to truth through frankness, a certain relationship to his own life through danger, a certain type of relation to himself or other people through criticism (self-criticism or criticism of other people), and a specific relation to moral law through freedom and duty. More precisely, parrhesia is a verbal activity in which a speaker expresses his personal relationship to truth, and risks his life because he recognizes truth-telling as a duty to improve or help other people (as well as himself).[100]

Prince Andrei Bolkonsky is given so little opportunity to deliver his message that he is unable even to begin to make claims about its epistemological status, but Bilibin, in giving his own news to Bolkonsky about the French treachery at the Tabor bridge, is obliged to insist that he is 'not jesting': 'Nothing could be truer or more melancholy'.[101] (Further examples of parrhesia from Shakespeare's war reporting scenes are given below.) Another means of conveying the trustworthiness of an account is by petitioning an external authority. By Homer's time, it was already a convention that the poet had been placed by his Muse in a position to tell the audience everything[102] and modern-day journalism also utilises quasi-supernatural practices, drawing, as Jean Seaton has it, on an 'evangelical tradition of revealed truth' in which affliction has its own authority and the reporting figure acts as a kind of intercessor.[103] In both these cases, accountability is diverted from the reporter to an unimpeachable outside authority. When such an authority is (as is usually the case) unavailable, its substitute has traditionally been the crucial attribute of *ethos*. 'Ethos', an Aristotelian term,

---

[99] Parrhesia has affinities with testimony, as analysed by Dori Laub and Shoshana Felman: 'To testify – to *vow to tell*, to *promise* and *produce* one's own speech as material evidence for truth – is to accomplish a *speech act*, rather than to simply formulate a statement' (*Testimony: Crises of Witnessing in Literature, Psychoanalysis, and History* (New York and London: Routledge, 1992), 5, original emphasis).

[100] Michel Foucault, *Fearless Speech*, ed. Joseph Pearson (Los Angeles: Semiotext(e), 2001), 19–20.

[101] Tolstoy, *War and Peace*, 171.

[102] E. V. Rieu, 'Introduction', *The Iliad*, trans. E. V. Rieu (Harmondsworth: Penguin, 1983), xi.

[103] Seaton, *Carnage and the Media*, 88, 97.

signifies the persuasive appeal that resides in character:[104] an amalgam of traits pointing to authoritativeness, trustworthiness and accountability of which the most prominent is good breeding. Reference to this last quality begins with Diomedes in the *Iliad* who bases his very claim to be heard on his noble lineage (14.113–14, 126–7). Hence, in the second paragraph of Defoe's *Memoirs of a Cavalier*, the protagonist states that 'My Father was a Gentleman of a very plentiful Fortune, having an Estate of about 5000 Pounds *per Annum*, of a Family nearly allied to several of the principal Nobility, and lived about six Miles from the Town',[105] data intended to function not only as the Cavalier's pedigree, but also that of his text. But breeding is a trivial factor when compared with another source of ethos. In his war-reporting scenes, Shakespeare explicitly makes the comparison. It is to a close scrutiny of these scenes – and the irresistible claims of first-hand experience – that this chapter now turns.

The many scenes of battle reporting in drama spring from the simple practical difficulty of enacting large-scale warfare on stage.[106] News-bearers (or 'posts') necessarily appear apart from the fighting, creating a lacuna in time and space which immediately historicises their accounts. Shakespeare's scenes of war reportage focus on the tripartite interaction between envoy, news and recipient(s), with a consequent emphasis on arrival and delivery. This emphasis renders two questions crucial: *why should I believe what you tell me?* and *how can I make you believe me?*

With a few exceptions (Mountjoy in *Henry V*, for example: 'so for my king and master; so much my office' (3.6.131)), Shakespeare's war reporters are more than couriers who merely reproduce messages verbatim. Rather, they participate in complex engagements with other characters and provoke a wide range of responses. Their function has been characterised as dramatic 'interruption',[107] but 'interruption' suggests an intervention that temporarily suspends a scene without changing it. Instead, to use a musical analogy, Shakespeare's messengers function more like 'accidentals' who 'modulate' the scenes they infiltrate, irrevocably altering their timbre, tone and dynamic by means of abrupt entries, attention-distracting stratagems and the delivery of important data. The arrival of the messenger Chatillon at an emotionally charged moment in *King John*, for example, converts a warm scene of fealty-swearing into a frosty reception: 'We coldly pause for thee' (2.1.53).

---

[104] See Sheppard, 'Tongues of War', 35.   [105] Defoe, *Memoirs*, colophon, 1.
[106] See Irene J. F. De Jong, *Narrative in Drama: The Art of the Euripidean Messenger-Speech* (Leiden: E. J. Brill, 1991), 117; Sheppard, 'Tongues of War', 59.
[107] Sheppard, 'Tongues of War', 186.

Typically, Shakespeare's dramatisation of war reporting begins with the envoy hailing the recipient(s) of his communication. *1 Henry VI* opens with several English lords mourning the death of Henry V. As Bedford invokes the late king's ghost to protect the realm, he is interrupted mid-line by a messenger, who announces:

> My honourable lords, health to you all!
> Sad tidings bring I to you out of France,
> Of loss, of slaughter and discomfiture.
>
> (1.1.57–9)

The greeting 'my honourable lords, health to you all' engages the envoy's interlocutors, acknowledges their status, indicates goodwill and creates the beginnings of a relationship of trust. The next two lines prepare the recipients for what is to come by alerting them to the gravity of the tidings through foreshadowing or 'implicit prolepsis'.[108] These mechanisms are also used extensively in *Richard II* in the scene in which Salisbury and Scroop inform the king of his devastating losses. Salisbury temporarily disarms Richard with his opening words: 'discomfort guides my tongue, / And bids me speak of nothing but despair' (3.2.65–6). But when it is Scroop's turn to give the bad tidings, Richard must be steeled once more: 'More health and happiness betide my liege / Than can my care-tuned tongue deliver him' (3.2.91–2). Richard professes himself ready – 'mine ear is open, and my heart prepared' (3.2.93) – but the onslaught from Scroop is relentless. Thrice more must he steady the king as bad news becomes the prelude to worse: 'I play the torturer by small and small / To lengthen out the worst that must be spoken' (3.2.198–9). These prolepses are examples of parrhesia: by suggesting that the news he is about to impart is negative, Scroop effectively requests permission to reveal it. But as parrhesiastes, Scroop does not cut such an elevated figure as Foucault's analysis (quoted above) implies: his concern is his own immediate wellbeing rather than any commitment to 'truth-telling as a duty'.

In some scenes, the recipient performs the task of preparation himself by anticipating bad tidings – often after observing the demeanour of the individual relaying them. 'What art thou whose heavy looks foretell / Some dreadful story hanging on thy tongue?' asks Richard of a hapless messenger in *3 Henry VI* (2.1.43–4). In the first scene of *2 Henry IV*, Northumberland, eager for news of the battle in which his son Hotspur is participating, remarks that 'every minute now / Should be the father of some stratagem'

---

[108] De Jong, *Narrative in Drama*, 46.

(1.1.7–8), creating an immediate expectation of a series of stop-presses. Bardolph having announced that he has 'certain news from Shrewsbury', Northumberland attempts to influence the communication in advance with his petition 'Good, an God will!' (1.1.13, 14). Later, observing Morton, he comments that 'this man's brow, like to a title-leaf, / Foretells the nature of a tragic volume . . . Thou tremblest; and the whiteness in thy cheek / Is apter than thy tongue to tell thy errand' (1.1.60–1, 78–9). The guessing and apotropaeic attempts to avert catastrophe by stifling its telling culminate in a desperate Northumberland unable either to hear or not to hear the news:

> Yet, for all this, say not that Percy's dead,
> I see a strange confession in thine eye,
> Thou shak'st thy head, and hold'st it fear or sin
> To speak a truth: if he be slain, say so.
> The tongue offends not that reports his death,
> And he doth sin that doth belie the dead,
> Not he which says the dead is not alive.
> Yet the first bringer of unwelcome news
> Hath but a losing office, and his tongue
> Sounds ever after as a sullen bell,
> Remembered tolling a departing friend.
>
> (1.1.93–103)

Immediately after this, Bardolph slips in, 'I cannot think, my lord, your son is dead' (1.1.104), an intervention which, by adding another swing to the 'is he / isn't he' pendulum, prolongs the suspense until the last possible moment and renders the true news, delivered by Morton, the graver.

Bardolph is an unreliable messenger, whose credentials are immediately, and successfully, challenged. When he delivers his erroneous report stating that Prince Harry has been 'slain outright', Hotspur victorious, Northumberland immediately questions, 'How is this deriv'd? / Saw you the field? came you from Shrewsbury?' (1.1.16, 23–4) (It is worth noting that the scene immediately follows the Prologue, in which Rumour has undermined conventional epistemology: 'I speak of peace, while covert enmity / Under the smile of safety wounds the world' (lines 9–10).) Such questions – *did you see it? were you there?* – lie at the heart of the war reporter's ethos. Bardolph, who has not seen the field but merely 'spake with one . . . that came from thence' (1.1.25), asserts the ethos of his source conventionally, by citing his high social standing: 'a gentleman well bred and of good name / That freely rend'red me these news for true' (1.1.25–7) ('good name' suggests both a title of rank and an unsullied reputation). In an attempt at epistemological one-upmanship, he then attacks the character of the source encountered by Northumberland's servant, Travers, dismissing him as 'some hilding person, that had stol'n the horse he rode on, and upon my life / Spoke at a venture'.[109] But what enhances the status of Travers's source's account is not his social standing but the fact that his horse is 'bloodied' and 'panting' and he himself wears 'arméd heels' (1.1.38, 45, 44) – indisputable signs of first-hand participation in the fray.[110] That the information passed on by Bardolph turns out to be worthless hearsay comes as no surprise to those in the audience who have just seen *1 Henry IV* and therefore witnessed Prince Harry slay Hotspur and Falstaff stab the corpse in the thigh for good measure (5.4.88, 129–30). In a scene throughout which successive instalments of news are delivered and contradicted, such superior knowledge on the part of the audience works to undermine confidence not only in Bardolph's capabilities as a bringer-of-messages but also in the epistemological premises on which he asserts those messages' validity. In a redefinition, rather than rejection, of the claims of ethos, the audience is assured that first-hand experience makes for more reliable witnessing than good breeding.

First-hand experience or autopsy is indeed the crucial ingredient of authority, legitimacy and credibility in war reporting.[111] The eye-witness offers the epistemological guarantee *you can believe it because I saw it happen*. This guarantee is a variation on the 'autobiographical pact' proposed by Philippe Lejeune in 1974, a pact signed by the autobiographer in the form of his or her name on the title page and warranting that the contents comprise a retrospective narrative made by a real person out of his or her own existence.[112] In the war reporter's case, the pact becomes embodied, its signature the various indications of the messenger's presence at war – and, just as Lejeune modified his position to claim that the autobiographer is not necessarily 'someone who speaks the truth about himself, but someone who says that he speaks it',[113] the tropes of autopsy should be regarded as constructions of presence and authority.[114]

---

[109] 1.1.57–8. A 'hilding person' is a good-for-nothing.
[110] Cf. 'What bloody man is that? He can report / As seemeth by his plight, of the revolt / The newest state' (*Macbeth* 1.2.1–3).
[111] The etymology of 'autopsy' includes both 'auto' and 'optic': its primary sense of 'seeing with one's own eyes, eye-witnessing; personal observation or inspection' (*OED* 1) has been superseded by the derived meaning of 'dissection of a dead body, so as to ascertain by actual inspection its internal structure, and *esp.* to find out the cause or seat of disease; post-mortem examination' (*OED* 2).
[112] Philippe Lejeune, *Le Pacte autobiographique* (Paris: Seuil, 1974), 14.
[113] Philippe Lejeune, *Les Brouillons de soi* (Paris: Seuil, 1998), 125.
[114] Nonetheless, the war reporter's autopsy pact is one of *uberrimae fides*, so that vitiating it through false claims is an act of extreme bad faith. The corollary of this is the inscribing of combat

The autopsy pact privileges what James Campbell calls 'combat gnosticism': 'a construction that gives us war experience as a kind of gnosis, a secret knowledge which only an initiated elite knows'.[115] Campbell describes the 'epistemological trap'[116] to which this construction gives rise:

[T]hey [combatant-poets] cannot truly inform an audience who lacks the experiential basis for understanding their work, and the only way an audience can acquire such a basis is to experience combat, at which point they are no longer the noncombatant audience the poetry assumes.[117]

Though Campbell is right to find fault with a critical tendency that erects a canon of war writing on the basis of combat knowledge, there is no getting round the fact that battle *is* a unique order of experience, able to confer a particular authority on those who have undergone and seek to represent it. (And, it should be said, experiences such as living as a civilian in a city under bombardment and war-caused bereavement, loss and displacement are also unique experiences, conferring similar authority.) Whether this authority results in more insightful, accurate or useful accounts of war is here irrelevant as well as undecidable:[118] what matters in the present context is the widespread perception by reporters and recipients of information about war that the signs of combat experience enhance their accounts.

---

*ag*nosticism in war texts, as, for example, Thomas Hardy does in his references to the unfamiliar in 'Drummer Hodge' (1899). The unglossed words 'karoo', 'kopje' and 'veldt' (Hardy, *The Complete Poetical Works*, 122) convey Hardy's lack of personal experience of the Boer Wars as much as the strangeness of South Africa to Hodge.

[115] James Campbell, 'Combat Gnosticism: The Ideology of First World War Criticism', *New Literary History* 30 (1999), 204.

[116] *Ibid.*, 210.   [117] *Ibid.*

[118] That the two orders of experience are qualitatively different cannot be doubted. By 1915, Freud was convinced of their qualitative psychological difference: 'A distinction should be made between two groups – those who themselves risk their lives in battle, and those who have stayed at home and have only to wait for the loss of one of their dear ones' (Sigmund Freud, 'Thoughts for the Times on War and Death', trans. under the supervision of Joan Rivière, *Collected Papers*, ed. Ernest Jones (London: The Hogarth Press / The Institute for Psycho-Analysis, 1950), 291) (a generation later, the lives of those staying at home were also at risk). But this is not the same as saying that representations by the former group should be privileged over those by the latter. Indeed, there is support for the view that the combatant's viewpoint is flawed as participation in battle can distort the senses and preclude a synoptic account: as Robert Graves remarked in a letter to the *Times Literary Supplement* on 26 June 1930, 'what is meant by the *truthfulness* of war books? . . . I would even paradoxically say that the memoirs of a man who went through some of the worst experiences of trench warfare are not truthful if they do not contain a high proportion of falsities. High explosive barrages will make a temporary liar or visionary of anyone' (Robert Graves, 'The Garlands Wither', *The Times Literary Supplement* (26 June 1930), 534). On the implications for women war writers of combat gnosticism, see Susan Schweik, 'Writing War Poetry Like a Woman', *Critical Inquiry* 13.3 (1987), 532–56: particularly 534, 540, 541. For a fuller discussion of the issues, see McLoughlin, *Martha Gellhorn*, 95–101.

The tropes of autopsy, then, are the war reporter's ultimate credentials. Hence, at the start of the set of scenes in which Bolkonsky delivers his message, his own combat experience is explicitly adverted to: 'Prince Andrei during the battle had been in attendance on the Austrian general Schmidt, who was killed in action. He himself had had his horse wounded under him and his hand slightly grazed by a bullet.'[119] In George Gascoigne's motto, 'Tam Marti, quam Mercurio' ('as much for Mars as Mercury'),[120] the warrior and the messenger are perfectly aligned. References to experience – and the lack of it – figure prominently in Gascoigne's *The Fruites of Warre*, creating dialectical tension. The colophon states that the work is 'written upon this Theame, Dulce Bellum inexpertis', a phrase loosely translated as 'war is sweet to those who know nothing about it'. *The Fruites of Warre*'s paratexts give notice that the work was 'written by peecemeale at sundrye tymes, as the Aucthour had vacant leysures from service' (colophon), 'written by stelth at such times as we loytered from service' (dedication). This, then, is the product of lulls in action, temporally and spatially surrounded by battle.

Yet, curiously, the poem proper opens with a statement of lack of combat experience, with the narrator disclaiming any personal knowledge of war:

> To write of Warre and wot not what it is,
> Nor ever yet could march where Warre was made,
> May well be thought a worke begonne amis,
> A rash attempt in worthlesse verse to wade:
> To tell the triall, knowing not the trade.
> [...]
> And herewithal I cannot but confesse,
> Howe unexpert I am in feates of warre:
> For more than writing doth the same expresse,
> I may not boast of any cruell iarre,
> Nor vaunt to see full valiant facts from farre;
> I have nor bene in Turkie, Denmarke, Greece,
> Ne yet in Colch to winne a Golden fleece.[121]

This series of apparent self-disqualifications unsettles the reader, who is hardly consoled by the speaker's reassurance that 'nathelesse I some what read in writte / Of high exploits by Martiall men ydone'.[122] But this must suffice for the majority of the poem, until the rhetorical trick is revealed:

---

[119] Tolstoy, *War and Peace*, 171.   [120] Gascoigne, *The Complete Works*, 196.
[121] *Ibid.*, lines 1–5, 8–14.   [122] *Ibid.*, line 16.

Therefore (say some) how fonde a foole is he,
That takes in hande to write of worthy warre,
Which never yet hath come in any iarre?
No iarre (good sir?) yes, yes, and many iarres,
For though my penne of curtesie did putte
A difference twixt broyles and bloudie warres,
Yet have I shot at maister Bellums butte,
And throwen his ball, although I toucht no tutte:
I have percase as deeply dealt the dole,
As he that hit the marke and gat the gole.[123]

Raising and then answering an imaginary objection (the anthypophora trope), Gascoigne converts his battle inexperience into experience by collapsing the semantic distinction between 'broyles' and 'warres' (the opposite linguistic sleight-of-hand is employed today when governments resort to various euphemisms to avoid the term 'war' and its consequences in international law). The succeeding stanzas detail Gascoigne's participation in battles at Flushing, Flanders, Bruges, Aardenburgh, Tergoes, Zeeland, Holland, Waterland and Ramykins. The poem's pay-off, therefore, is that experience *does* uniquely qualify the speaker to pronounce on war – and, for its time, this was unusual. According to C. T. Prouty, the practice of writing verse about personal experiences – rather than about mythical adventures, in the tradition of existing martial literature – was inaugurated by Gascoigne in *The Fruites of Warre*.[124]

By Daniel Defoe's time, as Michael McKeon explains, 'claims to historicity had . . . become far more elaborate, exploiting techniques of authentication'.[125] Such techniques, adopted from travel narratives, included invocations of the authority of 'original documentation'; citations of confirmatory evidence; prioritising eye-witness over hearsay reports; and plainness of style.[126] The premise of *Memoirs of a Cavalier*, according to the title page, is that the work comprises the manuscript of a 'military journal' of the Thirty Years' War and English Civil War written 'by an *English* Gentleman, who served first in the Army of *Gustavus Adolphus*, the glorious King of *Sweden*, till his Death; and after that, in the Royal Army of King *Charles* the First, from the Beginning of the Rebellion, to the End of that War'.[127] The Preface claims that the manuscript of the body of the work (the memoirs) was 'long ago found by great Accident, among other valuable Papers in the Closet of an eminent publick Minister', accompanied by

---

[123] *Ibid.*, lines 649–58. [124] Prouty, *George Gascoigne*, 228–9.
[125] Michael McKeon, *The Origins of the English Novel 1600–1740* (London: Radius, 1988), 47.
[126] *Ibid.*, 108. [127] Defoe, *Memoirs*, iii.

an anonymous note saying that it was 'got . . . as Plunder, at, or after, the Fight at Worcester'.[128] According to his bibliographers, Defoe did claim on more than one occasion to have in his possession a manuscript by an English gentleman who had served under Gustavus Adolphus.[129] Other scholars suggest that the memoirs themselves are the work of Defoe, who reconstructed data from a number of written sources 'to create the illusion of a personal account';[130] in this regard, John Mullan points out that many eighteenth-century works of fiction present themselves as fortunately dis-covered manuscripts and that all Defoe's novels are fabrications of personal histories.[131]

It is most likely, therefore, that *Memoirs* is a fictional work by Defoe, liberally adorned with truth tropes to increase its credibility. The extraordi-nary Preface is peppered with words relating to accountability: 'reputation' (which, in 1720, could mean 'high reputation'); 'sanction' (authorisation); 'credit' (good name). Defoe makes liberal use of techniques that convey the fact of witnessing. The Cavalier constantly adverts to the link between par-ticipation and accurate reporting: 'I can be more particular in it than other Accounts, having been an Eye-witness to every part of it', he remarks[132] (the word 'particular', in its eighteenth-century sense, signifies 'precise' and 'specific'). Use of the present tense casts a clear light on the battle scenes. Descriptions are detailed, technical, tactical; numbers, troop movements, manoeuvres and formations are carefully recorded.[133]

In the Preface, Defoe claims specifically that 'all the Histories of the Times' give 'sufficient Sanction' to the 'Actions here mentioned' but that 'admirable Manner of relating them' adds 'Lustre, as well to the Accounts themselves, as to the Person who was the Actor'.[134] In the course of this privileging of experience over established authority, certain further nuances creep into the accreditation process. The 'Soldierly Stile' is a bonus not

---

[128] *Ibid.*, vii, viii.
[129] P. N. Furbank and W. R. Owens, *A Critical Bibliography of Daniel Defoe* (London: Pickering & Chatto, 1998), 194.
[130] J. R. Hammond, *A Defoe Companion* (Basingstoke: Macmillan, 1993), 80.
[131] John Mullan, 'Introduction', in Daniel Defoe, *Memoirs of a Cavalier, or A Military Journal of the Wars in Germany and the Wars in England from the Year 1632, to the Year 1648*, ed. James T. Boulton (Oxford: Oxford University Press, 1991), vii, viii.
[132] Defoe, *Memoirs* (1974 edn), 95.
[133] This would have earned the approval of Thomas Blundeville, who believed that the information historians should give about war must include 'how the hoste was ordered in marching through the Countries in being incamped, in skirmuching, in fighting battels, eyther in playne field, or in place strongly trenched' (*The True Order and Methods of Wryting and Reading Hysteries* (London: William Seres, 1574), CIr; quoted in Sheppard, 'Tongues of War', 4).
[134] Defoe, *Memoirs* (1974 edn), vii.

to be found in conventional histories, but it also has the effect of making seem 'impossible any Thing, but the very Person who was present in every Action here related, could be the Relator of them'.[135] The logic of this is that it is the work itself which confirms the authenticity of the work, but this self-evident stylistic persuasiveness is founded on veterancy. It is the combatant credentials of the reporter which enhance the believability and hence acceptability of the account.

The tropes of autopsy continue to be indispensable to war reportage. In present-day TV news reports from conflict zones, it is conventional to show the reporter in the picture, a practice originating in early silent newsreels in which the presence of such figures proved that library footage was not being used.[136] 'Being there' can even acquire quasi-mystical significance, with the figure of the war reporter providing apotropaeic protection, as Allan and Zelizer note:

> Being there suggests that the violence, devastation, suffering, and death that inevitably constitute war's underside will somehow be rendered different – more amenable to response and perhaps less likely to occur – just because journalists are somewhere nearby.[137]

But, like singularity, autopsy has its pitfalls: it is possible to get *too* close. The culmination of first-hand experience is the phenomenon of embedding.[138] For the *Der Spiegel* correspondent Carolin Emcke, embedding makes critical reporting 'nearly impossible', an insight she gained when realising that she was willing the side protecting her to kill.[139] As this demonstrates, partiality – even emotional involvement – can quickly overtake the war reporter, as Defoe's Cavalier discovers:

> I had been used enough to Blood, and to see the Destruction of People, sacking of Towns, and plundering of the Country; yet 'twas in Germany and among Strangers; but I found a strange secret and unacceptable Sadness upon my Spirits to see this acting in my own native Country.[140]

---

[135] *Ibid.*, viii.   [136] Seaton, *Carnage and the Media*, 187.

[137] Stuart Allan and Barbie Zelizer, 'Rules of Engagement: Journalism and War', in *Reporting War*, ed. Allan and Zelizer, 5.

[138] Though associated with the Second War in Iraq, during which 660 journalists were embedded with the American military and 150 with the British (Emily Nelson and Matthew Rose, 'Media Reassess Risks to Reporters in Iraq', *The Wall Street Journal*, 9 April 2003, sec. Marketplace, B1), the practice can be traced in earlier conflicts: Agnes Smedley, for example, travelled with the Eighth Route Army in China during the Sino-Japanese War, referring to its members in her account of the experience as 'my beloved brothers and comrades' (*China Fights Back: An American Woman with the Eighth Route Army* (London: Victor Gollancz, 1938), 5). See further McLoughlin, *Martha Gellhorn*, 96–7.

[139] Emcke, *Echoes of Violence*, 292.   [140] Defoe, *Memoirs* (1974 edn), 184.

Proximity to the fighting action can lead the war reporter to question his or her own purpose. The First World War artist William Orpen came to feel like 'a mere looker-on',[141] while Augustus John described the experience as being 'a fish out of water . . . wondering who I am'.[142]

As these remarks indicate, the difficult question raised by presence in warfare concerns the usefulness of representation, an ongoing issue that becomes particularly acute in the midst of killing and dying. A written account or painting or photograph or film is evidence of what is happening in war but also a record of the fact that the writer, painter, photographer or film-maker did not stop to intervene or contribute humanitarian assistance.[143] (In this context, Prince Andrei's decision to interrupt his mission and hand out gold to the wounded soldiers he encounters en route subtly questions the worth of his own envoy assignment.) In a complex paragraph, Mary Seacole makes the point:

> Just as a spectator seeing one of the battles from a hill, as I did the Tchernaya, knows more about it than the combatant in the valley below, who only thinks of the enemy whom it is his immediate duty to repel; so you, through the valuable aid of the cleverest man in the whole camp [William Howard Russell, legendary *Times* war correspondent], read in the *Times'* columns the details of that great campaign, while we, the actors in it, had enough to do to discharge our own duties well, and rarely concerned ourselves in what seemed of such importance for you.[144]

While acknowledging Russell's 'cleverness' and even conceding that the spectator's view may be better informed than the combatant's, Seacole simultaneously insists on the distinction between observer and 'actor', a distinction reinforced by her constant references to her own usefulness and her approval of the fact that Russell did find time 'even in his busiest moments, to lend a helping hand to the wounded'.[145] 'The burden of the witness', according to Carolin Emcke, is 'to remain with a feeling of failure, of emptiness.'[146] Failure may be experienced as the realisation that no account can completely convey conflict, but it may also be felt as practical impotence; the inability to make a difference; a sense of worthlessness beside those who actually fight.

---

[141] William Orpen, *An Onlooker in France* (London: Williams and Norgate, 1921), v; quoted in Sue Malvern, *Modern Art, Britain and the Great War: Witnessing, Testimony and Remembrance* (New Haven and London: Yale University Press, 2004), 91.

[142] Augustus John, *Chiaroscuro: Fragments of Autobiography, First Series* (London: Jonathan Cape, 1952), 93; quoted in Malvern, *Modern Art*, 91.

[143] See McLoughlin, *Martha Gellhorn*, 172–9, for further discussion.

[144] Seacole, *Wonderful Adventures*, 128–9.   [145] *Ibid.*, 129, 148.

[146] Emcke, *Echoes of Violence*, 4.

Beyond this, there are instances in which the war reporter actively becomes a nuisance, for example by requiring special attention in the manner of the young Cavalier or the amateurish Auden and Isherwood; by distorting the course of events through certain journalistic practices; by spreading pessimism;[147] by failing to be reliable;[148] even by attempting to stop the carnage, an intervention which, according to Joanna Bourke, causes disquiet as it exposes 'the possibility of humanity in hellish circumstances'.[149] *1 Henry IV* features a particularly noisome war reporter in the form of a certain lord, 'perfumed like a milliner', who attempts to interview Hotspur about the casualty figures:

> he made me mad
> To see him shine so brisk, and smell so sweet,
> And talk so like a waiting-gentlewoman
> Of guns, and drums, and wounds.
>
> (1.3.37, 54–6)

At this point, the war reporter occasions revulsion. But it is worth noting that Hotspur's contempt focuses particularly on the fact that the 'certain lord' has avoided combatant status himself (1.3.64–5). Autopsy, this indicates, means as much to those who entrust the representation of their war experiences to others as to those who are the recipients.

The reception of Prince Andrei Bolkonsky's news seems to him flawed. In a series of apostrophes,[150] he attempts to find approbatory or even sympathetic hearing but is greeted with 'extravagant politeness' on the part of the adjutant and a 'stupid smile' from the minister.[151] His own response to the information relayed to him by Bilibin – a fuzzy inability to process the data – is no better. In another scene in *War and Peace*, Kutuzov's reaction to Wolzogen's news of the routing is even more disparaging:

'How . . . how dare you! . . .' he shouted, choking and making a threatening gesture with his trembling arms. 'How dare you, sir, say that to *me*? You know nothing about it. Tell General Barclay from me that his information is wrong, and that the real course of the battle is better known to me, the commander-in-chief, than to him.'[152]

---

[147] Joanna Bourke, *An Intimate History of Killing: Face-to-Face Killing in Twentieth-Century Warfare* (London: Granta, 1999), 211.
[148] Seaton, *Carnage and the Media*, 34.   [149] Bourke, *An Intimate History of Killing*, 214.
[150] Apostrophe, in its strict sense, is, as here, the re-direction of a speech from one hearer to another (see J. Douglas Kneale, 'Romantic Aversions: Apostrophe Reconsidered', *English Literary History* 58 (Spring 1991), 141–65).
[151] Tolstoy, *War and Peace*, 173, 174.   [152] *Ibid.*, 959.

Even when the reporter of war carries his message efficiently, achieves singularity and possesses both an excellent pedigree and first-hand experience, there is no guarantee that reception will be smooth. From the recipient's point of view, the interaction may be equally disappointing. The term 'war story' has taken on the negative connotations of a potentially dismal and lengthy tale recounted by someone who has (usually metaphorically) been 'in the wars', a tale whose prospect makes captive listeners groan. Alongside logorrhoeic, Ancient Mariner-like war reporters who buttonhole the unfortunate recipients of their complaints, there exist others who inexplicably clam up. Though aware of his prurience, the narrator of Wordsworth's *The Prelude* cannot repress his curiosity on meeting a discharged soldier but, while the responses he receives to his questions may attest to the veteran's numbed state of trauma, they otherwise give little away:

> Nor could I, while we journeyed thus, forbear
> To turn from present hardships to the past,
> And speak of war, battle, and pestilence,
> Sprinkling this talk with questions, better spared,
> On what he might himself have seen or felt.
> He all the while was in demeanour calm,
> Concise in answer; solemn and sublime
> He might have seemed, but that in all he said
> There was a strange half-absence, as of one
> Knowing too well the importance of his theme,
> But feeling it no longer.[153]

Wordsworth's veteran is unwilling or unable to satisfy his interlocutor's appetite for gory details of conflict. Autopsy and singularity avail nothing if other requisites of war representation are not in place.

Failure to deliver makes for some of the bleakest scenes in war writing. Even the most impeccable credentials cannot guarantee successful conveyance. Nonetheless, they can at least enhance the chances of smooth carriage, delivery and acceptance of information about conflict, which is why they are still, as in Homer's time, eagerly sought and stated.

---

[153] Wordsworth, *The Fourteen-Book Prelude*, lines 435–45.

CHAPTER 2

Details

Fifty million people died as a result of the Second World War.[1] Fourteen million died as a result of the First,[2] including, on the first day of the Battle of the Somme, some twenty thousand British soldiers – the greatest loss ever suffered in a single day by the British Army and equivalent to all British losses in the Boer War.[3] In the Thirty Years' War, eight million people died; in the French Revolutionary and Napoleonic Wars, five million; in the Mongol invasions of the thirteenth century, thirty-five million. One and a half million people died at the Battle of Stalingrad; six thousand, six hundred and fifty-five at the Battle of Gettysburg; eleven thousand at the Battle of Flodden.[4]

Death on this scale is ungraspable. But there is more to take in. The Second World War spread over five continents and lasted six years. The Hundred Years' War lasted one hundred and sixteen years, the Peloponnesian War twenty-seven. The Napoleonic Wars stretched from Russia and the Ottoman Empire, through Europe, to Latin America and the Indian Ocean. War is colossal and chronic in its effects: it reconfigures nations, displaces peoples, disrupts families, razes cities, devastates landscapes. Huge quantities are its hallmark; indeed, the military defines and presents itself in

---

[1] Martin Gilbert, *Second World War* (London: Phoenix Press, 1989), 1.

[2] Martin Gilbert, *First World War* (London: HarperCollins, 1994), xv.

[3] David Cannadine, 'War and Death, Grief and Mourning in Modern Britain', in *Mirrors of Mortality: Studies in the Social History of Death*, ed. Joachim Whaley (London: Europa, 1981), 197.

[4] These figures are taken from the following sources, but the difficulties of calculation are great and other authorities give different statistics: Micheal Clodfelter, *Warfare and Armed Conflicts: A Statistical Reference to Casualty and Other Figures, 1500–2000* (Jefferson: McFarland, 2002), 5; Greg Cashman and Leonard C. Robinson, *An Introduction to the Causes of War: Patterns of Interstate Conflict from World War I to Iraq* (Lanham: Rowman & Littlefield, 2007), 2; E. L. Jones, *Growth Recurring: Economic Change in World History* (Ann Arbor: University of Michigan Press, 2000), 109; Michael S. Neiberg, *Warfare in World History* (London: Routledge, 2001), 74; Jeffrey C. Hall, *The Stand of the U. S. Army at Gettysburg* (Bloomington: Indiana University Press, 2003), 246; Jenny Wormald, 'Scotland: Reformation and Inflation', in *The Cambridge Historical Encyclopaedia of Great Britain and Ireland*, ed. Christopher Haigh (Cambridge: Cambridge University Press, 1990), 164.

the copiousness of its human legions[5] and material resources, as depicted in T. S. Eliot's 'Triumphal March' (1931) from his unfinished 'Coriolan' sequence:

> Stone, bronze, stone, steel, stone, oakleaves, horses' heels
> Over the paving
> And the flags. And the trumpets. And so many eagles.
> How many? Count them.
> [. . .]
> What comes first? Can you see? Tell us. It is
>
>   5,800,000 rifles and carbines,
>   102,000 machine guns,
>   28,000 trench mortars,
>   53,000 field and heavy guns,
>   I cannot tell how many projectiles, mines and fuses,
>   13,000 aeroplanes,
>   24,000 aeroplane engines,
>   50,000 ammunition waggons
>   now 55,000 army waggons,
>   11,000 field kitchens,
>   1,150 field bakeries.[6]

Surrounded by words, the numbers here are conspicuous, precisely aligned to march down the page *en bloc*.[7] Massed ranks are a show of force, but the most significant figures – quieting, disquieting – remain the vast numbers of the dead.

The challenge explored in this chapter is how to frame the huge scale of war for human comprehension. How can such large quantities (primarily of the slaughtered) be calibrated and represented? For, as Quintillian noted in *Institutio Oratoria*, simply to state the case is insufficient:

No doubt, simply to say 'the city was stormed' is to embrace everything implicit in such a disaster, but this brief communiqué, as it were, does not touch the emotions. If you expand everything which was implicit in the one word, there will come into view flames racing through houses and temples, the crash of falling

---

[5] The word 'legion' comes from 'legere' – to choose or levy (an army) (*OED* 1a). Its association with copiousness is derived from Mark 5.9: 'My name is Legion, for we are many.'

[6] T. S. Eliot, *The Complete Poems and Plays* (London: Faber, 1969), 127.

[7] The same effect is evident in Tom Paulin's reprise of 'Triumphal March', 'Chancellor Hitler's Speech' (2002). Here, though, the figures, now in their millions, refer not to a military parade but to German armaments destroyed under the Treaty of Versailles. Alluding to 'Triumphal March', Paulin recalibrates its scale (a technique described later in this chapter): the tens and hundreds of thousands in Eliot's poem are multiplied and on them will soon be heaped *further* destruction: 'the lives / and the cities that I / the modern Coriolanus / will soon lay waste' (*The Invasion Handbook* (London: Faber, 2002, 100)).

roofs, the single sound made up of many cries, the blind flight of some, others clinging to their dear ones in a last embrace, shrieks of children and women, the old men whom an unkind fate has allowed to live to see this day ... 'Sack of a city' does, as I said, comprise all these things; but to state the whole is less than to state all the parts. (8.3.67–70)

The flaw in this aesthetic is that expanding 'everything which was implicit in the one word' would, in most wars, be beyond the scope of enumeration. The attempt, though, is characteristic of the first of the two main modes of response to the problems of scale explored in this chapter. This mode, which might be called taliation[8] nominatim or the 'name-tallying approach', directs effort towards accounting for every element of the event, every one of the lost. The second mode is what might be called the 'synecdochic approach': a single individual or detail comes to stand for the many or the whole.

'Detail' is a military term signifying the distribution of the duties of the day for the entirety of the forces ('grand' or 'general' detail) and for its subdivisions ('particular' detail).[9] It also refers to the small party 'told off' for a special task. In his Boer War poem 'Bridge-Guard in the Karroo' (1901), Kipling refers to a particular detail and to its executors when he cites a line from the 'District Orders: Lines of Communication': 'and will supply details to guard the Blood River Bridge'.[10] The opening of the poem marks the point at which, in theatrical style, the lights go down on the grand 'pageant' of battle. The brilliantly lit 'Ramparts of slaughter and peril – / Blazing, amazing, aglow' fade in the twilight and the guard detail is illuminated only by the faint spotlights of a few stars. Alone on the dark karroo, the watchers are 'Few, forgotten and lonely' and their lowly standing is stated three times: 'No, not combatants – only / Details guarding the line'.[11]

In this poem, the military sense of 'detail' serves to dehumanise the members of the guard-party (they are brought to life only briefly by the arrival of the north-bound train and its offer of 'a handful of week-old papers / And a mouthful of human speech').[12] As a military detail, they represent a tiny cog in the vast war machine. But 'detail' has another signification, deriving from the French root of its verb form: *détailler* means

---

[8] 'Taliation', deriving from the Latin *talis* (such, like), signifies a return of like for like and hence conveys the idea of one-to-one correspondence. It also evokes the idea of repaying an injury in kind ('retaliation') – a not inapposite function of war representation.

[9] *OED* 5a.

[10] Rudyard Kipling, *Rudyard Kipling: Selected Poems*, ed. Peter Keating (London: Penguin, 2000), 91.

[11] *Ibid.*, 91, 92, 93.   [12] *Ibid.*, 92.

'to cut into pieces'[13] – pieces then ready to be retailed, or retold. Despite its obscurity, Kipling's detail discharges a vital task in guarding the bridge: similarly, in aesthetic terms, it also shoulders the burden of conveying the Boer War. Like other military sectiuncules, such as the platoon in Norman Mailer's *The Naked and the Dead* (1948), it is a synecdochic representation of a greater phenomenon.

This chapter begins by investigating how war writing can suggest war's enormity and then considers in turn the name-tallying approach and the synecdochic approach as methods of reframing it to a more manageable size (both are illustrated with reference to well-known war memorials: the Vietnam War Memorial in the case of the former, the Unknown Warrior in the case of the latter). Considering specific synecdoches – the offcuts of wholesale war such as dead bodies, body parts and single combat – it concludes that the synecdochic mode has a natural affinity with the subject matter of conflict. The main texts for discussion are speeches from *1 Henry VI* (*c.*1588–90) and *Henry V* (*c.*1599); Milton's *Paradise Lost* (1667, 1674); Byron's *Don Juan* (1819–24) and naming-poems by Southey (1827), Day Lewis (1940) and George Orwell (1943); Siegfried Sassoon's 'The Effect' (1918); Dalton Trumbo's *Johnny Got His Gun* (1939); and Keith Douglas's '*Vergissmeinnicht*' (1943).

One technique for conveying the enormity of conflict is to express the difficulties of measurement. In 'The Effect' (1918), Siegfried Sassoon suggests that the dead are unaccountably uncountable. The poem takes as its epigraph the words of a 'War Correspondent': 'The effect of our bombardment was terrific. One man told me he had never seen so many dead before.'[14] A soldier trudging along a body-strewn road is assailed by the disturbing effect of huge quantities:

> '*He'd never seen so many dead before.*'
> The lilting words danced up and down his brain,
> While corpses jumped and capered in the rain.
> No, no; he wouldn't count them any more . . .

The rained-on dead actively resist numbering in their distressing refusal to lie still and be counted, but also in their very numerousness. Repetition again gives a sense of magnitude as the last stanza reiterates the impossibility of enumeration: '*How many dead? As many as ever you wish. / Don't count 'em; they're too many*'.

---

[13] *OED.*   [14] Siegfried Sassoon, *Collected Poems 1908–1956* (London: Faber, 1961), 73.

'The Effect' dramatises the limits of the ability to 'subitise' or grasp a precise quantity.[15] When the quantity is in the thousands or hundreds of thousands, the problems of estimation come to the fore, as Homer notes as he addresses the task of counting the Greek forces:

The multitude I could not tell or name, not even if ten tongues were mine and ten mouths and a voice unwearying, and the heart within me were of bronze.[16]

The impact of the uncountable is what Kant termed the mathematical sublime. Chapters 5 and 6 discuss the Kantian sublime in detail, but this particular version is relevant here. For Kant, the mathematical sublime makes apparent 'the very inadequacy of our faculty for estimating the magnitude of the things of the sensible world'.[17] Kant further explains:

For the mathematical estimation of magnitude there is, to be sure, no greatest (for the power of numbers goes on to infinity); but for the aesthetic estimation of magnitude there is certainly a greatest; and about this I say that if it is judged as an absolute measure, beyond which no greater is subjectively (for the judging subject) possible, it brings with it the idea of the sublime, and produces that emotion which no mathematical estimation of magnitudes by means of numbers can produce (except insofar as that aesthetic basic measure is vividly preserved in the imagination), since the latter always presents only relative magnitude through comparison with others of the same species, but the former presents magnitude absolutely, so far as the mind can grasp it in one intuition.[18]

For Sassoon's soldier – as for the speaker in Eliot's 'Triumphal March' who cannot assess the figures of 'projectiles, mines and fuses' – the sense of his inability to estimate the quantity of corpses is simultaneously an apprehension of their apparently limitless numbers. Indeed, the precise count becomes less important than the impression of 'many': 'How many

---

[15] According to George A. Miller, loss of the ability to subitise occurs at the number seven (plus or minus two), after which it is only possible to estimate ('The Magical Number Seven, Plus or Minus Two: Some Limits on our Capacity for Processing Information', in *Essential Sources in the Scientific Study of Consciousness*, ed. Bernard J. Baars, William P. Banks and James B. Newman (Boston: MIT Press, 2003), 365). The effect of moving from subitisation to estimation is exploited in James Fenton's poem 'Cambodia' (published in a 1982 collection): 'One man shall wake from terror in his bed. / Five men shall be dead. / One man to five. A million men to one. / And still they die. And still the war goes on' (*The Memory of War and Children in Exile: Poems 1968–1983* (London: Penguin, 1983), 23).

[16] *Iliad*, 2.488f. As Chapter 6 argues, Homer is here using the trope of adynaton to liberate the audience's imaginative grasp of the numbers. Similarly, Edmund Burke points to the enumeration of forces in Shakespeare's *1 Henry IV* (4.1.97–104) as an example of the sublime (*A Philosophical Enquiry into the Origin of Our Ideas of the Sublime and the Beautiful*, ed. Adam Phillips (Oxford: Oxford University Press, 1990), 72).

[17] Immanuel Kant, *Critique of the Power of Judgment*, trans. Paul Guyer and Eric Matthews, ed. Paul Guyer (Cambridge: Cambridge University Press, 2000), 134.

[18] *Ibid.*, 135.

dead? As many as ever you wish'. The effect of 'The Effect', in Kant's terms, is to present 'magnitude absolutely'.[19]

Refusing to put a figure on the total, 'The Effect' encourages the reader to make a macabre estimate. But another technique for conveying vast quantities is explicitly to mention numbers, as Eliot does in 'Triumphal March'. War seems to encourage this in its susceptibility to framing in such terms as death tolls and body counts.[20] Enumeration is, as W. T. J. Mitchell points out, a form of narration: reckoning is recounting, telling is giving an account.[21] In war literature, numbers are used to induce consternation. One of the most famous numbers in writing about conflict is Tennyson's 'six hundred', the group-protagonist of 'The Charge of the Light Brigade' (1854). The amphibrachic 'six hundred', mentioned seven times in the poem, echoes the galloping charge of its riders and assumes an aura of greatness. But the impact of the poem lies in the trope of the diminishing troops: the discrepancy between those who ride out and those who come back. Tennyson is not specific about the exact fraction: the phrases 'not the six hundred' and 'all that was left of them' allow the reader unlimited speculation as to the losses.[22]

The giving of figures in war texts may in some cases be traced to an overriding wish to witness accurately, to record with scientific exactitude in order to diminish the chances of the data being challenged or doubted. Yet the statistics can have the opposing effect: instead of sharpening awareness, numbers become numb-ers;[23] instead of communicating with certainty,

---

[19] *Ibid.*

[20] 'Counting is the epistemology of war. War is bounded by the referential extremes of the prebattle roll call and the postbattle body count, and is constituted within by the mundane and innumerable calculations . . . that make war in theoretical writings so susceptible to formulation as a mathematical contest . . . Indeed, counting is a speech act so pervasive during wartime that it approaches an ideology: it is thus not simply a formal or typological question (What shall I count? How shall I count?) but also a fundamentally ethical one (Who counts? Do I count?)' (Dawes, *The Language of War*, 29–30 and see ch. 1 *passim*).

[21] W. T. J. Mitchell, *Picture Theory: Essays on Verbal and Visual Representation* (Chicago: University of Chicago, 1994), 195. Cf. Fluellen in *Henry V*, who claims that 'the pig [big], or the great, or the mighty, or the huge, or the magnanimous, are all one reckonings' (4.7.15–18). Interrupted in the process of drawing an extended analogy between King Henry and Alexander the Great, Fluellen protests, 'It is not well done, mark you now, to take the tales out of my mouth ere it is made an end and finished. I speak but in the figures and comparisons of it' (4.7.40–2). The 'figures and comparisons' suggest that 'tales' is a pun, not only on tails (see Patricia Parker, 'Uncertain Unions: Welsh Leeks in *Henry V*', in *British Identities and English Renaissance Literature*, ed. David J. Baker and Willy Maley (Cambridge: Cambridge University Press, 2002), 89) but on tallies (for a discussion of tallies, see later in this chapter).

[22] *The Poems of Tennyson*, ed. Christopher Ricks, 3 vols. (London: Longman, 1969), vol. II, 512, 513.

[23] 'In the presence of such multitudes [of the dead] the psychic defense called numbing quickly sets in; our imaginations simply can't encompass all those armies on all those battlefields' (Samuel Hynes, *The Soldiers' Tale. Bearing Witness to Modern War* (London: Pimlico, 1998), xii).

they confound. Integers obscure individuals. To make the quantities real and meaningful, it may be necessary to resort to the kind of arithmetic used by Martin Amis when describing the potential yield of the Soviet H-Bomb:

A train carrying the Hiroshima yield in TNT form would take up four miles of track. A train carrying the equivalent of the Soviet H-bomb would put a girdle round the earth at the latitude of London with a three-thousand-mile overlap.[24]

But images like this are arbitrary and baffling in themselves. 'The estimation of the magnitude of the basic measure', writes Kant, 'must consist simply in the fact that one can immediately grasp it in an intuition and use it by means of imagination for the presentation of numerical concepts.'[25] Amis's measures, and others like them, are not 'immediately graspable'. The mind, trying to imagine 'four miles of track' or 'a three-thousand-mile overlap', is again left struggling with the significance.

In Kantian terms, Amis's measures push comprehension beyond its maximum: 'the aesthetically greatest basic measure for the estimation of magnitude'.[26] At this point, it is impossible to see the wood for the trees, or, in Kant's own spatial analogy, the pyramids for the stones:

In order to get the full emotional effect of the magnitude of the pyramids one must neither come too close to them nor be too far away. For in the latter case, the parts that are apprehended (the stones piled on top of one another) are represented only obscurely, and their representation has no effect on the aesthetic judgement of the subject. In the former case, however, the eye requires some time to complete its apprehension from the base level to the apex, but during this time the former always partly fades before the imagination has taken in the latter, and the comprehension is never complete.[27]

This effect of the mathematical sublime is noted by Freud in his essay 'Thoughts for the Times on War and Death' (1915), in which spatial imagery of proximity is again the means of conveying incomprehensibility:

Swept as we are into the vortex of this war-time, our information is one-sided, ourselves too near to focus the mighty transformations which have already taken place or are beginning to take place, and without a glimmering of the inchoate future, we are incapable of apprehending the significance of the thronging impressions, and know not what value to attach to the judgements we form.[28]

[24] Martin Amis, *Visiting Mrs Nabokov and Other Excursions* (London: Jonathan Cape, 1993), 16.
[25] Kant, *Critique*, 135. [26] *Ibid.*, 135. [27] *Ibid.*, 135–6.
[28] Freud, 'Thoughts for the Times on War and Death', trans. under the supervision of Joan Rivière, *Collected Papers*, ed. Ernest Jones (London: The Hogarth Press / The Institute for Psycho-Analysis, 1950), 288.

War is too huge to see close-up: both geographical and temporal distance
are required for reliable judgement. This point has significant consequences
for the depiction of conflict by the combatant, as Donald Bain notes in his
undated Second World War poem 'War Poet':

> We in our haste can only see the small components of the scene
> We cannot tell what incidents will focus on the final screen.
> A barrage of disruptive sound, a petal on a sleeping face,
> Both must be noted, both must have their place.[29]

Later, in 'Thoughts for the Times', Freud turns to the issue of mass death:
'People are really dying, and now not one by one, but many at a time, often
ten thousand in a single day.'[30] Death 'one by one' might be emotionally
manageable, but 'ten thousand in a single day' is unthinkable.[31] The figure
is simply too large to make sense of and therefore dehumanising.[32] And
numbers, as one 'memory expert' points out,[33] are, as abstractions, difficult
to remember.

The techniques of expressing the difficulties of measurement and giving
actual numbers have, therefore, some limitations in their effectiveness as
means of conveying the scale of war. Hence, in addition to numbers,
writers turn to *names*. War and onomastics are closely connected. Battle is
an opportunity to make one's name, to become a household name: 'many
a darkness into the light shall leap, / And shine in the sudden making of
splendid names'.[34] Outstanding martial deeds bring fame to a name – the
Greek concept of *kleos* – a fame which allows its bearer to live, as Hector
says, 'immortal, ageless all my days, and . . . honoured just as are Athena
and Apollo'.[35] In his essay 'On Names' (1580, 1592), Montaigne also equates

---

[29] Donald Bain, 'War Poet', *The Terrible Rain. The War Poets 1939–1945*, ed. Brian Gardner (London: Methuen, 1966), 159.

[30] Freud, 'Thoughts for the Times', 307.

[31] When Ezra Pound uses the same statistic in 'Hugh Selwyn Mauberley' (1920) – 'there died a myriad' (*Selected Poems 1908–1959* (London: Faber, 1975), 101) – he invokes both connotations of the word 'myriad': 'ten thousand' and 'countless' (*OED* 1a, 2a). Ten thousand, or the myriad, was the highest figure for which the Greeks had a word (Geoffrey Ifrah, *The Universal History of Numbers: From Prehistory to the Invention of the Computer*, trans. David Bellos *et al.* (London: Harvill, 1998), 427).

[32] Cf. 'Winterbourne heard them constantly using the phrase "three hundred thousand men," as if they were cows or pence or radishes . . . The phrase "Division smashed to pieces" rang in his brain. He wanted to seize the people in the room, the people in authority, everyone not directly in the War, and shout to them: "Division smashed to pieces! Do you know what that means?"' (Richard Aldington, *Death of a Hero* (London: Penguin, 1929), 276).

[33] Ron Fry, *Improve Your Memory* (London: Kogan Page, 1997), 66.

[34] Alfred, Lord Tennyson, 'Maud: A Monodrama' (1855), *The Poems of Tennyson*, vol. II, 584.

[35] *Iliad.*, 8.538–41.

'a good name' with 'renown and reputation'.[36] 'Renown' is re-nouning or re-naming – the *reinforcement* of a name – while 'reputation' is the sum of what is thought about a person.

Shakespeare's *1 Henry VI* deftly conveys the complex connection between deeds, name, report, repute and renown in a scene attesting to Talbot's fame:

> MESSENGER: All hail, my lords! which of this princely train
> Call ye the warlike Talbot, for his acts
> So much applauded through the realm of France?
> TALBOT: Here is the Talbot; who would speak with him?
> MESSENGER: The virtuous lady, Countess of Auvergne,
> With modesty admiring thy renown,
> By me entreats, great lord, thou wouldst vouchsafe
> To visit her poor castle where she lies,
> That she may boast she hath beheld the man
> Whose glory fills the world with loud report. (2.2.34–43)

Significantly, in its reporting, Talbot's name has been reinforced – or renowned – with the epithet 'warlike'. His deeds have, similarly, been reiterated: 'much applauded through the realm of France'; 'fills the world with loud report'. So augmented, both the name and the deeds it connotes have an *inflationary* effect on the battles Talbot has fought in. Expanding his name magnifies them. The same effect can be observed in *Coriolanus* and *Macbeth*. In the former, Caius Martius is cognominated 'Coriolanus' after his victory over the Volscians at Corioli:

> HERALD: Know, Rome, that all alone Martius did fight
> Within Corioli gates, where he hath won,
> With fame, a name to Caius Martius; these
> In honour follows Coriolanus.
> Welcome to Rome, renowned Coriolanus! (2.2.153–7)

Here conspicuous individualism – 'all alone ... did fight' – results in Martius being both 'renowned' and 're-nouned', given another proper noun, a to-name, as a signifier. Macbeth, too, is given extra names in recognition of his renown. Described by his sergeant as 'brave' – 'well he deserves that name' (1.2.16) – he is nominated bearer of the title 'Thane of Cawdor'. Ross brings the news of this antonomasia from the king:

---

[36] Michel de Montaigne, *The Complete Essays*, trans. and ed. M. A. Screech (London: Penguin, 1987), 308.

> And, for an earnest of a greater honour,
> He bade me, from him, call thee Thane of Cawdor;
> In which addition, hail, most worthy Thane!
> For it is thine.   (1.3.104–7)

This is, again, a literal augmentation of a name, the 'addition' of a title. In French, the word for *noms-de-guerre* like 'Coriolanus' is 'surnom':[37] a nickname, title or epithet added to someone's name – what might be thought of as a 'super-name', 'over-name' or 'hyper-name'.[38] Such renowned or reinforced names, cognomens, to-names, surnames, hyper-names: all these have an enlarging effect, both on the individual who is nominated and on the battle in which he fights. Naming a few outstanding warriors – as is the case with single combat, discussed later in the chapter – conjures up titanic clashes and large-scale encounters.

But hyper-naming is not the only kind of nominal response to war. Lines from *Henry V* suggest an alternative. After the Battle of Agincourt, Henry seeks an account of the encounter in the form of a body count:

> KING HARRY: Now, herald, are the dead numbered?
> HERALD: Here is the number of the slaughtered French.
>   (4.8.73–4)

Immediately after this, Exeter accounts for the French prisoners as follows:

> EXETER:
> Charles Duke of Orleans, nephew to the King;
> John Duke of Bourbon, and Lord Bouciqualt;
> Of other lords and barons, knights and squires,
> Full fifteen hundred, besides common men.
>   (4.8.76–7)

Reading from the herald's note, the King continues:

---

[37] The apparent English equivalent of *surnom* – 'surname' – has a different meaning, but one that also associates 'name' with 'renown': it refers to the system of family nomenclature, or hereditary last names, introduced with the Norman Conquest (Thomas Dutoit, 'Translating the Name?', in Jacques Derrida, *On the Name* (Stanford: Stanford University Press, 1995), x). It is this kind of name which is referred to in the battle report which opens *Much Ado About Nothing* (1.1.5–7) and in Henry V's reading of the roll-call of English dead (*Henry V* 4.8.103–5) (the note in the 1995 Arden edition glosses 'name' in this passage as 'notable family'). Henry, in his imaginative prolepsis of Agincourt veterans remembering the battle, reinforces the distinction when he predicts that only the names of the (aristocratic) military leaders will live on (a two-tier onomastics that undermines his other attempts to forge national unity as part of the war effort): see 4.3.60–6.
[38] Dutoit, 'Translating the Name?', ix, xi.

KING HARRY:
        This note doth tell me of ten thousand French
        That in the field lie slain. Of princes in this number
        And nobles bearing banners, there lie dead
        One hundred twenty-six; added to these,
        Of knights, esquires, and gallant gentlemen,
        Eight thousand and four hundred, of the which
        Five hundred were but yesterday dubbed knights.
        So that in these ten thousand they have lost
        There are but sixteen hundred mercenaries;
        The rest are princes, barons, lords, knights, squires,
        And gentlemen of blood and quality.
        The names of those their nobles that lie dead:
        Charles Delabret, High Constable of France;
        Jacques of Châtillon, Admiral of France;
        The Master of the Crossbows, Lord Rambures;
        Great-Master of France, the brave Sir Guiscard Dauphin;
        Jean, Duke of Alençon; Antony, Duke of Brabant,
        The brother to the Duke of Burgundy;
        And Édouard, Duke of Bar; of lusty earls,
        Grandpré and Roussi, Fauconbridge and Foix,
        Beaumont and Marle, Vaudemont and Lestrelles.
        Here was a royal fellowship of death.
        Where is the number of our English dead?
        He is given another paper
        Edward the Duke of York, the Earl of Suffolk,
        Sir Richard Keighley, Davy Gam Esquire;
        None else of name, and of all other men
        But five-and-twenty.   (4.8.80–106)

Naming is a sensitive issue in the play; as Thomas Healy points out, Henry's St Crispian's Eve claim that 'be he ne'er so vile / This day shall gentle his condition' (4.3.62–3) is an empty promise given that the majority of the band of brothers remain 'anonymous casualties'.[39] But more important for present purposes is to observe the two methods of accounting that are in operation in Exeter's and Henry's speeches. In the former, the lords, barons, knights and squires are *counted*, all of them represented by the single number 'fifteen hundred'. The same is true of the princes, barons, lords, knights, squires and gentlemen mentioned by Henry. 'Fifteen hundred', 'ten thousand', 'one hundred and twenty-six', 'eight thousand and four hundred',

---

[39] Tom Healy, 'Remembering with Advantages: Nation and Ideology in *Henry V*', in *Shakespeare in the New Europe*, ed. Michael Hattaway, Boika Sokolova and Derek Roper (Sheffield: Sheffield Academic Press, 1994), 175.

'sixteen hundred' are literal responses to the query 'are the dead numbered?'
They are also, like the other large numbers already encountered, virtually
meaningless. There is an arbitrariness about them: why fifteen hundred
rather than fourteen or sixteen hundred? The nobles, by contrast, are in
both speeches effectively *tallied*. Tallying is the simplest form of number
notation. A tally (which has the same etymological root as 'detail') was
originally a stick notched to represent an amount: this was a method used
in ancient societies to compare the number of soldiers who returned from
a military foray with the number who had gone out (the grim calculation
at the base of Tennyson's 'Light Brigade').[40] To tally, therefore, is not so
much to count as to *mark*: it involves a one-to-one correspondence in
which each element is not subsumed within an integer but represented by
its own notch.

   In these lines, though, the tally is not of notches but of names. Though
there is some hyper-naming present and Henry's 'Here was a royal fellow-
ship of death' displays an unmistakeable pride in the taking of prized scalps,
'Charles Duke of Orleans', 'John Duke of Bourbon', 'Lord Bouciqualt'
and the others are not solely inflationary indices but signs in one-to-one
correspondence with their referents. To appreciate the effects of such name-
tallying, it is important to remember that names are more often lost, than
made, in war. Soldiers 'surrender' their given names on joining the forces,
becoming surnames, ranks and serial numbers. The uniformed member of
the military is an anonymous social type par excellence. The experience of
combat, argues one sociologist, is so overwhelming ('sublime') as to involve
the loss of ego.[41]

   Taliation nominatim is what arises in response: an intense counter-urge
to recuperate, catalogue and enunciate lost names. Her motivation for
writing, states the *Der Spiegel* war correspondent Carolin Emcke, is 'to give
each of these stinking, faceless bodies a name again'.[42] Similar motivation
lies behind the kind of war memorials in which the names of all the dead

---

[40] Ifrah, *The Universal History of Numbers*, xxi. 'I counted them all out and I counted them all
back' became a phrase associated with the Falklands War of 1982. It was spoken by the BBC's
correspondent, Brian Hanrahan, in order to circumvent the reporting restrictions which forbade
him giving the exact number of British Sea Harrier jets which had returned from their bombing
mission to HMS *Hermes* safely: 'I'm not allowed to say how many planes joined the raid, but I
counted them all out, and I counted them all back' (Brian Hanrahan and Robert Fox, *'I counted
them all out and I counted them all back': The Battle for the Falklands* (London: BBC Books, 1982),
21). British viewers were to take comfort from the fact that the tallies tallied. Cf. George Gascoigne,
'of our owne, we lost but three by tale' (*The Fruites of Warre*, line 1125).
[41] Harvie Ferguson, 'The Sublime and the Subliminal: Modern Identities and the Aesthetics of
Combat', *Theory, Culture and Society* 21.3 (2004), 1–33: 4, 6, 21.
[42] Emcke, *Echoes of Violence*, 10.

and missing are listed.[43] One of the most extensive of these – a cultural artefact whose name might stand for the name-tallying approach[44] – is the Vietnam Veterans' Memorial in Washington, DC. Reflecting on this monument reveals what name-tallying can achieve. Inspiration for the memorial came to a Vietnam veteran, Jan C. Scruggs, in a dream he had in March 1979. Scruggs was present at an explosion when mortar rounds hit an ammunition truck which twelve of his comrades were unloading:

Organs and pieces of bodies were scattered along the ground. They belonged to his friends. He had only one bandage. He stood and screamed for help.

The flashbacks ended, but the faces continued to pile up in front of him. The names, he thought. The names. No one remembers their names.[45]

The key feature of this dream is that individuals have become un-differentiated, blasted into body parts. There is a hint that one might be saved ('He had only one bandage' suggests at least the possibility of using it once, whereas 'He had only a bandage' would suggest the total inadequacy of medical supplies), but Scruggs rejects any such first-aid synecdoche. All his friends must be saved – through their names. Scruggs's waking vision of a memorial that would 'have the name of everyone killed'[46] in Vietnam (the name, that is, of every American serviceman killed there) was realised by the design by Maya Ying Lin of two polished black granite walls meeting at an apex, set into a slope on the Mall in Washington, DC. From 10 to 14 November 1982, a National Salute to Vietnam Veterans was held in the city, during which time volunteers read out the names on the Wall. *Newsweek* editor-in-chief and Vietnam veteran William Broyles reflected:

[43] Naming as a form of war memorialisation is a topic too vast to go into here. The following works, covering memorial naming from ancient times until the present, are recommended: Alan Borg, *War Memorials. From Antiquity to the Present* (London: Leo Cooper, 1991); Bob Bushaway, 'Name upon Name: The Great War and Remembrance', in *Myths of the English*, ed. Roy Porter (Cambridge: Polity Press, 1992), 136–67; Joseph Clarke, *Commemorating the Dead in Revolutionary France: Revolution and Remembrance 1789–1799* (Cambridge: Cambridge University Press, 2007); Geoff Dyer, *The Missing of the Somme* (London: Hamish Hamilton, 1994); Adrian Gregory, *The Silence of Memory: Armistice Day 1919–1946* (Oxford and Providence: Berg, 1994); Thomas Laqueur, 'Memory and Naming in the Great War', in *Commemorations: The Politics of National Identity*, ed. John R. Gillis (Princeton: Princeton University Press, 1994), 150–67; James E. Young, *The Texture of Memory: Holocaust Memorials and Meaning* (New Haven: Yale University Press, 1993).

[44] It is not the only name-bearing war memorial, nor the one with the most names: cf. the Menin Gate (54,896 names), Tyne Cot (34,888), Vimy Ridge (11,000), Thiepval (73,367). The Central Database of Shoah Victims' Names at Yad Vashem, Jerusalem, contains some 3 million names. See Borg, *War Memorials*, xi-xii; Bushaway, 'Name upon Name', 137; Laqueur, 'Memory and Naming in the Great War', 154–5.

[45] Jan C. Scruggs and Joel L. Swerdlow, *To Heal a Nation: The Vietnam Veterans' Memorial* (New York: Harper & Row, 1985), 7.

[46] *Ibid.*, 8.

Rhythmic Spanish names. Tongue-twisting Polish names, guttural German, exotic African, homely Anglo-Saxon names. Chinese, Polynesian, Indian and Russian names... to hear the names being read... is to remember. The war was about names, each name a special human being who never came home.[47]

When the monument itself was unveiled, it was clear that the names – and the fact that viewers saw their own reflections behind them in the polished granite – had extraordinary power: 'As you saw your living reflection mixed up with the names, a strong bond, a sharing, came forth.'[48] Above all, people touched the names. 'Fingertips traced out each letter. Lips said a name over and over, and then stretched up to kiss it.'[49]

These reactions suggest that name-tallying has two main effects. The first is to retain a trace of the individual in the world.[50] The urge to caress the carved names of a loved one indicates that names function as referents, somehow embodying the lost individuals. By contrast, the second effect of the name-tallying approach depends on the fact that the names also function as signs, referencing those individuals on the principle of one-to-one correspondence. Listed in full, the names convey the scale of the conflict in which those referred to have been lost. Monumental onomasticons, that is, force the human imagination 'to see, as concretely as possible, what a million dead men look like'.[51]

Now, a literary work, not being a stone wall, cannot list fifty-eight thousand names, let alone a million ('For fifty thousand heroes, name by name, / Though all deserving equally to turn / A couplet, or an elegy to claim, / Would form a lengthy lexicon of glory / And what is worse still a much longer story').[52] But similar effects of tracing and taliation are possible, even when fewer names are cited. *Don Juan* exhibits intense interest in naming (and name loss). Byron's naming strategies in the poem are of two kinds. Naming to achieve (mock-)inflation of the battle is evident in his (tongue-in-cheek) listing of the names of notable Cossack fighters: 'Strongenoff and Strokonoff, / Meknop, Serge Lwow, Arseniew of modern

---

[47] Quoted in *ibid.*, 142.   [48] Quoted in *ibid.*, 147.

[49] *Ibid.*, 146, 147. It should be acknowledged that, despite the power of the name incised on stone or listed in newspapers, there was and is a widely expressed sense that it is an inadequate recompense. In *Don Juan*, Byron, evoking 'a whole gazette of slaughter' (canto 7, stanza 31, line 8, questions, 'I wonder... if a man's name in a *bulletin* / May make up for a *bullet in* his body?' (7.21.1–3) (this stanza notes that the same question is asked in *Hamlet* (4.4.56–62)). *Don Juan* (8.125), Siegfried Sassoon's 'Base Details' (1918), 'Memorial Tablet' (1919) and 'On Passing the New Menin Gate' (1927), Gavin Ewart's 'War Dead' (1945) and Geoffrey Hill's 'The Distant Fury of Battle' (1959) ('Named, Anonymous' (Geoffrey Hill, *Collected Poems* (Harmondsworth: Penguin, 1985), 26)) all castigate the easy reading of names of the lost.

[50] The idea of name as trace goes back at least as far as Plato's *Cratylus* (360 BCE): 'everything has a right name of its own, which comes by nature... an inherent correctness' (384E, 383A).

[51] Laqueur, 'Memory and Naming in the Great War', 160.   [52] Byron, *Don Juan*, 8.17.4–8.

Greece, / And Tschitsshakoff and Roguenoff and Chokenoff' (7.15.2–4).
In contrast to this is the listing of the names of the English participants:

> 'Mongst them were several Englishmen of pith,
> Sixteen called Thomson and nineteen named Smith.
> Jack Thomson and Bill Thomson – all the rest
> Had been called Jemmy, after the great bard.[53]
> [. . .]
> Three of the Smiths were Peters [. . .]
> The rest were Jacks and Gills and Wills and Bills;
> But when I've added that the elder Jack Smith
> Was born in Cumberland among the hills
> And that his father was an honest blacksmith,
> I've said all *I* know of a name that fills
> Three lines of the dispatch in taking Schmaksmith.
>
> (7.18.7–7.20.6)

Rather than an inflationary effect, these names have a tallying function, albeit that the tallying is interrupted by counting (true tallying would entail writing out 'Smith' nineteen times). In a sense, these are unknown names (the last stanza quoted reveals that these individuals are not very familiar to the speaker): their purpose is to convey a sense of *multitude*. But this is not to underestimate Byron's concern for the name as referent. The siege cantos of *Don Juan*, indeed, reveal a preoccupation with the spoken and written articulation of a name, with getting it right. The Cossack names – 'of twelve consonants apiece' – 'want nothing but pronunciation' (7.15.5, 7.14.8). Byron categorises them by their endings – 'ischskin, ousckin, iffskchy, ouski' (7.16.7) – a play that recalls Southey's onomastical tomfoolery with Russian names in 'The March to Moscow' (1814).[54] Canto VIII expresses sympathy for a man whose name was misspelled in a dispatch: 'I knew a man whose loss / Was printed Grove, although his name was Grose'

---

[53] I.e. James Thomson, author of *The Seasons*.

[54]
> And Platoff he play'd them off,
> And Shouvaloff he shovell'd them off,
> And Markoff he mark'd them off,
> And Krosnoff he cross'd them off,
> And Tuchkoff he touch'd them off,
> And Boroskoff he bored them off,
> And Kutusoff he cut them off,
> And Parenzoff he pared them off,
> And Worronzoff he worried them off,
> And Doctoroff he doctor'd them off,
> And Rodionoff he flogg'd them off.

(Robert Southey, *Poems of Robert Southey*, ed. Maurice H. Fitzgerald (Oxford: Oxford University Press, 1909), 362.) Similar play on German names appears in *Don Juan* at 8.49.1–2.

(18.18.7–8). Such concern for the proper writing and speaking of names reflects Byron's urge to ensure that even here, in mock-heroic, the dead are properly recognised ('But here are men who fought in gallant actions / As gallantly as ever heroes fought, / But buried in the heap of such trans-actions / Their names are rarely found nor often sought' (7.34.1–4)) – but such recognition must comprise both acknowledgement of service and preservation of name. Conjoining these two effects, *Don Juan* is a literary forebear to the Vietnam Wall, a literary monument which both recuperates name as trace and demonstrates the effect of tallying.

These effects are again observable in two twentieth-century naming-poems: Cecil Day Lewis's 'The Stand-To' (1940) and the verses at the end of George Orwell's essay, 'Looking Back on the Spanish War' (published 1943). In 'The Stand-To', Day Lewis rejects for 'men maddened by numbers' such terms as 'Destiny, History, Duty, Fortitude, Honour'.[55] Instead:

> I write this verse to record the men who have watched with me –
> Spot who is good at darts, Squibby at repartee,
> Mark and Cyril, the dead shots, Ralph with a ploughman's gait,
> Gibson, Harris and Long, old hands for the barricade,
> Whiller the lorry-driver, Francis and Rattlesnake,
> Fred and Charl and Stan.

In the face of 'all / The words of the politicians', which 'seem too big or too small', only this listing of names has value. The naming is deliberate and explicitly drawn attention to. Notably, the names are single names: though there is a hint of hyper-naming, these are given names and nicknames with a working-class ring to them. If they are fictional, at least the act of naming, with all its significance, is accomplished: the men are recorded and a clue to their numerousness is given (twelve names are mentioned in five lines). The same impetus and effect are evident in Orwell's verse, which cites names that, in the Spanish system of nomenclature, are down-to-earth:

> For where is Manuel Gonzalez,
> And where is Pedro Aguilar,
> And where is Ramon Fenellosa?
> The earthworms know where they are.
> Your name and your deeds were forgotten
> Before your bones were dry.[56]

---

[55] Cecil Day Lewis, *The Complete Poems* (London: Sinclair-Stevenson, 1992), 333, 334.
[56] George Orwell, 'Looking Back on the Spanish War', *All Propaganda is Lies 1941–1942*, in *The Complete Works of George Orwell*, ed. Peter Davison, 20 vols. (London: Secker & Warburg, 1986–7), vol. XIII, 497–511: 511.

Explicitly citing the disappearance of the body in these *ubi sunt* lines, Orwell, like Day Lewis, suggests that the name is a substitute: not just a sign, but a trace, an incision in the monument of the poem.

But alongside the functions of salvaging and tallying, another effect begins to be felt in these poems that is not present in *Don Juan*. The twelve names in 'The Stand-To' and the three names in Orwell's verses imply numerousness by suggesting that those named are only a small fraction. Unlike hyper-names, these names are relatively common and undistinguished: there might only be one Caius Martius Coriolanus but there will be many more Freds and Stans, Ramons and Pedros. In these instances, the synecdochic function begins to emerge. This function is evident in a poem by Southey which mentions but a single name: 'Thomas'. In the Peninsular Wars, the Duke of Wellington lost eight hundred soldiers at Crimiera, one thousand at Corunna, seven thousand at Albuera, five thousand at Badajoz, seven thousand at Burgos and seven thousand in the Battle of the Pyrenees. None of the names of these dead men were recorded,[57] a state of affairs which Southey redressed in a series of poetic 'Inscriptions'. 'Epitaph' (1827) names a standard-bearer at Albuera:

> Then too in the front
> Of battle did it flap exultingly,
> When Douro, with its wide stream interposed,
> Saved not the French invaders from attack,
> Discomfiture, and ignominious rout.
> My name is Thomas: undisgraced have I
> Transmitted it. He who in days to come
> May bear the honour'd banner to the field,
> Will think of Albuhera [*sic*], and of me.[58]

Naming, in this poem, achieves a number of the effects already encountered. The namelessness (ignominy) of the shamefully defeated is contrasted with the ongoing name of the valiant, though, un-augmented by any cognomen and shorn of a surname (or first name), 'Thomas' does not inflate the battle with associations of renown but rather condenses it to a six-letter trace. Deftly, the lines work to make the banner and 'Thomas' coincide. The individual alluded to bears both standard and name; 'it' in the seventh line quoted may refer to either. Like the flag, Southey therefore suggests, the name is a concrete synecdoche as well as a sign: it functions as both tally (albeit of one) and trace. Naming, then, can adjust the scale of conflict for human comprehension: both augmenting it by invoking a

---

[57] Laqueur, 'Memory and Naming in the Great War', 151. [58] Southey, *Poems*, 352.

few notables' renown and reducing it to the more manageable size of a few specified participants. And if, as Karl Shapiro says, 'the final aggregate is *one*',[59] let *one* be the focus of attention.[60]

While taliation nominatim relies on the principle of one-to-one signification, the ratio underpinning the synecdochic approach is one-to-many. This approach, too, can be illustrated with reference to a war memorial: the Unknown Warrior, interred in Westminster Abbey on 11 November 1920. Promoting the idea of 'known though unknown', the words inscribed on the Warrior's tomb made the representative aesthetics clear: 'Thus are commemorated the many'. *The Times* reported that those who heard the words of the state funeral service 'felt that they were uttered also for all the hundreds of thousands, his comrades in death as in life, who rest in far-off graves from Flanders to Mesopotamia, or who sleep their last sleep beneath our guardian seas'.[61] The theme was widely taken up in literature responding to the monument.[62] A poem published in 1926, 'The Unknown Warrior' by E. C. Dee, claims:

> Not alone in our sorrow we stand;
> In this one we honour those others who fell,
> And rest in a foreigner's land.[63]

In similar vein, W. H. Abbott's poem 'The Unknown Warrior in Westminster Abbey' (1929) calls the figure 'the cynosure and passion of all eyes', 'type and peak of all who died'.[64] The Warrior's missing identity prompted massive imaginative speculation. Abbott finds tantalising the conundrum that the corpse might equally be of high or low birth:

---

[59] Karl Shapiro, 'Elegy for a Dead Soldier' (1944), *Selected Poems* (New York: Random House, 1968), 105.

[60] Cf. Aldington's *Death of a Hero*: 'How could the Army individually mourn a million "heroes"? How could the little bit of Army which knew George mourn him? . . . How can we atone for the lost millions and millions of years of life, how atone for those lakes and seas of blood? . . . Headstones and wreaths and memorials and speeches and the Cenotaph – no, no; it has got to be something *in* us . . . That is why I am writing the life of George Winterbourne, a unit, one human body murdered, but to me a symbol' (32). Winterbourne might be intended as symbol, but functions as synecdoche.

[61] 'The Quick and the Dead', *The Times*, 12 November 1919, 13.

[62] The deference given to the Unknown Warrior provoked cynicism: cf. 'The Body of an American' section of John Dos Passos's *Nineteen Nineteen* (1932):

> In the tarpaper morgue at Châlons-sur-Marne in the reek of chloride of lime and the dead, they picked out the pine box that held all that was left of
> Enie menie minie moe plenty other pine boxes stacked up there containing what they'd scraped up of Richard Roe.

(John Dos Passos, *U.S.A.* (Boston: Houghton Mifflin, 1946), 407, 411–12.)

[63] E. C. Dee, *The Unknown Warrior and Other Poems* (London: Arthur H. Stockwell), 1926, 3.

[64] W. H. Abbott, *The Unknown Warrior and Other Poems* (London: Erskine Macdonald, 1929), 29.

Who was he? What crowned mother's son is here,
Warrior unknown, who has for place of bier
This hallowed shrine? What rests beneath
That slab of death?
Is it rough hands and feet, coarse body, born
To task and need, or does some high dame, lorn
Because he is not, out-bid Rachel's tears?[65]

E. H. Carrier's 'The Unknown Warrior' (1926) develops this idea in its account of a young boy whose aspiration is that 'So too might he as famous be, / And with his Country's heroes rest!'[66] Coningsby Dawson, who had fought in the trenches with the Canadians, goes even further in his novella *The Unknown Soldier* (1920), which imagines that the nameless warriors buried by the various different nations are in fact the same entity: Christ.

Above all, the universality of anonymity offered scope for intense personal identification with the 'unknown and yet well known'.[67] The Warrior 'might be the child of any one of a million mothers', claimed *The Times*. 'Therefore, all could mourn for him the better because he was unknown.'[68] On the day of the interment an anonymous pamphlet was published by Hodder & Stoughton in London, New York and Toronto, presumably for mass distribution. *To My 'Unknown' Warrior* is an extended monologue by a widow or bereaved fiancée. It opens, 'Boy dear, I am so happy. I have found you at last'.[69] With utter certainty, the speaker addresses the occupant of the Unknown Warrior's tomb as her lost lover, thankful that she will 'never again have to read those cruel words, "*Regret – No trace*"'.[70] Notable about this publication – aside from the unswerving conviction with which it identifies the Unknown Warrior – is the way in which it appropriates the aesthetics of universal applicability. The soldier is simply named 'John' and no other details are given. Facilitating the transfer of its sentiments to the readers' personal situations, the pamphlet provides a template of grieving in which uniqueness of sorrow and the dead soldier's individuality are emphasised (numbering is reclaimed from military practice to become a mark of private affection):

[65] *Ibid.*, 29.
[66] E. H. Carrier, *The Unknown Warrior and Other Poems* (London: Unknown Publisher, 1926), 1.
[67] Cf. *Catch-22*: 'Yossarian, on the other hand, knew exactly who Mudd was. Mudd was the unknown soldier who had never had a chance, for that was the only thing anyone ever did know about all the unknown soldiers – they never had a chance. They had to be dead' (Joseph Heller, *Catch-22* (London: Jonathan Cape, 1962), 141).
[68] 'The Burial of the Unknown Warrior', *The Times*, 12 November 1920, sec. Supplement, i.
[69] *To My 'Unknown' Warrior* (London, New York, Toronto: Hodder & Stoughton, 1920), 7.
[70] *Ibid.*, 8.

I have tried not to be altogether selfish in my grief, and mine are tears in a sea of tears which lies behind the great army of the other figures, but, surely, there has been no sorrow quite like my sorrow over just one number. Do you remember how angry I was about those figures on your identification disc when first I noticed them on your wrist – how I hate your being a number at all? And how you said – it was just like you to understand and not to laugh at me then – 'Why, as long as I'm Number One to you what in the world does it matter what number I am to the Army?'[71]

What this and the other literary reactions to the Unknown Warrior suggest is perhaps surprising, given the importance of naming already discussed in this chapter. They indicate that, if long lists of names blur into meaning-lessness, the one unnamed and unknown permits unlimited significance – significance that may be both universal and deeply personal.

And this is how the synecdochic approach works. It is, in effect, the metonymic mode identified by Roman Jakobson in his classic essay, 'Two Types of Language and Two Types of Aphasic Disturbances' (1956). Jakobson argues that the linguistic sign involves two kinds of arrangement: combination, which takes place on the vertical plane of the sentence, and selection, which takes place on the horizontal plane of the set of possibilities for each word.[72] Aphasics with 'contiguity disorder' find it difficult to combine simpler linguistic entities into more complex units, so the grammar of their sentences begins to disintegrate, while those with 'selection deficiency' forget key words and replace them with 'abstract anaphoric substitutes' or metonyms.[73] Metonymy, Jakobson concludes, underlies the 'realistic' tendency in literature.[74] Unlike metaphor, a figure based on something's similarity with a different thing, metonym – or, more accurately, synecdoche – works figuratively by representing a thing by part of itself.[75] As David Lodge, commenting on Jakobson, remarks, a metonymic text 'seems to offer itself as a representative *bit* of reality'.[76]

Realism is a literary trend associated with the eighteenth- and nineteenth-century novel. The realist novel is based on the principle of exemplification, presenting a specific situation 'as though it were a universal

[71] *Ibid.*, 8–10.
[72] Roman Jakobson, 'Two Aspects of Language and Two Types of Aphasic Disturbance', in *Fundamentals of Language*, eds. Roman Jakobson and Morris Halle ('S-Gravenhage: Mouton, 1956), 53–82: 60.
[73] *Ibid.*, 71, 64.   [74] *Ibid.*, 78.
[75] See George Puttenham, *The Arte of English Poesie*, ed. Gladys Dodge Willcock and Alice Walker (Cambridge: Cambridge University Press, 1936), 180, 185, 195.
[76] David Lodge, *The Modes of Modern Writing: Metaphor, Metonymy, and the Typology of Modern Literature* (London: Edward Arnold, 1977), 108.

truth'.[77] The exemplary thrust is reinforced by an accumulation of details producing what Roland Barthes has called 'the reality effect'.[78] Realism meets the overriding need for authenticity in war representation[79] and its synecdochic tendencies have a natural affinity with the subject matter of conflict. It is not just that the war zone is littered with details – arms and legs and guns and clothes – grotesque fragments that have been described as 'battlefield gothic'.[80] Violence quickly disanimates. Simone Weil defines 'force' as:

That *x* that turns anybody who is subjected to it into a thing. Exercised to the limit, it turns man into a thing in the most literal sense: it makes a corpse out of him.[81]

Conflict, then, is peculiarly about 'things'. In addition, battle has a pointillist character. In the arrhythmia of war, periods of monotonous waiting are punctuated by bursts of intensive action. The sounds of ordnance sharply rend the air. A corpse, or body part, is happened upon suddenly. There are vivid, split-second events. All these phenomena are accentuated in the hypervigilance typical of those under fire.[82] The effect is what Freud, in 'Beyond the Pleasure Principle' (1921), placing it in opposition to *Angst* (apprehension) and *Furcht* (fear), called *Schreck* (fright). *Schreck* is 'the condition to which one is reduced if one encounters a danger without being prepared for it' and the most likely to result in traumatic neuroses.[83] Writing on Freud's piece in his essay 'Some Motifs in Baudelaire' (1939), Walter Benjamin finds *Schreck* at the heart of Baudelaire's poetic practice, encapsulated in his image of the poet-as-fencer.[84] Fencing provides an apt martial image for the hallmark of war representation: the detail's rapier-thrust. It is a representation which is fundamentally tmetic, cut through by interjections and interruptions. As John Taylor writes:

---

[77] Terry Eagleton, *The English Novel* (Oxford: Blackwell, 2005), 13.
[78] Roland Barthes, 'The Photographic Message', in *A Barthes Reader*, ed. Susan Sontag (London: Jonathan Cape, 1982), 194–210.
[79] See James Knibb, 'Literary Strategies of War, Strategies of Literary War', in *Literature and War*, ed. David Bevan (Atlanta: Rodopi, 1990), 7, 12.
[80] Hynes, *The Soldiers' Tale*, 26.
[81] Simone Weil, *War and The Iliad*, trans. Mary McCarthy (New York: New York Review Books, 2005), 3.
[82] On hypervigilance, see Chapter 3.
[83] Sigmund Freud, *Beyond the Pleasure Principle*, trans. C. J. M. Hubback, in *Collected Papers*, ed. Ernest Jones (London: The Hogarth Press / The Institute for Psycho-Analysis, 1942), 9.
[84] Walter Benjamin, *Charles Baudelaire: A Lyric Poet in the Era of High Capitalism*, trans. Harry Zohn (London: NLB, 1973), 117–18.

Fright makes the blood run cold, the senses faint, the sinews stiffen. Horror may electrify the body, forcing screams and fits. Disgust can provoke involuntary physical signs such as tics, winces or grimaces.[85]

But the detail does not need to be gruesome to stay in the mind: it just needs to be a detail. The single orphan inhabits the memory in the way that fifty-eight thousand names do not.[86] One severed arm – seen or described – imprints itself on a mind reeling from a sea of bodies.

Paradoxically, then, the massive scale of war finds its best communication in localised, focused images recuperated from the generality. The rest of this chapter explores the most salient synecdoches of conflict: the tiny physical effects, the single encounters and, above all, the dead body and the detached body part.

In 'Range-Finding' (1916), Robert Frost condenses a battle to a rip in a cobweb:

> The battle rent a cobweb diamond-strung
> And cut a flower beside a ground bird's nest
> Before it stained a single human breast.
> [. . .]
> On the bare upland pasture there had spread
> O'ernight 'twixt mullein stalks a wheel of thread
> And straining cables wet with silver dew.
> A sudden passing bullet shook it dry.
> The indwelling spider ran to greet the fly,
> But finding nothing, sullenly withdrew.[87]

The poem readjusts the scale of war, but the readjustment is itself unsettling. The single bullet, arriving and departing suddenly, shakes (for the spider) a world ('straining cables' turns gossamer into an endeavour of industrial proportions). As the title of the poem indicates, 'range-finding' is an ongoing project, requiring delicate balance: war's fleeting, devastating nature makes it difficult to keep in view. Frost's torn cobweb is an example of a tendency in war synecdoche to the tiny. At times, *War and Peace* distils the Napoleonic Wars into such minute details as Napoleon's hand ('plump', 'little', 'soft' and 'white'); the 'twitching of his left leg'; the bulging vein in

---

[85] John Taylor, *Body Horror: Photojournalism, Catastrophe and War* (Manchester: Manchester University Press, 1998), 1.

[86] This is the principle underlying both the documentary and the journalistic 'human interest' story. Jean Seaton writes, 'the preference for saving the single known victim . . . can be defended if it leads to a wider engagement in which the fate of one child focuses attention and delivers care for others' (Seaton, *Carnage and the Media*, 274).

[87] Robert Frost, *The Poetry of Robert Frost*, ed. Edward Connery Lathem (London: Jonathan Cape, 1971), 126.

the neck of Vereshchagin; Rostopchin's twitching jaw.[88] In *Her Privates We* (1929), Frederic Manning draws attention to the 'dark patches' of sweat on the soldiers' khaki where equipment has pressed on the cloth;[89] *For Whom the Bell Tolls* transfixes the reader with the drop of iodine on the razor-cut on Maria's ear.[90] Cobwebs, sweat patches and iodine stings are not irrelevant details, but rapier lunges at the reader's attention.

Looming larger in texts about war is the dead body; indeed, to read war literature is constantly to stumble over corpses.[91] How might this body language be interpreted? Battlefield dead, distended by internal gases, have the potential to become grotesque, Bakhtinian bodies, literally bloated and swollen. In the following passage by Hemingway, corpses are associated with the fantastic ('unbelievable') and the carnivalesque ('balloons'):

The dead grow larger each day until sometimes they become quite too big for their uniforms, filling these until they seem blown tight enough to burst. The individual members may increase in girth to an unbelievable extent and faces fill as taut and globular as balloons.[92]

But, while such bodies might be viewed, after Bakhtin, as contributors to a festive fecundity,[93] the reading seems strained. The war fatality does not belong to carnival. It has more in common with what Kelly Hurley calls 'the Gothic body'. '[Fin-de-siècle] Gothic', argues Hurley, 'offers the spectacle of a body metamorphic and undifferentiated... in place of a unitary and securely bounded human subjectivity, one that is both fragmented and permeable... a not-quite human subject... continually in danger of becoming not-itself, becoming other'.[94] The corpse 'sprawling in the sun' in Keith Douglas's '*Vergissmeinnicht*' fulfils these criteria: the stomach burst open like a 'cave', the eye turned to 'paper', the skin 'swart' and fly-blown ('mocked at by his own equipment / that's hard and good when he's decayed' also suggests a projection of penis onto gun barrel, a suggestion made stronger by Douglas changing 'durable' in an earlier draft to 'own').[95] Fragmented, permeated and metamorphic, there is also a

---

[88] Tolstoy, *War and Peace*, 486, 488, 502, 1189, 735, 1055.

[89] Manning, *Her Privates We* (London: Serpent's Tail, 1999), 47.

[90] Ernest Hemingway, *For Whom the Bell Tolls* (London: Arrow, 1994), 376.

[91] See Aristotle, *Poetics* 4, on the delight taken in artistic representations of the dead body.

[92] Ernest Hemingway, 'A Natural History of the Dead', *The First Forty-Nine Stories* (London: Arrow, 1993), 420.

[93] Mikhail Bakhtin, *Rabelais and His World*, trans. Hélène Iswolsky (Bloomington: Indiana University Press, 1984), 317.

[94] Kelly Hurley, *The Gothic Body: Sexuality, Materialism, and Degeneration at the Fin de Siècle* (Cambridge: Cambridge University Press, 1996), 34.

[95] Keith Douglas, *The Complete Poems*, ed. Desmond Graham (Oxford: Oxford University Press, 1998), 140.

sense in which this body refuses the category 'dead', as Douglas makes the German and his girlfriend Steffi seem to coincide. The lines 'here the lover and killer are mingled / who had one body and one heart' most obviously suggest that the dead man was both a lover and a warrior, but also hint that the mingling is of the dead man ('killer') and the absent woman (to whom 'lover' may also refer). Though death has 'singled' the soldier, it has also had a doubling effect in that it has done 'mortal hurt' to the lover. In an early version, Douglas added a couplet at the end of the poem – two lines which Steffi might have written on the photograph: 'Mein Mund ist stumm, aber mein Aug'es spricht / Und was es sagt ist kurz – Vergissmeinnicht'.[96] These lines give rise to further coincidences between the corpse and woman or, at least, her photographic image: the mouths of both are silent, the eyes of both are paper (potential 'speaking' texts as the word 'spricht' suggests) and, just as the corpse is 'abased' and 'decayed', the picture is 'dishonoured' in the 'spoil' of the gunpit. Roland Barthes argues that a photograph of a dead body evokes horror because 'it certifies that the corpse is alive, as corpse: it is the living image of a dead thing':[97] in '*Vergissmeinnicht*', the photograph of a living person is dying, too. Strangely un-dead, and demonic while alive, Douglas's German 'explode[s] crucial binarisms that lie at the foundations of human identity'.[98] In ascribing this function to Gothic (and to *fin-de-siècle* Gothic in particular), Hurley notes that the genre re-emerges 'cyclically, at periods of cultural stress, to negotiate the anxieties that accompany social and epistemological transformations and crises'.[99] War is a period of cultural stress par excellence, a time when identity is radically threatened. But it is also important to note that the dead of war are not always characterised by the metamorphic qualities of the Gothic or carnivalesque body. These are immoveable bodies, gross and unmanageable. Not easily dragged away – the corpse in '*Vergissmeinnicht*' has lain unmoved in the desert for three weeks – these heavy dead bodies clog up the text, difficult to avoid or circumvent. Again, like photographs, they are traces, memories, silent reproaches.

As Douglas's paper eye and burst stomach indicate, bodies shatter into further shards of significance, are 'packaged and sent home in parts'.[100] If the reader of war literature is constantly tripping over corpses, he or she is also assailed on every side by body parts. Jerky stumps and phantom

---

[96] 'My mouth is silent but my eye speaks / And what it says is short – Forget-me-not'.
[97] Roland Barthes, *Camera Lucida*, trans. Richard Howard (London: Fontana, 1984), 35.
[98] Hurley, *The Gothic Body*, 25.   [99] *Ibid.*, 5.
[100] Louis Simpson, 'The Heroes' (undated), *Selected Poems* (Oxford: Oxford University Press, 1966), 20.

limbs startle and pester the reader,[101] while trunks clutter up texts: so many reminders of the etymology of 'detail' – to cut into pieces for retail (the sale of commodities in small quantities). Detached limbs are similarly retailed in war texts, offered as counters of the conflict which has detached them. But how might they be interpreted?

Dismemberment is, again, a stock image of the Bakhtinian grotesque, an assault on the confines of the body which opens it up, assuaging anxieties about corporeal limitations and causing laughter.[102] But the body in pieces in the war text is not easily slotted into the medieval traditions of mythologising and relic-worship adduced by Bakhtin. A more apposite way of viewing them can be illustrated with reference to Dalton Trumbo's *Johnny Got His Gun* (1939), which imagines a First World War American soldier, Joe Bonham, lying in a French hospital. Joe has lost not only both legs and both arms, but eyes, nose, mouth, tongue and hearing as well. Reduced to head and trunk, he is a synecdoche of a person. Joe realises his horrific losses incrementally, as though being slowly stripped of his corporeality. When he is fully aware of what has gone, he thinks:

He was alive alive. He was nothing but a piece of meat like the chunks of cartilage old Prof Vogel used to have in biology. Chunks of cartilage that didn't have anything except life so they grew on chemicals. But he was one up on the cartilage. He had a mind and it was thinking . . . He was thinking and he was just a thing.[103]

The 'rhetoric of Thing-ness' is a feature of Gothic, a rhetoric 'deployed to signal the loss of human specificity, the becoming-abhuman of the human body'.[104] But, as this passage makes clear, Joe's thing-ness is mitigated by his thinking. Rather than offering merely a Gothic object of horror, troubling classifications and undermining perceptions of the human, Trumbo encourages the reader to respond to Joe's missing limbs in a specific way. The way this response works is once more illuminated by Kant's 'Analytic

---

[101] Some of these even assume a life of their own: truant and wilful synecdoches. Cf. *Henry V* 4.1.131–5: 'WILLIAMS: But if the cause be not good, the King himself hath a heavy reckoning to make, when all those legs and arms and heads chopped off in a battle shall join together at the latter day, and cry all, "We died at such a place" – some swearing, some crying for a surgeon'; Louisa May Alcott's *Hospital Sketches* (1863): 'Lord! what a scramble there'll be for arms and legs, when we old boys come out of our graves, on the Judgment Day: wonder if we shall get our own again? If we do, my leg will have to tramp from Fredericksburg, my arm from here, I suppose, and meet my body, wherever it may be' (ed. Bessie Z. Jones (Cambridge, MA: The Belknap Press of Harvard University Press, 1960), 32); and Silas Weir Mitchell's 'The Case of George Dedlow', *Atlantic Monthly* 18.105 (July 1866), 1–11, in which a quadruple amputee is visited by the ghosts of his legs at a séance.

[102] Bakhtin, *Rabelais and His World*, 318, 339, 347.

[103] Dalton Trumbo, *Johnny Got His Gun* (New York: Citadel, 2007), 64.

[104] Hurley, *The Gothic Body*, 30.

of the Sublime' (1790). Discussing how aesthetic judgement of the sublime functions (a subject explored in depth in Chapters 5 and 6), Kant
proscribes consideration of 'ends' or purposes. In the specific case of the
'human figure', he writes:

We do not look to concepts of the ends for which all its members exist for
determining grounds of our judgment and must not let agreement with them
influence our aesthetic judgment (which in that case would no longer be pure),
though that they do not conflict with those ends is of course a necessary condition
even of aesthetic satisfaction.[105]

Paul de Man interprets this as follows:

We must, in short, consider our limbs, our hands, our toes, our breasts, or what
Montaigne so cheerfully referred to as '*Monsieur ma partie,*' in themselves, severed
from the organic unity of the body, the way the poets look at the oceans severed
from their geographical place on earth. We must, in other words, disarticulate,
mutilate, the body.[106]

For de Man, a non-purposive aesthetic judgement of the human figure
requires dismemberment: a hand, removed from the body, ceases to have
any hand-like function. And yet, the opposite effect seems to be produced
by Joe Bonham's missing limbs. To 'sever' the oceans from their 'geographical place' may be to permit an apprehension of them unencumbered by
the preoccupations of earth science, but to 'disarticulate' the body is precisely to reduce its constituent parts to their roles. Joe's missing arms and
legs are apotheoses of arms and legs; his lost eyes, nose, mouth and ears
the epitomes of eyes, noses, mouths and ears.[107] As he feels them, the
absences loudly proclaim the (lost) ability to touch, to feel, to carry, to
sense.

Amputation in *Johnny Got His Gun* leads the reader to substitute purposive for aesthetic judgement. But the key body parts in this regard are
not strictly the missing limbs. The crucial purposive organ is Joe Bonham's
skin. Through sensing the nurse's hands manipulating him and the warmth
of the sunrise, he is eventually able to tell the time and count the days and
years:

---

[105] Kant, *Critique*, 153. See earlier.
[106] Paul de Man, 'Phenomenality and Materiality in Kant', in *The Textual Sublime. Deconstruction
and Its Differences*, eds. Hugh J. Silverman and Gary E. Aylesworth (New York: State University of
New York Press, 1990), 106.
[107] The same is true of the subject of Denise Levertov's poem, 'The Weeping Woman' (1975): 'She is
weeping for her lost right arm. / She cannot write the alphabet any more / on the kindergarten
blackboard' (*Poems 1972–1982* (New York: New Directions, 2001), 17).

Although he knew that he was in a sheltered hospital room as far removed as possible from changes in temperature it seemed to him when it came that it came in a blaze of heat. It felt like his neck was seared burned scorched by the heat of the rising sun.[108]

As a result of his keen desire to mark time, Joe's skin has become hyper-sensitive and ultra-functional. Now a sunrise sensed through glass in a northern clime is a 'blaze': the feeling of heat can be calibrated as sear-ing, burning or scorching. With the arrival of a new nurse, a further set of extraordinary acts of communication through skin occurs. From the vibrations of her footsteps, Joe is able to work out that she is shorter and younger than the usual nurse.[109] She puts her hand to his forehead and he tries to 'ripple his skin to show her how much he appreciated the way she had done it'.[110] Then he realises that she has opened his nightshirt and is 'moving the tip of her finger against the skin of his breast'.[111] After a while, it dawns on him that she is tracing letters and he 'tighten[s] the skin on his chest so that he [can] better receive the impression of her finger'.[112]

Are these communications received with or on the skin? The question cuts to the ambivalent status of the organ: does the skin enclose the self or is it equivalent to the self? Didier Anzieu has proposed a metaphorical 'Skin Ego' – 'a mental image of which the Ego of the child makes use during the early phases of its development to represent itself as an Ego containing psychical contents, on the basis of its experience of the surface of the body'.[113] Equating the skin with the subject allows it to 'stand metonymically for the whole human body'.[114] And skin as synecdoche is strikingly apt in the context of war representation. In *Dichtung und Wahrheit* (1811–33), Goethe writes:

[A] man's name is not like a cloak, which merely hangs about him, and which, perchance, may be twitched and pulled with impunity; but is a perfectly fitting garment, which has grown over and around him like his very skin, and which one cannot scratch and scrape without wounding the man himself.[115]

---

[108] Trumbo, *Johnny Got His Gun*, 142.   [109] *Ibid.*, 203.

[110] *Ibid.*, 204.   [111] *Ibid.*, 205.   [112] *Ibid.*, 207.

[113] Didier Anzieu, *The Skin Ego*, trans. Chris Turner (New Haven: Yale University Press, 1989), 40. Anzieu cites the novel and film versions of *Johnny Got His Gun*: in the latter (1971 dir. Trumbo), Joe is masturbated by the nurse and as a result, Anzieu argues, 'regains the will to survive, because he feels himself recognized and his need for communication and his virile desire satisfied' (*ibid.*, 39).

[114] Claudia Benthien, *Skin. On the Cultural Border Between Self and the World*, trans. Thomas Dunlap (New York: Columbia University Press, 2002), 17.

[115] Johann Wolfgang von. Goethe, *Poetry and Truth from My Own Life*, trans. Minna Steele Smith, 2 vols. (London: George Bell, 1908), vol. I, 364.

Like the name, the skin gathers together, summates the individual: both are 'indispensable components of identity';[116] both susceptible to attack. 'Skin' shares with 'shame' the Indo-Germanic root meaning 'to cover':[117] 'covering oneself is a natural expression of shame'. When the skin is understood, not as the self's integument but as its equivalent, nakedness becomes, like namelessness, a form of ignominy. Little more than skin, and unable to communicate his name, Joe Bonham is ashamed to be looked at: 'he didn't want anybody he had ever known to see him . . . He only wanted to hide his face to turn his blind sockets away from them to keep them from seeing the chewed up hole that used to be a nose and mouth that used to be a living human face.'[118]

Joe's skin is a thing of pure purpose: a record of war, a receptor of vibrations, a piece of parchment for finger-writing (Anzieu argues that one function of the skin is as 'a site and primary means of communicating with others, of establishing signifying relations . . . an "inscribing surface" for the marks left by those others').[119] As such, it resists aesthetic judgement and instead induces the reader to ponder corporeal functionality and focus on its loss. The result is a kind of readerly hyper-sensitivity, easily rubbed raw.

The final synecdoche to be noted is monomachy: the clash between two warriors. Battle scenes in the *Iliad*[120] involve a cinematic technique in which the focus moves from individual encounter to individual encounter, intermittently panning out over the entire field of fighting. One critical line of thinking is that this constitutes a bi-angled depiction of promachos-style warfare.[121] In this mode of battle, the *promachoi*, or foremost fighters, engage in a kind of 'hit-and-run' tactic,[122] falling back between bouts into the mass of men (*plethus*) behind them. In addition to promachos warfare, the *Iliad* features set-piece duels (Paris against Menelaus, Hector against Aias, Hector against Achilles), which tend to take place at the outset of mass battles. Historians account for the ancient institution of monomachy by suggesting that it provided an opportunity for a warrior to prove his qualities of leadership and legitimise his status[123] or to win fame (rather than wars) and thereby provide a service to the state.[124] But what is the

---

[116] Benthien, *Skin*, 95. See also Anzieu: 'The Skin Ego performs a function of individuating the Self, thus giving the Self a sense of its own uniqueness' (*The Skin Ego*, 103).

[117] Benthien, *Skin*, 100.   [118] Trumbo, *Johnny Got His Gun*, 163.

[119] Anzieu, *The Skin Ego*, 40.   [120] See, for example, those beginning at 4.457.

[121] Hans van Wees, 'Kings in Combat: Battles and Heroes in the *Iliad*', *The Classical Quarterly* 38.1 (1988), 12.

[122] *Ibid.*, 5.   [123] *Ibid.*, 17, 19.

[124] S. P. Oakley, 'Single Combat in the Roman Republic', *The Classical Quarterly* 35.2 (1985), 399, 405.

literary effect of monomachy? Most obviously, a fierce clash between named warriors demonstrates the *personalised* nature of war:[125] in this sense, the scenes have a condensing effect on scale (that they also have an inflationary effect was noted earlier in the discussion of hyper-names). These brief encounters are quanta of dramatic energy, providing for the reader suspense and *Schreck seriatim*. They involve fighters of extraordinary valour (heroes in the Homeric sense of 'men of superhuman strength, courage, or ability, favoured by the gods'),[126] serial cynosures in the text who loom larger-than-life for the reader or audience.

The risk with the larger-than-life approach is oversimplification: epic monomachy can all too easily become a reductive and distorting clash between agents of pure good and evil. In *Paradise Lost*, all the problems of scale discussed in this chapter are magnified since this is a cosmic battle which must be represented; nonetheless, this is *nuanced* monomachy. Milton adopts Homer's techniques of interspersing promachos-style fighting (though he names fewer individual encounters (see 6.373–5 for the explanation)) with set-piece duels: Satan versus Abdiel, Satan versus Michael, Christ versus the entire horde of rebel angels.[127] Providing the backdrop against which these encounters are highlighted are the enormous armies of obedient and fallen angels, conveyed both by big numbers and by phrases expressing the impossibility of counting them: 'thousands and millions ranged for fight', 'innumerable', 'incessant armies', 'Millions of fierce encountering angels', 'Army against army numberless'.[128] Among these countless forces, Satan comes 'towering' (6.110). Milton emphasises

---

[125] For those who experience it, the huge phenomenon of war comes down to the deeply personal. This catches Nikolai Rostov unawares: '"Who are they? Are they coming at me? Can they be running at me? And why? To kill me? *Me* whom everyone is so fond of?" He thought of his mother's love for him, of his family's and his friends', and the enemy's intention of killing him seemed impossible' (Tolstoy, *War and Peace*, 216). See also the following exchange from Heller's *Catch-22*:

> 'They're trying to kill me,' Yossarian told him calmly.
> 'No one's trying to kill you,' Clevinger cried.
> 'Then why are they shooting at me?' Yossarian asked.
> 'They're shooting at *everyone*,' Clevinger answered. 'They're trying to kill everyone.'
> 'And what difference does that make?' (16)

[126] *OED* 1; see also R. Renehan, 'The Heldentod in Homer: One Heroic Ideal', *Classical Philology* 82.2 (April 1987), 100.

[127] For a thorough account of the influence of classical literature on *Paradise Lost*, see Charles Martindale, *John Milton and the Transformation of Ancient Epic* (Bristol: Bristol Classical Press, 2002). For the relationship between the war in heaven, early Christian hexameral poems and Renaissance epics, see Stella Purce Revard, *The War in Heaven: Paradise Lost and the Tradition of Satan's Rebellion* (Ithaca: Cornell University Press, 1980).

[128] John Milton, *Paradise Lost*, ed. Alastair Fowler (London: Longman, 1998), 6.48, 82, 138, 220, 187.

Satan's hugeness: exceeding any Homeric hero, he is as massive as a mountain – 'like Tenerife or Atlas unremoved'[129] – and greater than the greatest knights:

> Thus far these beyond
> Compare of mortal prowess yet observed
> Their dread commander. He, above the rest
> In shape and gesture proudly eminent,
> Stood like a tower.[130]

This passage demonstrates Milton's strategy of recalibration of scale. The arrayed ranks of rebel angels – already evoked in their innumerableness – are 'beyond compare of mortal prowess', but Satan is greater. His duel with Michael is compared – 'to set forth / Great things by small'[131] – to the collision of planets, but the duel is bigger. The warring angels pluck the 'seated hills' and throw them at each other, but when Christ rides over his 'prostrate' foe they are driven to wish 'the mountains now might be again / Thrown on them as a shelter from his ire' (6.664, 6.842–3). What seemed big must be re-viewed as small, so that the even bigger can be encompassed. The telescoping effect is, precisely, Kant's mathematical sublime: 'when apprehension has gone so far that the partial representations of the intuition of the senses that were apprehended first already begin to fade in the imagination as the latter proceeds on to the apprehension of further ones, then it loses on the one side as much as it gains on the other, and there is in the comprehension a greatest point beyond which it cannot go'.[132] As Milton inexorably cranks up the scale, comprehension is stretched to its limits.

The calibration and recalibration of his hugeness convey a salient fact about Satan, namely that he is *famous*. Standing out from the crowd, he is talked about and looked up to. Leo Braudy relates desire for fame with 'uncertainty of personal identity'[133] and Satan experiences doubt as to his stature when he realises his new realm is the burning lake:

> What matter where, if I be still the same
> And what I should be, all but less than he
> Whom thunder hath made greater?[134]

---

[129] *Ibid.*, 4.987. Cf. *Iliad.*, 13.754.

[130] Milton, *Paradise Lost* 1.587–91. Edmund Burke cites this description as an example of the sublime (*A Philosophical Enquiry*, 57).

[131] Milton, *Paradise Lost* 6.310–11.   [132] Kant, *Critique*, 135.

[133] Leo Braudy, *The Frenzy of Renown: Fame and Its History* (Oxford: Oxford University Press, 1986), 7.

[134] Milton, *Paradise Lost* 1.256–8.

In his duels with Abdiel and Michael,[135] Satan receives blows that lower him, literally and by wounding his pride and therefore his fame. Abdiel's strike forces him to recoil ten paces to his knees. Michael's leaves him 'Gnashing for anguish and despire and shame / To find himself not matchless and his pride / Humbled by such rebuke' (6.340–2). Milton draws a clear distinction between the angels who, 'contented with their fame in Heaven, / Seek not the praise of men' (6.375–6) and 'the other sort' who:

> In might though wondrous and in acts of war,
> Nor of renown less eager, yet by doom
> Cancelled from Heaven and sacred memory,
> Nameless in dark oblivion let them dwell.
> For strength from truth divided and from just,
> Illaudable, naught merits but dispraise
> And ignominy, yet to glory aspires
> Vainglorious, and through infamy seeks fame:
> Therefore eternal silence be their doom.
>
> (6.377–85)

Expressing a Christian preference for private virtue over public fame, Milton makes clear that the rebel angels' punishment is ignominy (a cognate also appears at 6.395).[136] Indeed, Satan's 'former name / Is heard no more in Heaven'[137] and the rebels are also now known by other names (1.374). The consequence is that they are lost without trace:

> Though of their names in heavenly records now
> Be no memorial, blotted out and razed
> By their rebellion from the books of life.
>
> (1.361–3)

This punishment is an ironic reversal of the Act of Indemnity and Oblivion 1660, which waived liability for revolutionary behaviour except for those actually involved in the regicide – a piece of legislation from which Milton himself benefited. The names of the rebel angels, by contrast, are forgotten though their deeds remain on the record. Through synecdochic monomachy on a grand scale, Milton brings off the feat, not just of conveying mass warfare, but of conveying *cosmic yet subtle* mass warfare. Juxtaposing the named and the nameless, he not only makes the theological point that pride is not to be rewarded through endurance as a name-trace but also

---

[135] *Ibid.*, 6.189–98, 6.296–353.
[136] For an exhaustive account of naming in Milton's works, see John Leonard, *Naming in Paradise: Milton and the Language of Adam and Eve* (Cambridge: Cambridge University Press, 1990).
[137] Milton, *Paradise Lost* 5.658–9; see also 1.82.

exploits the effects of different formal solutions to the enormity of conflict. If anonymity conveys un-differentiation and massification, a few ringing names inflate and focus.

In a 1945 poem, 'The One', Ida Proctor wrote:

> In the mass is the one.
> In the thousand drowned,
> In the hundred shot,
> In the five crashed,
> Is the one.
> Over the news
> Falls the shadow
> Of the one.
> We cannot weep
> At tragedy for millions
> But for one.
> In the mind
> For the mind's life
> The one lives on.[138]

Resonating with the physical and psychical experiences of conflict, detail – the one – is war's natural representative mode. As Proctor and the other writers discussed in this chapter point out, the mind blanks at war's massive numbers. Recuperating the individual – particularly the individual's name – is a counterthrust to the blankness, but the numbers have a tendency to mount up again. Concentration on detail is a means of focusing the endless losses. In *The Arte of English Poesie*, George Putten-ham cautioned that synecdoche, 'the figure of quick conceite', has a certain 'darkenes and duplicitie': 'it encombers the minde with a certaine imagi-nation what it may be that is meant and not expressed'.[139] Puttenham's is an apt warning that the devil is in the details. The single searing image can obscure the bigger picture, unfairly forcing other details to the background and suggesting that the referent is less than the sum of its parts. But forcing the mind to consider 'what it may be that is meant and not expressed' is literature's peculiar talent, and its best hope of conveying the unknown quantity of war's vast scale.

---

[138] Ida Proctor, 'The One', in *Chaos of the Night: Women's Poetry and Verse of the Second World War*, ed. Catherine Reilly (London: Virago, 1984), 102.
[139] Puttenham, *The Arte of English Poesie*, 195.

CHAPTER 3

Zones

In his account of the Battle of Schön Graben, Tolstoy goes beyond his usual practice of supplying details of military topography. He establishes a gap – 'unapproachable and intangible' – of some seven hundred yards between the French and Russian armies and configures it as a field of uncertainty, as curiously inviting as it is forbidding:

'One step beyond that line, which is like the bourne dividing the living from the dead, lies the Unknown of suffering and death. And what is there? Who is there? There beyond that field, beyond that tree, that roof gleaming in the sun? No one knows, but who does not long to know? You fear to cross that line, yet you long to cross it; and you know that sooner or later it will have to be crossed and you will find out what lies there on the other side of the line, just as you will inevitably have to learn what lies the other side of death. But you are strong, healthy, cheerful and excited, and surrounded by other men just as full of health and exuberant spirits.' Such are the sensations, if not the actual thoughts of every man who finds himself confronted by the enemy, and these feelings lend a singular vividness and happy distinctness of impression to everything that takes place at such moments.[1]

This passage illustrates the special relationship between war and space. War is fought over and in space, it alters irrevocably the space on and within which it occurs. But it also brings into being a unique situation, unclassifiable as either neutral 'space' or significant 'place', vital and intense yet temporary (lasting 'moments') and arbitrary, as much a product of experience as of geographical factors, transformative, requiring special consciousness ('singular vividness and happy distinctness of impression') from those within it. This is the war zone. In *War and Peace*, it features recurrently, delimited by 'that terrible dividing line of uncertainty and fear', 'this invisible line'.[2] The line demarcates a situation where knowledge and experience will be gained and from which there will therefore be no innocent return. In entering this situation – Keith Douglas likened it to walking through a

---

[1] Tolstoy, *War and Peace*, 162.   [2] *Ibid.*, 214.

looking-glass[3] – an individual immediately becomes different from those who have not entered it: hence the war zone becomes the locus in and on which the credentials of autopsy are grounded.

The challenge for war writing is to convey this charged space, to communicate the complex situation – part psycho-physiological, part geographical – that is conflict. What responses has this challenge elicited? Dunya Mikhail's poem 'O' (published in 2004) takes a concrete approach: a spiral of twelve repeated phrases that draws the reader, at acceleration, down a vortex of ambulances, emergency rooms, coffins and graves.[4] The shape of the poem, and of its title, dramatise the sense that, once entered, the mental and physical confinement of bombed Iraq cannot be left; the word / sound O – a cry of anguish – simultaneously functions as a commentary on the situation. Writers have also used metaphors and analogies to underscore the affinities between warfare and life on the land, drawing attention to war's *locative* quality, its close association to the territory it is fought on and over. Literature hints at what is encrypted in the warscape – what is buried or otherwise vanished – allowing the reader to unearth what has taken (the) place. Land is figured as a text of war, recording its prosecution in the script of damaged terrain and denuded vegetation. The special topographical awareness possessed by those in the war zone is recreated. Most importantly, the ancient literary mode of pastoral is pressed into service.

Now, the symbolic status of war has famously been called 'the ultimate anti-pastoral'[5] and, prima facie, this is correct. There is nothing Arcadian about warfare; its bleak and ravaged landscapes are *loci horribiles*. But, arguably, pastoral can do more than point up the desolation of the warscape through (ironic) contrast. Conceived of as a space of isolation and exceptional cognition, pastoral's rural retreat has surprising affinities with the psycho-geographical experience of the war zone. The zone emerges, not so much as anti-pastoral, as inverted pastoral: it requires proactive entry instead of withdrawal but still demands and produces a special consciousness. And as Annabel Patterson in *Pastoral and Ideology* (1988) and Terry Eagleton in his essay on William Empson, 'The Critic as Clown' (collected 1988), have noted, the security and isolation of pastoral raise questions as to the proper relationship of the pastoral commentator to his or her subject matter. Similar questions surround the authority of the individual who has experienced the war zone though, again, the pastoral situation is inverted.

[3] Keith Douglas, *Alamein to Zem-Zem*, ed. Desmond Graham (London: Faber, 1992), 16.
[4] Dunya Mikhail, *The War Works Hard*, trans. Elizabeth Winslow (Manchester: Carcanet, 2006), 23.
[5] Fussell, *The Great War and Modern Memory*, 231.

While the pastoral commentator may be disqualified from pronouncing upon a society he or she is unacceptably removed from, the insights of the individual who has entered the war zone are routinely accorded privileged status: the valorisation of combat gnosticism discussed in Chapter 1. In figuring the war zone, then, the writer engages with the fundamental epistemology of conflict representation. This chapter explores this engagement in Virgil's *Eclogues* (42–37 BCE), Joseph Addison's 'The Campaign' (1705), Ambrose Bierce's 'What I Saw at Shiloh' (1881), Rupert Brooke's 'The Soldier' (1914), Edward Thomas's 'As the team's head-brass' (1916) and Henry Reed's 'Lessons of the War' (1946–91).

What manner of space or place is the war zone? The terms embedded in this question derive from the distinction, of ancient standing, between a neutral and a charged location: space corresponds with Aristotle's idea of *topos*, place with Plato's idea of *chora*. Eugene Victor Walter explains:

In the classical [Greek] language, *topos* tended to suggest mere location or the objective features of a place, and Aristotle made it into an abstract term signifying pure position. The older word, *chora* – or sometimes *choros* – retained subjective meanings in the classical period. It appeared in emotional statements about places, and writers were inclined to call a sacred place a *chora* instead of a *topos*.[6]

The space/place dichotomy is a commonplace in contemporary geography. J. E. Malpas notes that 'place' is often distinguished from 'mere location' through being 'understood as a matter of the *human response* to physical surroundings of locations',[7] while the environmental psychologist Jonathan D. Sime writes that 'the term "place", as opposed to space, implies a strong emotional tie, temporary or more longlasting, between a person and a particular physical location'.[8] But, as Patricia Yaeger points out, the 'space/place binary' often becomes 'porous and provisional':[9] the exact nature of the response or tie to the location in question is in dispute, the idea of a location unaffected by human shaping is questionable and the dichotomy in any event risks overlooking those human interactions with the environment that are hidden or vanished.

The war zone itself defies easy classification as space or place. War involves a particularly intense attachment to location (most often expressed

[6] Eugene Victor Walter, *Placeways: A Theory of the Human Environment* (Chapel Hill: University of North Carolina Press, 1988), 120. See Aristotle, *The Physics* 4 *passim*; Plato, *Timaeus* 52.

[7] J. E. Malpas, *Place and Experience: A Philosophical Topography* (Cambridge: Cambridge University Press, 1999), 30.

[8] Jonathan D. Sime, 'Creating Places or Designing Spaces?' *Journal of Environmental Psychology* 6.1 (1986), 50.

[9] Patricia Yaeger, 'Introduction: Narrating Space', in *The Geography of Identity*, ed. Patricia Yaeger (Ann Arbor: The University of Michigan Press, 1996), 5n.

in terms of a relationship with the land) on the part of those fighting it, an attachment that is both cognitive and emotional. But the attachment is most often negative (the terrain is viewed as hostile), departing from standard models of 'place' which involve 'positive, satisfactory experience(s)';[10] moreover it is temporary and contingent. A location of great tactical importance, known with the intimacy required for survival by those within it, is abandoned, together with its significance, when battle moves on: the detritus of what Addison calls 'the moving war'.[11] Both conceptual category and literal territory, the war zone is highly regulated (including by the international law of armed conflict) but also highly lawless, a state of exception where peacetime laws and norms are suspended. An 'affective terrain',[12] it records the effects of battle in its temporary and permanent alterations; in Patricia Yaeger's terminology,[13] it is a realm of ghosts, encrypting the bodies and body parts that fall to ground. It is both *heimlich* and *unheimlich*, vividly known and constantly strange.

Resistant to categorisation in terms of space/place, how else might the war zone be understood? The French ethnologist Marc Augé applies the term 'non-place' (*non-lieu*) to those *loci* of transit and interchange which are simply there 'to be passed through'; entering the non-place, the individual is 'relieved of his usual determinants'.[14] The war zone's temporary, transitional and self-transforming qualities are those of the non-place, but this itself can only be a passing description. The zone has more in common with Edward W. Soja's concept of 'thirdspace': 'simultaneously real and imagined and more (both and also)'.[15] More effectively, it may be understood as a *situation*, a word that incorporates both terrain and experience: the horizontal and vertical axes, so to speak, of the locative.

How, then, is this situation conveyed in war writing and what is achieved in the process? Fundamental to the war/space relationship is that the latter is both subject and venue of the former. And though the *loci* of war may range from the ocean depths to the troposphere to cyberspace, conflict has a special affinity with land. Land is what is fought for: conquered,

[10] Sime, 'Creating Places?', 50.
[11] Joseph Addison, 'The Campaign', *The Miscellaneous Works of Joseph Addison*, ed. A. C. Guthkelch, 2 vols. (London: G. Bell, 1914), vol. I, line 57.
[12] Sara Blair, 'Cultural Geography and the Place of the Literary', *American Literary History* 10.3 (Autumn 1998), 545.
[13] Yaeger, 'Introduction', 6, 25.
[14] Marc Augé, *Non-Places: Introduction to an Anthropology of Supermodernity*, trans. John Howe (London: Verso, 1995), 107, 104, 103.
[15] Edward W. Soja, *Thirdspace: Journeys to Los Angeles and Other Real-and-Imagined Places* (Oxford: Blackwell, 1996), 11.

defended, loved. The use of descriptions and visual images of the English countryside as motivating propaganda in both world wars is well known,[16] appealing to individuals' sense of attachment towards the land (whether closely acquainted with it or not) to induce them to defend the nation. But beyond this, references to the land underscore war's *emplaced* quality. 'I see war (or should I say I feel war?) more as a territory than as a page of history', wrote Elizabeth Bowen,[17] and this sense pervades the specially grounded consciousness of those fighting.

The significance of land is linked to the fact that war takes place on its own subject matter. Wars are almost exclusively fought outdoors and involve a close relationship with the terrain. Use of the word 'field' to signify the ground on which battle is fought dates from *c.*1300 (*OED*) and the title of Addison's poem on the Duke of Marlborough's victory at Blenheim (Blindheim, Bavaria), 'The Campaign', alerts the reader to the ancient nexus between military expedition and open countryside.[18] The champaign enables the campaign, supporting the troops in the sense both of holding them up from below and of nourishing them:

> The growth of meadows, and the pride of fields,
> Whatever spoils Bavaria's summer yields,
> (The Danube's great increase) Britannia shares,
> The food of armies, and support of wars.[19]

With land cast as booty for despoliation ('a purchase to the sword' (line 60)), warfare is revealed as a perverse kind of planting that transforms the country physically as well as politically. Despoiled Bavaria will become the record of Marlborough's conquest. At first, this will be a temporary record of stripped crops, but later in the poem, permanent violation is described:

---

[16] See Fussell, *The Great War and Modern Memory* and David Matless, *Landscape and Englishness* (London: Reaktion, 1998).

[17] Elizabeth Bowen, *The Mulberry Tree*, ed. Hermione Lee (London: Vintage, 1999), 5.

[18] 'Campaign' has the military significance of 'the continuance and operations of an army "in the field" for a season or other definite portion of time, or while engaged in one continuous series of military operations constituting the whole, or a distinct part, of a war' (*OED* 3). The *OED* note continues: 'The name arose in the earlier conditions of warfare, according to which an army remained in quarters (in towns, garrisons, fortresses, or camps) during the winter, and on the approach of summer issued forth into the open country (*nella campagna*, *dans la campagne*) or "took the field", until the close of the season again suspended active operations. Hence the name properly signifying the "being in the field", was also applied, now to the season or time during which the army kept the field, and now to the series of operations performed during this time. In the changed conditions of modern warfare, the season of the year is of much less importance, and a campaign has now no direct reference to time or season, but to an expedition or continuous series of operations bearing upon a distinct object, the accomplishment or abandonment of which marks its end, whether in the course of a week or two, or after one or more years.'

[19] Addison, 'The Campaign', lines 204–7.

> [T]he soldier fills his hand
> With sword and fire, and ravages the land,
> A thousand villages to ashes turns,
> In crackling flames a thousand harvests burns.
> To the thick woods the woolly flocks retreat,
> And mixt with bellowing herds confus'dly bleat.
>
> (lines 232–7)

The verb 'ravage' suggests, in its etymology, both seizure and penetration.[20] But the earth-scorching policy[21] is not so much one of despoliation as of desertification. The campaign's progress is measured and recorded by the conversion of villages, crop-fields and pastures to ashland; the terrain becomes a vast map of conquest. Writing on cartography, J. B. Harley notes that military maps 'not only facilitate the conduct of warfare, but also palliate the sense of guilt which arises from its conduct: the silent lines of the paper landscape foster the notion of socially empty space'.[22] Converted into a map on, as it were, a one-to-one scale, Addison's Moselle region is likewise presented as a socially empty space, functioning as both metaphor and metonym for political domination:

> [T]he Moselle, appearing from afar,
> Retards the progress of the moving war.
> Delightful stream, had Nature bid her fall
> In distant climes, far from the perjur'd Gaul;
> But now a purchase to the sword she lyes,
> Her harvests for uncertain owners rise,
> Each vineyard doubtful of its master grows,
> And to the victor's bowl each vintage flows.[23]

As competing political claims are disguised as doubtfulness as to ownership on the part of the real estate itself, human existence and activity are effectively removed from the landscape.

The idea of war inscribing itself on the land informs Edward Thomas's 'As the team's head-brass', written on 27 May 1916, when Thomas was serving as a map-reading instructor before going out to fight in France.[24]

---

[20] The Old French *revagier* means to pull out vines.

[21] The term 'scorched earth policy' strictly refers to the devastation of the land by its inhabitants, to thwart an invading army (*OED* 1b).

[22] J. B. Harley, 'Maps, Knowledge, and Power', in *The Iconography of Landscape: Essays on the Symbolic Representation, Design and Use of Past Environments*, ed. Stephen Daniels and Denis Cosgrove (Cambridge: Cambridge University Press, 1988), 284.

[23] Addison, 'The Campaign', lines 56–63.

[24] Edward Thomas, *Selected Poems and Prose*, ed. David Wright (Harmondsworth: Penguin, 1981), 294. Edna Longley points out that this poem rewrites Hardy's 'In Time of "The Breaking of

The poem points to parallel universes whose alternative existences are marked by a fallen elm. In the real universe, the tree 'strew[s] the angle of the fallow' because the man who would have helped remove it has been killed in the First World War: 'Now if / He had stayed here we should have moved the tree'.[25] This line evokes 'another world' in which the war has not taken place and the tree has been taken away. The fallen elm therefore functions as a kind of worm-hole or wooden door between the two scenarios. In the poem various affinities between the ploughed field and the Western Front are accumulated: in both locations vegetation is being uprooted, metallic instruments cut and flash, lovers are banished and the soil is turned ('clods crumble and topple over'). More significantly, in both locations proprietorship is being incised and inscribed in the earth; as Cornelia Vismann puts it, 'incisions in the ground are overall inscriptions of property and identity'.[26] A title-deed is being drafted in the boustrophedonic script of the plough as it is in its twinned territory, the entrenched landscape of the Front; as the 'yellow square / Of charlock' is 'narrowed' by the furrowing plough, so battle encroaches on the fields of France and Flanders.[27] In building up these affinities between the ploughed field and the battlefield, Thomas is not so much establishing an ironic contrast as figuring the latter in the former: a kind of ghostly sub-stratum that the plough unearths. But there is, as it were, a zone within the zone. The speaker sits on the fallen elm where what is known in Germanic law as the *Pflugswenderecht* – the right to turn the plough on neighbour's ground[28] – is exercised ('the horses turned / Instead of treading me down'). The tree, lying across 'the angle of the fallow', itself presumably prevents the area beyond it from being ploughed. The perspective of the speaker

---

Nations"' (1915) ('The Great War, History, and the English Lyric', in *The Cambridge Companion to the Literature of the First World War*, ed. Vincent Sherry (Cambridge: Cambridge University Press, 2005), 75).

[25] Thomas, *Selected Poems*, 296–7.

[26] Cornelia Vismann, 'Starting from Scratch: Concepts of Order in No Man's Land', in *War, Violence and the Modern Condition*, ed. Bernd Hüppauf (Berlin and New York: Walter de Gruyter, 1997), 49.

[27] It is tempting to read the ploughed field, and the corner in which the poem's speaker sits, in terms of Deleuze and Guattari's 'striated' and 'smooth', concepts which have also been applied to the texture of the Western Front (see Becca Weir, '"Degrees in Nothingness": Battlefield Topography in the First World War', *Critical Quarterly* 49.4 (2007), 40–55). In particular, the narrowing yellow square of charlock fulfils their criterion that 'a striated space . . . is necessarily delimited . . . the necessity of a back and forth motion [in weaving a fabric] implies a closed space' (*A Thousand Plateaus. Capitalism and Schizophrenia*, trans. Brian Massumi (London and New York: Continuum, 2004), 524). But Deleuze and Guattari insist that striated space 'is constituted by two kinds of parallel elements; in the simplest case, there are vertical elements, and the two intertwine, intersecting perpendicularly' (524). Thomas's ploughed field is not striated because, so to speak, it lacks warp.

[28] Vismann, 'Starting from Scratch', 60.

is therefore from an uncharacteristically non-furrowed region – a corner of an English field that is forever foreign. The blank site in which he sits reflects the fact that he is not, and has not been, fighting ('Have you been out?' 'No.'); his knowledge of loss of life and limb is not grounded on first-hand experience but presumably gleaned from encounters with returning veterans or from reading the newspapers. Mirroring this are his encounters with the returning ploughman (the talk at ten-minute intervals is dramatised by the jerky enjambments) and his 'reading' of the script being ploughed into the earth. Constructing the trenched landscape of the Western Front and the ploughed field as linked alternative universes, Thomas establishes the field (in both places) as the legible text of war and the ground of knowledge concerning it.

Incised and inscribed, land is the durable record of conflict. But the close relationship between the individual fighter and the war zone – the relationship which permits the use of land as a figure for the special consciousness that characterises the war experience – goes beyond scratching the surface. In war, bodies and land become very close. Soldiers are inhabitants of the terrain, troglodytes in trenches or in foxholes, wrigglers through the undergrowth, camouflaged to match their environs. But beyond this, war requires humans to become particularly intimate with the land because it is both surface and substance on which the most private bodily functions are discharged. Soldiers eat and sleep, piss and shit, bleed and die on the soil. Evoking the First World War in *Storm of Steel* (*In Strahlgewittern*) (1920), Ernst Jünger refers to 'blood-bedewed meadows' and battle that is naturalised through being conducted to the rhythm of the seasons: 'Spring marked the beginning of a new year's fighting; intimations of a big offensive were as much part of the season as primroses and pussy-willow'.[29] The dead sink into the mud, 'their pale faces staring up out of water-filled craters, or already so covered with mud that their human identity [is] almost completely masked'.[30]

The idea of the body killed in war becoming part of the terrain on which it has fallen recurs in war writing. It underscores the need for what Yaeger calls 'a spatial cryptography', for cultural geography – and literary analysis – to function as 'ghost story'[31] or as exhumation. Probably the most famous expression of the idea is Rupert Brooke's sonnet 'The Soldier':[32]

---

[29] Ernst Jünger, *Storm of Steel*, trans. Michael Hofmann (London: Penguin, 2003), 5, 141.
[30] *Ibid.*, 201.   [31] Yaeger, 'Introduction', 7, 25.
[32] Brooke himself died on a French hospital ship from sepsis following a mosquito bite, en route to fighting at Gallipoli. His remains are buried on Skyros, Greece.

> If I should die, think only this of me;
> That there's some corner of a foreign field
> That is for ever England. There shall be
> In that rich dust a richer dust concealed;
> A dust whom England bore, shaped, made aware,
> Gave, once, her flowers to love, her ways to roam,
> A body of England's breathing English air,
> Washed by the rivers, blest by suns of home.[33]

Mixed with the motifs of rural England (and Caroline Dakers points out that only 20 per cent of the population lived in the countryside in 1914, so that appreciating wild flowers, taking country walks and bathing in rivers would have been minority pastimes)[34] and a 'candidly imperialist' attitude,[35] there is in these lines a surprisingly earthy approach to death. The 'richer dust' is human (post-)humus, a corpse-compost; the word 'roam' suggests its rhyme 'loam',[36] reinforcing the idea of a flesh-fertilizer. Death in battle has suddenly become not so much a heroic gesture as a horticultural event: a means of soil enrichment. But, unlike the soldiers' corpses in Hardy's 'Drummer Hodge' (1899), Allen Tate's 'Ode to the Confederate Dead' (1928) and Seamus Heaney's 'Requiem for the Croppies' (1966), this enriched soil does not give rise to any memorialising or redemptive new vegetative growth, but remains a paradoxically sterile compost in the rhizosphere. The sterility forms an ironic contrast with Brooke's vision of the heart, which, apparently disembodied and un-interred, can participate in a cosmic ecology in which thoughts, dreams, laughter and gentleness are *given back* to other individuals.[37]

But the war/land connection goes deeper than the merging of soldiers' bodies with the soil. Radically affecting its venue, war also demands a special approach to the terrain on the part of those waging it. This approach is best described as 'topographical'. Battle is allochthonous: it springs up on territory that is strategically significant but otherwise of no special quality – territory that becomes temporarily a 'strong place' or 'thickness', akin to a stopping-place on a journey[38] – and, once concluded, moves on again.

---

[33] Rupert Brooke, *The Poetical Works*, ed. Geoffrey Keynes (London: Faber, 1970), 23.

[34] Caroline Dakers, *The Countryside at War 1914–1918* (London: Constable, 1987), 15.

[35] Jon Silkin, 'Introduction', in *The Penguin Book of First World War Poetry*, ed. Jon Silkin, 2nd edn (London: Penguin, 1981), 30.

[36] Cf. Edmund Blunden's 'bone-fed loam' ('Rural Economy' (1917), *The Poems of Edmund Blunden* (London: Cobden-Sanderson, 1930), 149–50: 150).

[37] Wilfred Owen takes issue with Brooke's vision in at least three poems – 'An Imperial Elegy' (1915–16), 'Miners' (1918) and 'A Terre' (1917–18), as does Edward Thomas in 'No One Cares Less Than I' (1916).

[38] Michel Butor, 'Travel and Writing', *Mosaic* 8.1 (Fall 1974), 6, 12.

Otherwise unconnected with its location, it nonetheless requires both specialised knowledge and specialised awareness of it. Lawrence Buell points
out that 'place' is related to 'complacency' etymologically and psychologi-
cally, in the sense that, most of the time, people lapse into inattention with
regard to their surroundings.[39] By contrast, the soldier's relationship with
his or her surroundings must be 'active' and 'reciprocal'.[40] The passage
from *War and Peace* quoted at the outset of this chapter makes clear that
going into war is going into the 'Unknown'[41] – another phrase might be
'going out of one's comfort zone' – and there is a consequent need for extra
vigilance or 'heightened alertness'.[42] Indeed, the soldier's interaction with
his environment becomes that of 'a creature [with] its habitat',[43] existing,
in Kurt Vonnegut's description, 'like woods creatures, living from moment
to moment in useful terror, thinking brainlessly with their spinal cords'.[44]
In explaining habitat or 'prospect-refuge' theory, Jay Appleton writes:

> The spontaneous reactions to environmental objects, so important to survival
> under primitive conditions, may need to be resuscitated in conditions of war . . . we
> can find in the adjustment of a soldier to his field environment manifestations
> of attitudes, feelings and impulses recognisably related to those which regularly
> enter into landscape aesthetics. Manuals of infantry training . . . are concerned
> with camouflage and concealment, with assessing the lie of the land and with
> fostering an awareness of every detail of an environment, on the effective use of
> which a soldier's life may depend.[45]

Zoomorphised, the individual in war is hyper-aware (both optically and
haptically) of his environs; constantly alert to 'sign-stimuli indicative of
environmental conditions favourable to survival';[46] predatory practitioner
of the voyeuristic 'art of hiding from sight to see';[47] de Certeau-esque
tactician negotiating his way through the war zone.[48] The war reporter

---

[39] Lawrence Buell, *The Environmental Imagination: Thoreau, Nature Writing, and the Formation of American Culture* (Cambridge, MA: Harvard University Press, 1995), 261.

[40] *Ibid.*, 267.

[41] Tolstoy, *War and Peace*, 162. The Russian is 'neizvestnost'' (uncapitalised) (Tolstoy, *Voina i mir*, 173): uncertainty, the unknown.

[42] Jonathan Crary, *Suspensions of Perception: Attention, Spectacle, and Modern Culture* (Cambridge: MIT Press, 1999), 41.

[43] Jay Appleton, *The Experience of Landscape* (Chichester: John Wiley, 1996), 63.

[44] Kurt Vonnegut, *Slaughterhouse-Five* (London: Vintage, 2000), 35.

[45] Appleton, *The Experience of Landscape*, 167.   [46] *Ibid.*, 62.

[47] Paul Virilio, *War and Cinema: The Logistics of Perception*, trans. Patrick Camiller (London: Verso, 1989), 49.

[48] 'To walk is to lack a place. It is the indefinite process of being absent and in search of a proper' (Michel de Certeau, *The Practice of Everyday Life*, trans. Steven Rendall (Berkeley: University of California, 1984), 103). But the soldier moving through the war zone could equally be said to create a place at each successive juncture.

Carolin Emcke describes her experiences in Colombia in precisely these terms, using a jungle metaphor to express a sense of urban danger:

I felt terribly uncomfortable to be lost in the midst of this jungle of steps and houses, unable to understand the territory or its military logistics. I longed to be positioned somewhere where I could see the neighbourhood, seize its cartography, measure its dangers, sound its risks.[49]

Emcke's instinct is to discover a location where she can see without being seen: a key feature of prospect-refuge theory.[50] As Paul Rodaway points out, geographical (and topographical) experience 'is fundamentally mediated by the human body',[51] and Emcke's discomfort is both physical feeling and psychic state.

Nowhere is the hyper-sensuous relationship to terrain which war necessitates more expertly conveyed than in the writings of Ambrose Bierce. Bierce studied topographical engineering at the Kentucky Military Institute, later serving as regimental cartographer to the 9th Indiana Infantry Regiment during the American Civil War.[52] His accounts of the battles of that war are marked by extraordinary topographical detail and awareness of locale. Precise distances and lucid descriptions of layouts are given, so that the reader can not only appreciate their strategic relevance but glimpse the nature of a mindset with unusual areal consciousness. The following passage is from 'What I Saw of Shiloh', first published in the San Francisco-based *Wasp* magazine on 23 and 30 December 1881:

In subordination to the design of this narrative, as defined by its title, the incidents related necessarily group themselves about my own personality as a center; and, as this center, during the few terrible hours of the engagements, maintained a variably constant relation to the open field already mentioned, it is important that the reader should bear in mind the topographical and tactical features of the local situation. The hither side of the field was occupied by the front of my brigade – a length of two regiments in line, with proper intervals for field batteries. During the entire fight the enemy held the slight wooded acclivity beyond. The debatable ground to the right and left of the open was broken and thickly wooded for miles, in some places quite inaccessible to artillery and at very few points offering opportunities for its successful employment. As a consequence of this the two sides of the field were soon studded thickly with confronting guns, which flamed away at one another with amazing zeal and rather startling effect. Of course, an infantry

---

[49] Emcke, *Echoes of Violence*, 234.   [50] Appleton, *The Experience of Landscape*, 66.
[51] Paul Rodaway, *Sensuous Geographies. Body, Sense and Place* (London and New York: Routledge, 1994), 3, 31.
[52] Tom Quirk, 'Introduction', in *Ambrose Bierce: Tales of Soldiers and Civilians*, ed. Tom Quirk (Harmondsworth: Penguin, 2000), ix, i.

attack delivered from either side was not to be thought of when the covered
flanks offered inducements so unquestionably superior; and I believe the riddled
bodies of my poor skirmishers were the only ones left on this 'neutral ground' that
day . . . The configuration of the ground offered us no protection. By lying flat on
our faces between the guns we were screened from view by a straggling row of
brambles, which marked the course of an obsolete fence; but the enemy's grape
was sharper than his eyes, and it was poor consolation to know that his gunners
could not see what they were doing, so long as they did it.[53]

Essentially, this consciousness is Kantian. In his essay 'Concerning the Ultimate Ground of the Differentiation of Directions in Space' (1768), Kant,
working towards the concept of absolute space, argues that 'concerning
the things which exist outside ourselves: it is only insofar as they stand in
relation to ourselves that we have any cognition of them by means of the
senses at all'.[54] The 'ultimate ground' on which we form our concept of
directions in space derives from the relation of three intersecting planes
to our bodies. These three planes, which intersect physical space at right
angles, give rise to our sense of 'above' and 'below', 'right' and 'left' and
'in front' and 'behind'. Our most ordinary knowledge of the position of
places would be no use to us, Kant writes, 'unless we could also orientate
the things thus ordered, along with the entire system of their reciprocal
positions, by referring them to the sides of our body'.[55] In Bierce's account,
the scene at Shiloh is entirely understood in these terms: 'hither', 'front',
'beyond', 'right' and 'left' derive their meanings solely from his bodily
positioning and perception. Indeed, the title itself, 'What I Saw at Shiloh',
which Bierce describes as defining the design of the narrative and subordi-
nating the incidents recounted within it, may be understood, not merely
as a routine magazine headline with a standard claim to autopsy, but as
a very precise statement of Kantian orientation. Subject, object, verb and
adverbial phrase all give vital co-ordinates.

But the account contains more than a Kantian sense of physical space,
becoming an extended application of prospect-refuge theory. The central
and centring personality not only orders the terrain in terms of spatial perception but also gives it cognitive and emotional value. Ground is understood as 'tactical', 'debatable', 'inaccessible', 'offering opportunities', giving
rise to 'success' and configured; the idea of its being neutral is ridiculed

---

[53] Ambrose Bierce, *A Sole Survivor: Bits of Autobiography*, eds. S. T. Joshi and David E. Schultz
(Knoxville: University of Tennessee Press, 1998), 20.
[54] Immanuel Kant, 'Concerning the Ultimate Ground of the Differentiation of Directions in Space',
Theoretical Philosophy, 1755–1770, trans. and ed. David Walford (Cambridge: Cambridge University
Press, 1992), 366.
[55] *Ibid.*, 368.

by ironic speech marks. Its strategic usefulness is instantly perceived; with hazards, refuges, vistas and vantage-points noted in the manner posited by Appleton. There is cognisance of who can see and be seen. The account is high in 'situational awareness': 'the perception of the elements in the environment within a volume of time and space, the comprehension of their meaning, and the projection of their status in the near future'.[56] Able to read the field in a professional way, Bierce also 'writes' it, converting gaps in the trees into potential artillery points and a low hill into a 'slight wooded acclivity' held by the enemy. Flat on his face and hidden behind brambles, he also makes clear his personal, bodily engagement with the land and suggests a future stratum deeper than the physical contours in his reference to 'the riddled bodies of my poor skirmishers'.

In *Place and Experience: A Philosophical Topography* (1999), J. E. Malpas posits that:

we are the sort of thinking, remembering, experiencing creatures we are only in virtue of our active engagement in place; that the possibility of mental life is necessarily tied to such engagement, and so to the places in which we are so engaged; and that, when we come to give content to our concepts of ourselves and to the idea of our own self-identity, place and locality play a crucial role – our identities are . . . intricately and essentially place-bound.[57]

This symbiosis is evident in 'What I Saw at Shiloh'. Though Bierce establishes his personality as the 'center' around which incidents 'necessarily group themselves' and in relation to which the direction of topographical features are distributed, the battlefield he describes in turn constructs that personality by giving its experiences location. Assured in the 'situation', Bierce is grounded, at home; as much as he reads and writes the terrain, the terrain defines his consciousness. And this is the function of pastoral.

To appreciate the contribution of pastoral to war representation involves some rethinking of the mode. Defining pastoral, as Annabel Patterson points out, is 'a cause lost as early as the sixteenth century'.[58] But, as she goes on to note, it is still fruitful to explore how writers have '*used* pastoral for a range of functions and intentions'.[59] In what follows, this chapter aims to discover another, perhaps unexpected, use for the mode.

---

[56] Addie Johnson and Robert W. Proctor, *Attention: Theory and Practice* (Thousand Oaks, London and New Delhi: Sage Publications, 2004), 280.
[57] Malpas, *Place and Experience*, 177.
[58] Annabel Patterson, *Pastoral and Ideology: Virgil to Valéry* (Oxford: Clarendon, 1988), 7.
[59] *Ibid.*

The strongest statement of war as 'anti-pastoral' occurs in Paul Fussell's *The Great War and Modern Memory* (1975).[60] Fussell writes at the outset of his chapter 'Arcadian Resources':

If the opposite of war is peace, the opposite of experiencing moments of war is proposing moments of pastoral. Since war takes place outdoors and always within nature, its symbolic status is that of the ultimate anti-pastoral. In Northrop Frye's terms, it belongs to the demonic world, and no one engages in it or contemplates it without implicitly or explicitly bringing to bear the contrasting 'model world' by which its demonism is measured. When H. M. Tomlinson asks, 'What has the rathe primrose to do with old rags and bones on barbed wire?' we must answer, 'Everything.'[61]

As Fussell sees it, 'recourse to the pastoral [was] an English mode of both fully gauging the calamities of the Great War and imaginatively protecting oneself against them'.[62] Ruralism of the same kind that assuaged the homesickness of imperial exile or the pain of industrialism (whether it took the form of trench gardening or literary creation or mental invocations of '"home" and "the summer of 1914"') was both 'a way of invoking a code to hint by antithesis at the indescribable [and] a comfort in itself'.[63] Both these functions depend upon the *difference* ('antithesis') between the pastoral oasis and the experience of war. In a similar definition (though distinct in its emphasis on meaningfulness in pastoral space), Terry Gifford discerns 'anti-pastoral' in Matthew Arnold's 'Dover Beach' since the natural world it presents 'is a bleak battle for survival without divine purpose'.[64] This 'anti-pastoral' is also based on 'exposing the distance between reality and pastoral convention',[65] an exposure which a locale like the Western Front – in Samuel Hynes's phrase, an 'anti-landscape'[66] – would indubitably achieve.

Now, if the uses of pastoral are confined to traditional conceptions of the *locus amoenus*, these identifications of accounts of the horrors of war as anti-pastoral are correct. (Incidentally, they are of obvious service to propagandist constructions of 'innocent civil societ[ies] that [have] to be

---

[60] For other expressions of the view that warscapes are anti-pastoral, see Dawn Bellamy, '"Others Have Come Before You": The Influence of Great War Poetry on Second World War Poets', in *The Oxford Handbook of British and Irish War Poetry*, ed. Tim Kendall (Oxford: Oxford University Press, 2007), 307; Santanu Das, *Touch and Intimacy in First World War Literature* (Cambridge: Cambridge University Press, 2005), 66; Sandra Gilbert, '"Rats' Alley": The Great War, Modernism, and the (Anti)pastoral Elegy', *New Literary History* 30 (1999), 185, 191; and Andrew Rutherford, *The Literature of War: Five Studies in Heroic Virtue* (London and Basingstoke: Macmillan, 1978), 9.

[61] Fussell, *The Great War and Modern Memory*, 231.   [62] *Ibid.*, 235.   [63] *Ibid.*

[64] Terry Gifford, *Pastoral* (London and New York: Routledge, 1999), 120.   [65] *Ibid.*, 128.

[66] Samuel Hynes, *A War Imagined: The First World War and English Culture* (London: Pimlico, 1992), 7.

defended'; as Nick Mansfield notes, '[a]n innocent domain . . . is perpetually retrospectively reinvented by the wars it requires as the thing that war leaves behind'.)[67] In 'What is Pastoral?', Paul Alpers arrives at the conclusion that the genre's 'representative anecdote' is 'the lives of shepherds',[68] while Renato Poggioli argues that 'the psychological root of the pastoral is a double longing after innocence and happiness, to be recovered not through conversion or regeneration but merely through retreat'.[69] The traditional elements of pastoral are the shepherd's life, withdrawal and repose, and tranquil and beautiful natural settings. Nothing could be further from the experience of war.

And yet, as all these theorists acknowledge, pastoral can do more than this. Fussell notes in his 'Arcadian Resources' chapter the resonance of the classical tag *Et in Arcadia ego* – in Fussell's translation, 'Even in Arcadia I, Death, hold sway'.[70] The pastoral setting is never as blissful, or as innocent of horror, as it appears to be, and war is a frequent intruder. Indeed, it is possible to say that, in many instances, pastoral – or the pastoral life – is founded on, or enabled by, war. Virgil's *Eclogues*, one of the seminal works of the genre, open with Meliboeus comparing his lot with Tityrus':

You, Tityrus, lie under the canopy of a spreading beech, wooing the woodland Muse on slender reed, but we are leaving our country's bounds and sweet fields. We are outcasts from our country; you, Tityrus, at ease beneath the shade, teach the woods to re-echo 'fair Amaryllis'. (1.1–5)

This distractingly mellifluous opening in fact records the radical effects on Roman real estate of the civil wars between Brutus and Cassius and Antony and Octavian (later Augustus), namely the expropriation of lands by Octavian for the settlement of his discharged veterans in the course of which Virgil himself may have lost his Mantuan farm.[71] Meliboeus complains again:

Is a godless soldier to hold these well-tilled fallows? A barbarian these crops? See where strife has brought our unhappy citizens! For these we have sown our fields![72]

---

[67] Mansfield, 'War and Its Other', unpaginated.

[68] Paul Alpers, 'What Is Pastoral?', *Critical Inquiry* 8.3 (Spring 1982), 449.

[69] Renato Poggioli, *The Oaten Flute: Essays on Pastoral Poetry and the Pastoral Ideal* (Cambridge, MA: Harvard University Press, 1975), 1.

[70] Fussell, *The Great War and Modern Memory*, 245–6.

[71] E. V. Rieu, ed., *Virgil: The Pastoral Poems (The Eclogues)* (Harmondsworth: Penguin, 1954), 13, 123–6.

[72] 1.70–2. Expropriation of lands for discharged soldiers is also mentioned at 9.2–6. See also Alexander Pope, 'Windsor Forest' (1704, 1712), lines 65, 85, 91.

This conversation between the dispossessed Meliboeus and the more fortunate Tityrus – the crucial contrast between living in a hostile world, where goats have to be herded along the road and kids are born on the hard flint (1.12–15), and living in secure, easy pastoral – is therefore only possible because of martial events. It is important to note that war's effect is not one-sided: the existence of Tityrus' 'otium', as much as Meliboeus' hardships, is due to Octavian's policies (1.5–10). The claim at the beginning of the sixth *Eclogue* – since 'bards in plenty will you find eager to sing your praises, Varus, and build the story of grim war', the speaker 'will woo the rustic Muse on slender reed' (6.6–8) – is disingenuous, for the reason that, when 'such unrest is there on all sides in the land' (1.11–12), songs of war and songs of the countryside are indistinguishable. The ninth *Eclogue*, which praises Menalcas' skill as a poet by referring to his verse petition against the enforced evictions (9.27–9), reinforces this. Later, in the *Georgics*, another genre-setting work, the same connection between war and husbandry is maintained. In the concluding lines, the speaker invokes what is simultaneously happening beyond the woods and fields:

So much I sang in addition to the care of fields, of cattle, and of trees, while great Caesar thundered in war by deep Euphrates and bestowed a victor's laws on willing nations, and essayed the path to Heaven. In those days I, Virgil, was nursed by sweet Parthenope, and rejoiced in the arts of inglorious ease. (4.559–64)

Here Octavian's triumphal progress through the East following the Battle of Actium is explicitly set against 'inglorious ease'. But, again, the apparent division between farm life and war is misleading. The success of Roman arms overseas encouraged ranching back on the Italian peninsula by securing the importation of cereal; weeds and decay proliferated during the civil wars.[73] The very shape and texture of the land the husbandry of which the *Georgics* are devoted to expounding are determined by martial developments.

Intrusion and interaction, then, characterise the relationship between the bucolic and the bellicose. War is immanent in the rural, insofar as its sounds may penetrate the quietude at any moment, converting ready-made agricultural implements into weaponry. (The lurking land-mine is a perverted sort of immanence in the earth.) Erwin Panofsky, referring to Virgil, suggests that suffering creates a 'dissonance' in Arcady that must be

---

[73] L. P. Wilkinson, *The Georgics of Virgil: A Critical Survey* (Cambridge: Cambridge University Press, 1969), 50–2.

'resolved',[74] and yet it seems that such resolution is indefinitely deferred. Dissonance – the warlike – is ineradicable from Arcadia.

But, again, pastoral in relation to war representation means something more than a rural/martial interaction and certain elements in kind. The pastoral setting of Virgil's *Eclogues* is, crucially, 'procul' ('far-off') (1.76, 82). This is a distance not only in geographical terms but in the sense of removal from social constraints: indeed, the pastoral venue is where such constraints are (with licence) criticised, challenged and even temporarily reversed (typically, an unregulated outdoors community, often in a wood, is set in opposition to a formal indoor society, such as a court).[75] Pastoral, then, is aptly described as 'a mode of thought'[76] or as 'ideological theater'.[77] This view takes its most famous form in Empson's dictum that pastoral is a process 'of putting the complex into the simple'[78] – a dictum anticipated at least as far back as George Puttenham's *The Arte of English Poesie* (1585):

> The poet devised the Eglogue . . . not of purpose to counterfait or represent the rusticall manner of loves and communication; but under the vaile of homely persons, and in rude speeches to insinuate and glaunce at greater matters, and such as perchance had not bene safe to have disclosed in any other sort.[79]

The idea of pastoral as a critical space gives a special timbre, or charge, to the rural setting. Similarly, the war zone can be seen as a specially charged space, a place apart, a demarcated area subject to its own laws where things are different. Geographically, it is hyper-defined, subject to intense surveillance (alongside the war machine, as Paul Virilio points out, there has always existed a 'watching machine'),[80] imbued with strategic significance, its access restricted. David Jones calls it, in the introduction to *In Parenthesis*, 'a place of enchantment'.[81] This special/spatial charging of the war zone is evident in the following passage from Addison's 'The Campaign':

---

[74] Erwin Panofsky, *Meaning in the Visual Arts* (New York: Doubleday, 1955), 300; quoted in Alpers, 'What Is Pastoral?', 453.

[75] As Simon Schama writes on one emanation of pastoral, the greenwood: 'Greenwood . . . the upside-down world of the Renaissance court: a place where the conventions of gender and rank are *temporarily* reversed in the interest of discovering truth, love, freedom, and, above all, justice' (*Landscape and Memory* (London: Fontana, 1996), 141). Hence, in *As You Like It*, Duke Senior is described as living with 'many merry men' in the Forest of Arden 'like old Robin Hood of England . . . many young gentlemen flock to him every day, and fleet the time carelessly, as they did in the golden world' (1.1.109–14).

[76] Helen Cooper, *Pastoral: Mediaeval into Renaissance* (Ipswich: D. S. Brewer, 1977), 2.

[77] Buell, *The Environmental Imagination*, 35.

[78] William Empson, *Some Versions of Pastoral* (London: Chatto and Windus, 1950), 25.

[79] George Puttenham, *The Arte of English Poesie*, 38–9.

[80] Virilio, *War and Cinema*, 3.   [81] David Jones, *In Parenthesis*, x.

'Twas then great Marlbrô's mighty soul was prov'd,
That, in the shock of charging hosts unmov'd,
Amidst confusion, horror, and despair,
Examin'd all the dreadful scenes of war;
In peaceful thought the field of death survey'd,
To fainting squadrons sent the timely aid,
Inspir'd repuls'd battalions to engage,
And taught the doubtful battle where to rage.
So when an Angel by divine command
With rising tempests shakes a guilty land,
Such as of late o'er pale Britannia past,
Calm and serene he drives the furious blast;
And, pleas'd th'Almighty's orders to perform,
Rides in the whirl-wind, and directs the storm.

(lines 284–97)

In these lines, the field of operations is a delimited locale, the site of intensive activity, itself divided into 'scenes' and under the close surveillance of Marlborough himself. Indeed, the Duke's positioning as a kind of *genius loci*, watching, directing and modifying the arena of battle, is a major means by which the area is charged with significance, becoming distinct from those surrounding it. Terrain is transformed into a 'field of death', the space of combat experienced as a situation of otherness.

But beyond even the idea of a specially charged, delimited area, pastoral as thought-space suggests an existence of intellectual intensity, focused reflection in isolation. Indeed, pastoral can be understood not only as a flower-strewn retreat but as a psycho-physiologico-physical area for extended mental activity: concentration, contemplation, meditation, view-formation, creativity. When, in contemporary parlance, sports psychologists speak of pre-race athletes entering or being in 'the zone', a phrase defined by the *OED* as 'a state of perfect concentration leading to optimum mental or physical performance', it is such a psycho-physiologico-physical space that is being described. As has already been shown, the soldier entering or in the war zone must acquire similar mental focus, blocking out distractions, focusing, visualising what lies ahead, preparing and motivating the self, achieving and maintaining a hyper-vigilant outlook, experiencing and managing extreme physical and emotional feelings. In this sense, the war zone *is itself a version of pastoral.*

Affinities may therefore be pointed out, for example, between Virgil's Tityrus in his pastoral retreat and Ambrose Bierce at Shiloh. Both are sensitively attuned to, and possess a working knowledge of, their locales and are hence able to exploit them to advantage, for example by converting environmental features into shelter. Both are aware of weather patterns and experience the land haptically, Tityrus lying under 'the canopy of a spreading beech' (1.1), Bierce flat on his face behind the brambles.[82] Most importantly, though Tityrus may enjoy the freedom to play his pipe and allow his cattle to roam at large, he remains watchful, aware that his enviable existence is only licensed by Octavian's whim, which must therefore be propitiated with regular sacrifices (mentioned twice in forty-five lines). Bierce is similarly strained and vigilant. Though the contexts and forms are vastly different, the two texts describe similar (pastoral) consciousnesses: at home in their surroundings yet never off guard; alertly interactive with their environments.

As a cognitive space, pastoral may be associated with the isolated intellectual or artist, bringing to a head the question of the proper nature and extent of that figure's participation in society.[83] In his essay on *Some Versions of Pastoral*, 'The Critic as Clown', Terry Eagleton reads Empson's dictum that pastoral is the process of putting the complex into the simple into Empson's own experience as a literary critic in the 1930s, specifically in relation to 'the problem of the critical intellectual in modern bourgeois society'.[84] Configuring pastoral as a means of encrypting 'intellectual sophistication' within 'common wisdom', Eagleton argues, is 'Empson's way of coming to terms with the fraught relations between critic and text, intellectual and society; its ironic interchanges of refinement and simplicity are an allegory of the critic's own dilemma'.[85] The individual in the war zone also possesses special and sophisticated insight, a fact recognised by psychiatrists and psychologists. 'Deployment to a war zone is a transformative process for everyone connected with this enterprise', write Charles R. Figley and William P. Nash,[86] while Judith A. Lyons notes that 'a persona and reaction style become engrained and remain forever a part of that individual'.[87] Though it comprises topographical hyper-awareness and the understanding gained from unique experience (including proximity to mass death and destruction) rather than intellectual sophistication, it nonetheless marks off those with it from those without it. And, crucially, like that of the pastoral

---

[82] Bierce, *A Sole Survivor*, 20.   [83] See Patterson, *Pastoral and Ideology*, *passim*.

[84] Terry Eagleton, *Against the Grain. Essays 1975–1985* (London and New York: Verso, 1986), 155.

[85] *Ibid.*, 152, 150.

[86] Charles R. Figley and William P. Nash, 'Introduction: For Those Who Bear the Battle', in *Combat Stress Injury. Theory, Research, and Management*, ed. Charles R. Figley and William P. Nash (New York and London: Routledge, 2007), 2.

[87] Judith A. Lyons, 'The Returning Warrior: Advice for Family and Friends', in *Combat Stress Injury*, ed. Figley and Nash, 312.

commentator, this insight is derived from, defined by and figured through
a particular psycho-physiologico-physical space.

The equivalence between spatial positioning and experience serves again
to privilege 'combat gnosticism' (already discussed in Chapter 1): the idea
that entry into the war zone 'represents a qualitatively separate order of
experience'[88] (it was pointed out in Chapter 1 that war-related experiences
in addition to combat – bereavement, being under bombardment, etc. –
were also of a qualitatively separate order). James Campbell, who coined the
term, notes that the corollary is that combat becomes 'a secret knowledge
which only an initiated elite knows', 'difficult if not impossible to communicate to any who have not undergone an identical experience'.[89] In
conflict's equivalent of the intellectual's dilemma as characterised by Eagleton, the denizen of the war zone must mediate between his or her special
insight and the differently informed understanding of the non-combatant.
Such mediation may be achieved by drawing on the metaphorical potential of the war zone, using geographical space to figure experiential space.
Hence Edmund Blunden, aiming to recreate his memories of combat in
Undertones of War (1928), uses the phrase 'I must go over the ground again',
though he notes that those who have 'gone the same journey' will already
be aware of what he has to say and those who have not will neither read
nor understand it.[90] 'Ground' and 'journey' say 'I have been somewhere
you have not' and also 'I have experienced something you have not'.

The same figuring of experiential in geographical space occurs in Henry
Reed's six-part poem 'Lessons of the War'.[91] Like many texts of conflict, this
poem depicts entry to the war zone as dependent upon passage through a
temenos or dromos – an anticipatory or intermediary zone, that is – in this
case, the basic training intended to convert the civilian into the combatant.
A play on words in the adulterated quotation from Horace that serves as
the poem's epigraph demarcates the zone of military experience from that
of peacetime activities: Reed changes the word 'puellis' in Horace's *Ode*
3.26 to 'duellis' so that 'vixi puellis nuper ideoneus / et militavi non sine
gloria' ('I have lived up until recently fit for the girls / and I have served
not without distinction') becomes 'vixi duellis nuper ideoneus / et militavi

---

[88] Campbell, 'Combat Gnosticism', 203.
[89] *Ibid.*, 204, 203. The reverse is also possible: that the warrior is 'placed apart' to reduce his or her
threat to society. Eric J. Leed notes the images and rites of liminality that separate those fighting from
civilian society: soldiers may be constructed as invisible, 'dead', 'buried' or otherwise 'identified with
the earth' (*No Man's Land*, 17–19). Accordingly, the war zone can be read as an externally imposed
quarantine as much as a space of privileged experience.
[90] Edmund Blunden, *Undertones of War* (Harmondsworth: Penguin, 1982), 7.
[91] Henry Reed, *Collected Poems*, ed. Jon Stallworthy (Oxford: Oxford University Press, 1991), 47–60.

non sine gloria' ('I have lived up until recently fit for the wars / and I have served not without distinction').[92] The duellis/puellis distinction will be exploited throughout the poem's parts.

The first section, 'Naming of Parts', begins the process of transforming non-combatant experience and cognition through the replacement of civilian by military language and semantics: 'This is the lower sling swivel. And this / Is the upper sling swivel'.[93] Still in a transitional state, the recruits cannot, as yet, fully appreciate military significance: the use of the swivels will only become apparent 'When you are given your slings'.[94] The ambivalent phrase 'easing the Spring' is, like Edward Thomas's fallen elm, a worm-hole between the separately charged zones of battle drill and gardens of almond-blossom; the transitional state of the recruit-speaker's mind is evident in the fact that he perceives the bees' going backwards and forwards as both 'assaulting' (a military action) and 'fumbling' (a civilian action) the flowers.[95]

In the second section, 'Judging Distances', the special cognition required in the war zone becomes even more apparent as the sergeant instructs 'How to report on a landscape':

> The still white dwellings are like a mirage in the heat,
> And under the swaying elms a man and woman
> Lie gently together. Which is, perhaps, only to say
> That there is a row of houses to the left of arc,
> And that under some poplars a pair of what appear to be humans
> Appear to be loving.[96]

In army parlance, the houses are situated as Kant described in his analysis of directional differentiation: 'left of arc'. The couple making love only 'appear to be humans' because, in war, a soldier may not rely on visual appearances. The couple must also be situated directionally and when the recruit is asked 'in what direction are they / And how far away, would you say?', he is also reminded that there may be 'dead ground' in between: that is, land that cannot be seen and therefore cannot be exploited militarily.[97] The awkward nomenclature makes the point that in the war zone, perception is altered, contingent. 'Judging Distances' is also about judging differences in knowledge and experience. Notably, the recruit who is asked to describe the landscape must do so 'having first come to attention'; this not only suggests standing erect but a form of mental alertness. In the final stanza, the speaker explicitly divides himself from the couple making love:

[92] Reed, *Collected Poems*, 47. See Pitcher, 'Classical War Literature', 75.
[93] Reed, *Collected Poems*, 49.   [94] *Ibid.*   [95] *Ibid.*   [96] *Ibid.*, 50.   [97] *Ibid.*, 51.

> I will only venture
> A guess that perhaps between me and the apparent loves,
> (Who, incidentally, appear by now to have finished,)
> At seven o'clock from the houses, is roughly a distance
> Of about one year and a half.[98]

Establishing a space-time continuum (he has been instructed that 'maps are of time, not place' and the clock-face positioning amalgamates space and time),[99] the speaker introduces a fourth dimension – temporal, experiential – to the landscape. After basic training, the recruit is differently experienced and on the way to acquiring special means of perception: 'dead ground' is now what is unrepeatable, incapable of re-visitation.

Part III of the poem, 'Movement of Bodies', further exposes this fourth dimension. Now the sergeant explicitly addresses the tactical approach to terrain:

> This brown clay model is a characteristic terrain
> Of a simple and typical kind. Its general character
> Should be taken in at a glance, and its general character
> You can see at a glance it is somewhat hilly by nature,
> With a fair amount of typical vegetation
> Disposed at certain parts.[100]

By the third lesson, the sergeant expects the men's understanding of land to have altered; now they should be able to 'take in at a glance' the 'character' of the fighting territory. Emphasising that 'of course it will not be a tray you will fight on', and so re-introducing the possibility that the actual terrain may be experienced other than in a military sense, the sergeant advises the recruits to imagine moving over it 'Past a ruined tank or a gun, perhaps, or a recently dead friend'.[101] In the next stanza the sergeant notes that 'there is always someone at this particular lesson / Who always starts crying' and later conjectures that this is because he mentioned a dead friend.[102] For the men who cry, the cognitive transformation has been incomplete: dead

---

[98] *Ibid.*, 50, 51.

[99] *Ibid.*, 50. Reed's poem registers experience that is, in Mikhail Bakhtin's terminology, 'chronotopical': 'Time, as it were, thickens, takes on flesh, becomes artistically visible; likewise space becomes charged and responsive to the movements of time, plot and history' (Bakhtin, *The Dialogic Imagination: Four Essays*, trans. and ed. Michael Holquist (Austin: University of Texas Press, 1981), 84). The war zone is easily characterised as a chronotope: particularised space in which time both flies and hangs heavy. But a detailed 'chronotopic' analysis of the war zone is resisted here for a number of reasons: as explained earlier, the zone is not merely a 'space'; place and time are of such complexity in war writing as to deserve separate chapters; and the chronotope is ultimately a descriptive, rather than an analytical, category.

[100] Reed, *Collected Poems*, 52.   [101] *Ibid.*, 52.   [102] *Ibid.*, 53, 54.

friends cannot be seen as obstacles in the field, in the same way as ruined tanks or guns, but retain the power to move emotionally. The brown clay model on the tray figures the military – pastoral – consciousness that must be acquired.

Movement through anticipatory or intermediary zones is often matched in war texts with an equivalent movement through recovery or aftermath zones. (These variegated zones themselves render war representation eclogic (taking the first meaning of 'eclogue', which is 'selection') or idyllic (taking the first meaning of 'idyl', which is 'small picture') or cinematic: scenes (like crops) rotate *seriatim*.) The final part of 'Lessons of the War' is 'Returning of Issue', which takes the form of a discharge talk by the sergeant. The men are standing inside now because it is autumn, and through the window the recruit-speaker notes a coming down to earth of 'small things' turning and whirling on the wind.[103] He is unable to tell whether these small things are 'leaves or flowers':[104] it is as though his perception has been thoroughly militarised, so that he is no longer capable of appreciating the realm of almond-blossom, japonica – and love. Indeed, the sergeant remarks, 'I think / I can honestly say you are one and all of you now: / Soldiers'.[105] In this section, as in the others, Reed exploits the military and civilian meanings of a phrase: here, 'Returning of Issue' denotes not only the giving back of kit after service but the prodigal son's return to his father. The recruit-speaker is unable to return to his father – significantly, his parent's fields 'are sold and built on'[106] – and so elects to stay in the army. The actual terrain on which his peacetime identity was grounded has been irretrievably lost, and so he decides to remain, not a person, but 'a personnel'.[107] In turn, he will himself 'teach: / A rhetoric instead of words; instead of a love, the use / Of accoutrements'.[108] His consciousness has forever changed – 'I have no longer gift or want'[109] – and so his place must change too.

The war zone is geographical and psycho-physiological, somewhere between space and place. The individual who enters it is transformed permanently by its sights, experiences and demands. But the war zone is not only the ground in and on which such transformation is effected: it is also the ground on and through which it is figured. Hence the zone is both challenge and response in terms of war representation. And, though this chapter has concentrated on combat, it should be stressed again that other experiences of war also involve crossing into what Tolstoy called

---

[103] *Ibid.*, 57.   [104] *Ibid.*   [105] *Ibid.*   [106] *Ibid.*, 58.
[107] *Ibid.*   [108] *Ibid.*, 60.   [109] *Ibid.*, 59.

the 'Unknown'. Therefore, it may be helpful to conceive the war zone as a series of overlapping circles in the manner of Dunya Mikhail's 'O': a Venn diagram with battle at its heart but other, related phenomena – bereavement through conflict, being under bombardment, displacement etc – converging on it. These phenomena are of a unique order of experience, too, and can also give rise to special consciousness. This chapter has likened such consciousness to the intellectual intensity and strained wariness of traditional pastoral. Like the insights of pastoral, the insights of the war zone require careful mediation: in configuring the zone as a charged space, writers both give special consciousness a location and convey that it is not on general access. As a corollary, the text about conflict – unlike 'the moving war' – remains linked to its territory, recording its transformation, mourning its scars.

CHAPTER 4

Duration

War reconfigures time as well as space. Conflict calls forth an increase in temporal expressions: 'for the duration', 'never again', 'back by Christmas'. If the war zone demands a special topography, wartime demands a bespoke narratology, or even, given the importance to it of (lack of) endings, a bespoke eschatology or theology. Wartime is twofold: both the duration of a conflict and how time is experienced within it. Defining the former and characterising the latter are both problematic. To ascribe a start and an end to a conflict is to emplot it, and emplotment is the beginning of interpretation and hence controversy (a point Tolstoy makes repeatedly in his examples of events being quickly rendered into historical accounts). Frank Kermode analyses emplotted time using the simple model of a clock's *tick-tock*:

All such plotting presupposes and requires that an end will bestow upon the whole duration and meaning. To put it another way, the interval must be purged of simple chronicity, of the emptiness of *tock-tick*, humanly uninteresting successiveness . . . that which was conceived of as simply successive becomes charged with past and future; what was *chronos* [passing or waiting time] must become *kairos* [the season, a point in time filled with significance, charged with a meaning derived from its relation to the end].[1]

Wartime, in its exceptional fashion, diverges from this. It is both chronos and kairos; moreover, its kaironic qualities are brought about as much by an absence of ending as by a definitive conclusion. The fact that, while a war is in progress, it is not known when, or how, or if it is going to end gives wartime its special property of *open-endedness* or *endinglessness* (an acute form of endlessness): a situation in which various possible outcomes exist simultaneously in, to borrow a concept from quantum physics, *superposition*. In the superposition of states, as this chapter will illustrate,

---

[1] Frank Kermode, *The Sense of an Ending: Studies in the Theory of Fiction* (Oxford: Oxford University Press, 1967), 46. Definitions in square brackets are taken from *ibid.*, 47.

time is synchronic; diachronic temporal expressions are thrown into confusion. Philosophers from Augustine to Derrida have noted the elusiveness of 'now'[2] but, no longer pre-war and not yet post-war, wartime is a radical, *sui generis* extended present.[3]

One of the challenges for war representation is, accordingly, to communicate and even exploit the peculiarities of this extraordinary temporal state. This chapter explores the techniques – including some radical narratological experiments – that writers have deployed to convey the nature and impact of the perpetual present; the functioning of synchronic time; the significance of outcomes hanging in the balance; the effects of time constraints; and the distinctions between pre-, in- and post-war literature. The main texts for discussion are Henry Vaughan's 'An Elegie on the Death of Mr. R. W. slain in the Late Unfortunate Differences at Routon Heath, near Chester, 1645' (1646); Henri Barbusse's First World War autobiographical novel *Under Fire* (*Le Feu*) (1916); Antoine de Saint-Exupéry's Second World War pilot narrative, *Flight to Arras* (*Pilote de guerre*) (1942); Kurt Vonnegut's *Slaughterhouse-Five* (1969) and Ian McEwan's *Atonement* (2001).

The complex nature of wartime is evident from the beginning. Defining a war's duration is notoriously difficult. The starts of wars can be messy; justifications for initiating them are often ambiguous or manufactured (examples include the sinking of the *USS Maine* that precipitated the Spanish-American War, the Tonkin Gulf Resolution that inaugurated Vietnam, the supposed existence of weapons of mass destruction that formed the pretext for the 2003 invasion of Iraq).[4] Historians frequently fail to agree on the precise moment of initiation; indeed, wartime may begin in advance of official declarations. Waiting for a war to begin – or, more precisely, waiting to see whether a war will begin – has features in

---

[2] Mark Currie helpfully summarises these as 'Augustine's puzzle of the vanishing present, Husserl's account of the present as a crossed structure of protentions and retentions, and Heidegger's priority for the future in being-towards-death' (*About Time: Narrative, Fiction and the Philosophy of Time* (Edinburgh: Edinburgh University Press, 2007), 22). To these can be added Henri Bergson's argument that 'the present consists, in large measure, in the immediate past' (*Matter and Memory*, trans. Nancy Margaret Paul and W. Scott Palmer (London: Allen & Unwin, 1919), 193); Paul Ricoeur's dialectic between memory and expectation that he characterises as the experience of the present (*Time and Narrative*, trans. Kathleen McLaughlin and David Pellauer, 3 vols. (Chicago: University of Chicago Press, 1984), vol. I, 8–11); and Derrida's 'logic of supplementarity' (*Speech and Phenomena and Other Essays on Husserl's Theory of Signs*, trans. David B. Allison (Evanston: Northwestern University Press, 1973), 89).

[3] As in the previous chapter, Bakhtin's notion of the chronotope, the fusion of spatial and temporal indicators (*The Dialogic Imagination*, 84) seems, prima facie, relevant. Again, a 'chronotopic' account of wartime is resisted here, not least because the special temporal property of war with which this chapter is most concerned – open-endedness – does not easily fall within its scope.

[4] See Keeble, 'Information Warfare in an Age of Hyper-Militarism', 43.

common with the temporal experience of wartime itself though, crucially, pre-war has a stronger sense of likely outcome: 'erotic with the / might-be of disaster',[5] tension will be building, warnings and responses may have been issued, discussion is likely to be intense and the momentum towards fighting becomes irresistible. Pre-war waiting is another example of the sublime (a phenomenon which this book considers crucial to the representation of armed conflict, and discusses further in Chapters 2, 5 and 6), a sublimity which has been termed comic apocalypse: the thought, *something disastrous will happen but it is unclear what or when* (as opposed to tragic apocalypse which claims that *this particular disaster will happen at this precise time*).[6] Writing on one extreme threat, the bomb (a subject whose vast narratology is beyond the scope of this chapter), Martin Amis notes:

When nuclear weapons become real to you, when they stop buzzing around your ears and actually move into your head, hardly an hour passes without some throb or flash, some heavy pulse of imagined catastrophe.[7]

But the 'imagined catastrophe' is simultaneously unimaginable, 'beyond belief', 'a pullulating reality dependent upon thousands of assumptions, all of them untested, all of them untestable'.[8] It is also, crucially, un-witnessable: 'no one will "see" the bursting city . . . what *we* cannot get, is the simultaneity: everything becoming nothing, all at once'.[9] The result is that nuclear war cannot be written about but informs all writing produced within its shadow. The difference between conventional pre-war anticipation and anticipation of nuclear war is that the latter holds out no future from which the present might be retrospectively contemplated. And this is also what distinguishes wartime itself.

To explain this proposition, some philosophical models of time need to be appreciated. In his virtuosic *About Time* (2007), Mark Currie, drawing on theories of the elusive pure present from Augustine, Husserl, Heidegger and Derrida, writes, '[t]he present is the object of a future memory, and we live it as such, in anticipation of the story we will tell later, envisaging the present as past'.[10] 'Archive fever' (Derrida's term) and 'accelerated recontextualisation' describe in further detail how the present is experienced as the object of potential future retrospect, immediately transformed into the past by anticipation of its memory.[11] In a highly developed media capitalist

[5] Elaine Feinstein, 'A Quiet War in Leicester' (1971), *Selected Poems* (Manchester: Carcanet, 1994), 61.
[6] Greg Garrard, *Ecocriticism* (London: Routledge, 2004), 87–8; Stephen D. O'Leary, *Arguing the Apocalypse: A Theory of Millennial Rhetoric* (Oxford: Oxford University Press, 1994), 83–4.
[7] Amis, *Visiting Mrs Nabokov*, 13.   [8] *Ibid.*, 16, 18.   [9] *Ibid.*, 14.
[10] Currie, *About Time*, 5.   [11] *Ibid.*, 9–11.

society, 'an event is recorded not because it happens, but it happens because it is recorded':[12] indeed, when an event is brought about because of its anticipated representation, it is possible to say that the present has been created by the (envisaged) future (Derrida's logic of supplementarity in which 'by delayed reaction, a possibility produces that to which it is said to be added on').[13] The term coined by Daniel Boorstin for the created-for-future-retrospect phenomenon is 'pseudo-event': his examples include the planned 'synthetic novelty' such as the interview or press conference.[14] Given the relative eventlessness of long stretches of conflict, pseudo-events proliferate in wartime: indeed, Jean Baudrillard has argued that the events of (post)modern warfare are none other than simulacra stage-managed for the media.[15] In fact, as suggested by the discussion of hyper-naming in Chapter 2, war has always been fought with an eye to remembrance, though the increasing sophistication of communications technology and the large-scale conflict memorialisation industry now in existence have doubtless exacerbated the tendency. In relation to the First World War, for example, Geoff Dyer has identified a prevailing 'anticipation of remembrance', describing that conflict's 'characteristic attitude' as 'look[ing] forward to the time when it would be remembered'. Dyer notes that perhaps the most famous of all First World War poems, Laurence Binyon's 'For the Fallen', was written in September 1914, well before the majority of the 'fallen' actually fell: its line 'we will remember them' therefore has the character more of an uncannily accurate prediction of mass commemoration than of a staunch vow to lost comrades.[16] In relation to the Second World War, Patricia Rae has also remarked the prevalence of 'proleptic elegy', the hoarding up of 'compensatory resources'.[17] In a 1937 poem called 'Remembrance Day', W. T. Nettlefold was already thinking ahead to the future memorialisation of 'the potential dead': 'Purchase the poppies while you may / For whom the next Remembrance Day?'[18]

But, while the pseudo-event and other phenomena of accelerated recontextualisation have shaped and continue to shape the representation of war, the model of anticipated retrospect is ultimately inapt to characterise

[12] *Ibid.*, 11–12.   [13] Derrida, *Speech and Phenomena*, 89; Currie, *About Time*, 42.
[14] Daniel J. Boorstin, *The Image* (London: Weidenfeld and Nicholson, 1961), 9.
[15] Jean Baudrillard, *The Gulf War Did Not Take Place*, trans. Paul Patton (London: Power Publications, 1994).
[16] Geoff Dyer, *The Missing of the Somme* (London: Hamish Hamilton, 1994), 7, 15, 7.
[17] Patricia Rae, 'Proleptic Elegy and the End of Arcadianism in 1930s Britain', *Twentieth Century Literature* 49.2 (Summer 2003), 265.
[18] W. T. Nettlefold, 'Remembrance Day', *Left Review* 3 (December 1937): 661; quoted in Rae, 'Proleptic Elegy', 249.

wartime. The reason is simple: wartime doubts the future and therefore denies a temporal space in and from which retrospect and memory can be effected. Keith Douglas figured this state of affairs in terms of looking through the wrong end of a telescope: the resulting view is shrunken and reductive:

> Time's wrong-way telescope will show
> a minute man ten years hence
> and by distance simplified.[19]

But, in the middle of a conflict, the idea that even 'ten years hence' will afford an observatory platform from which to turn a telescope back on a current war might seem optimistic. Once conflict has been initiated, the sense that '[i]t is war, and no man can see an end to it'[20] is pervasive. Paul Fussell points out that, in the First World War, 'one did not have to be a lunatic or a particularly despondent visionary to conceive quite seriously that the war would literally never end and would become the permanent condition of mankind'.[21] In this vein, Vera Brittain's brother remarked to her in 1915: 'I can never imagine the end of the War or what it'll be like; I believe now it'll last for years and I've no notion of what I would do if it were ended.'[22] In 1918, Brittain herself felt that '[t]he War had gone on for such centuries; its end seemed as distant as ever'; 'I had ceased to think of the War as ever ending'.[23] A related thought is that the war will end, but in annihilation. Beatrice Webb wrote in her diary on 19 April 1943:

[I]f my reasoning is right, we shall all disappear, including the *Germans themselves from the territory which they have conquered*. There will be no Jews, no conquered peoples, no refugees. The garden will disappear and all our furniture, the earth and the sun and the moon... We should merely – not exist (never even have existed). It all seems incredible and therefore is worth noting. Even Churchill and Roosevelt, states and kingdoms, would disappear![24]

---

[19] Keith Douglas, 'Simplify Me When I'm Dead' (1941), *The Complete Poems*, ed. Desmond Graham (Oxford: Oxford University Press, 1998), 74.

[20] Robinson Jeffers, 'Shine, Empire' (1944), *The Collected Poetry of Robinson Jeffers*, ed. Tim Hunt, 3 vols. (Palo Alto: Stanford University Press, 1991), vol. III, 17.

[21] Fussell, *The Great War and Modern Memory*, 71.

[22] Vera Brittain, *Testament of Youth* (London: Weidenfeld and Nicolson, 2009), 130.

[23] *Ibid.*, 346, 398. Cf. Ivor Gurney's 'Time and the Soldier' (1917): criticising Time for its slowness, the speaker defiantly claims that 'Some day I shall again, / For all your scheming, / See Severn valley clouds / Like banners streaming'. Nonetheless, this putative future must itself take place in time which, as the last line of the poem repeats, is 'SO SLOW!!!' (Gurney, *Collected Poems*, 34).

[24] Beatrice Webb, *The Diaries of Beatrice Webb*, ed. Norman MacKenzie and Jeanne MacKenzie (London: Virago in association with The London School of Economics and Political Science, 2000), 608. This and other diary entries quoted in this chapter can be found in Irene Taylor and

Importantly, these feelings of war-in-perpetuity or of impending annihilation express something other than the general openness and unknowability of the future in everyday life in peacetime. With the future conceived as nothing, the experience of wartime is intense and radical uncertainty about what is to come.

Currie uses the Heideggerian term 'hermeneutic circle'[25] to describe the interactive temporal effect of living life and reading literature:

> When we read a novel we make present events that are in the past, and when we live life we often do the opposite: we live the present as if it were already in the past, as if it were the object of a future memory. If in reading a narrative we decode the preterite as a kind of present, the process is one of presentification, whereas in living we use a kind of envisaged preterite to deprive the today of its character as present.[26]

Constantly asking *when will it end?*, *how will it end?* and, deadliest of all, *will it end?*, wartime refuses or is unable to imagine post-war. This breaks the hermeneutic circle: specifically, the removal of the future past forecloses the bringing of the past into the present ('presentification'). Nor may wartime turn to pre-war for self-definition as pre-war, by now, is itself too ineffably other. This unavailability of post-war and pre-war in turn crucially affects wartime, rendering it, *pace* the philosophers of the elusive 'now', an extended present. This is the Duration: past-less and future-less.

From within, the Duration is variously felt. In one of the first psychological studies to focus on time sense in trauma, Lenore C. Terr identified a number of temporal distortions, amongst them misperception of duration, gross confusion of sequencing, foreshortening of the future and retrospective presifting.[27] A perception of time slowing down accompanied by a sense of detailed remembrance characterise misperception of duration.[28] Richard Aldington writes, in *Death of a Hero*:

> To Winterbourne, as to so many others, the time element was of extreme importance during the war years. The hour-goddesses who had danced along so gaily before, and have fled from us since with such mocking swiftness, then paced by in a slow, monotonous file as if intolerably burdened. People at a distance thought of the fighting as heroic and exciting, in terms of cheering bayonet charges or little knots of determined men holding out to the last Lewis gun. That is rather

---

Alan Taylor, eds., *The Secret Annexe: An Anthology of the World's Greatest War Diarists* (Edinburgh: Canongate, 2004).

[25] Currie, *About Time*, 21.   [26] *Ibid.*, 30.

[27] Lenore C. Terr, 'Time Sense Following Psychic Trauma: A Clinical Study of Ten Adults and Twenty Children', *American Journal of Orthopsychiatry* 53.2 (April 1983), 244.

[28] *Ibid.*, 249.

like counting life by its champagne suppers and forgetting all the rest.[29] The qualities needed were determination and endurance, inhuman endurance. It would be much more practical to fight modern wars with mechanical robots than with men . . . the trouble is that men have feelings; to attain the perfect soldier, we must eliminate feelings. To the human robots of the last war, time seemed indefinitely and most unpleasantly prolonged. The dimension then measured as a 'day' in its apparent duration approached what we now call a 'month.' And the long series of violent stalemates on the Western Front made any decision seem impossible.[30]

This analysis highlights monotony, intermittency, a sense of temporal elongation and an accompanying automatism. But how can these phenomena be *conveyed*, as opposed to reported? Prolongation is often communicated by a concentration of what Seymour Chatman terms 'stasis statements': statements which expose, present, identify or qualify rather than enact or recount.[31] In *Under Fire*, Henri Barbusse uses stasis statements to convey the prevailing sense of endlessness among the *poilus* in the trenches:

The flaming and melancholy storm never, never ends. For more than fifteen months, for five hundred days in this part of the world where we are, the rifles and the big guns have gone on from morning to night and from night to morning. We are buried deep in an everlasting battlefield; but like the ticking of the clocks at home in the days gone by – in the now almost legendary Past – you only hear the noise when you listen.[32]

The present tense, the repetition of 'never', the anaphora of 'for', the repetitive chiasmus of 'from morning to night and from night to morning', the word 'everlasting' ('éternal' in the French),[33] the description of the past as 'legendary' ('quasi légendair')[34] – belonging, as it were, to another time zone, like the clocks of home: all these reinforce the impression of stasis. And, in likening occurrences on the battlefield to the ticking ('le tic-tac') of a clock (Kermode's model for narrative, as quoted above), Barbusse communicates the habituation that has set in among the men in this chronic now: events are no longer 'noisy' or kaironic but unremarked

---

[29] Cf. Spike Milligan's account of service in the Second World War: 'The war was now an accepted daily routine, we had "periods of utter boredom then bursts of sudden excitement", as Colonel Grant had told us, from then on we went about saying "Hello Dick, are you in an 'utter boredom period'?" "Oh no. I'm right in the middle of a 'sudden burst of excitement'"' (*Milligan's War: The Selected War Memoirs of Spike Milligan*, ed. Jack Hobbs (London: Penguin, 1989), 92–3).

[30] Aldington, *Death of a Hero*, 206–7.

[31] Seymour Chatman, *Story and Discourse: Narrative Structure in Fiction and Film* (Ithaca: Cornell University Press, 1978), 32–3.

[32] Henri Barbusse, *Under Fire: The Story of a Squad*, trans. Fitzwater Wray (London: J. M. Dent, 1926), 6.

[33] Henri Barbusse, *Le Feu: journal d'une escouade* (Paris: Gallimard, 2007), 15.   [34] *Ibid.*, 15.

in the more immediate sensation of being trapped in the present. Stasis statements contribute to the effect of 'stretch' (Chatman's term for an account that is longer than the events it narrates and so elongates real time).[35] Barbusse describes a couple of explosions:

The last two explosions are quite near. Above the battered ground they take shape like vast balls of black and tawny dust; and as they deploy and leisurely depart at the wind's will, having finished their task, they have the outline of fabled dragons.[36]

These explosions, extended by stasis statements, are in no hurry to disperse and Barbusse again uses an 'out-of-time' image ('fabled dragons' – 'dragons fabuleux' in the French)[37] to elongate the moment.

The first English translation of *Le Feu*, by Fitzwater Wray in 1926, translated the work's subtitle as 'The story of a squad'. The generic implications are of a narratology not present in the original French subtitle. *Journal d'une escouade* suggests nothing so teleological as a story but rather the open-endedness of a gazette, the primary meaning of *journal* in French being, according to *Le Robert micro*, 'relation quotidienne des événements' (daily relating of events). What Barbusse makes clear is that the quotidian includes the banal and monotonous as well as the diurnal. A common, if unexpected, feature of warfare, with which the sense of temporal arrest is associated, is boredom. As the passage quoted earlier from *Death of a Hero* makes clear, though conflict is obviously replete with danger and excitement, it can also, for long periods, be intensely tedious. This is not Siegfried Kracauer's 'extraordinary, radical boredom',[38] but a brittle existence on a spectrum ranging from the anxiegenic to the mundane ('inertia is frustrated despair' remarked de Saint-Exupéry).[39] William James defined boredom, in *Psychology: Briefer Course* (1892), as the state that comes about 'whenever, from the relative emptiness of content of a tract of time, we grow attentive to the passage of the time itself'.[40] This is the state of Barbusse's *poilus*, whose sole focus is on the next event to intervene in the tedium of life in the trenches when not under bombardment:

[35] Chatman, *Story and Discourse*, 67–8; see also Gerald Prince, *Narratology: The Form and Functioning of Narrative* (Berlin, New York and Amsterdam: Mouton, 1982), 56. 'And therefore all we have related in / Two long octaves passed in a little minute' (*Don Juan* 8.59.1–2).

[36] Barbusse, *Under Fire*, 209.   [37] Barbusse, *Le Feu*, 242.

[38] Siegfried Kracauer, *The Mass Ornament: Weimar Essays*, trans. and ed. Thomas Y. Levin (Cambridge: Harvard University Press, 1995), 331–4.

[39] Antoine de Saint-Exupéry, *Flight to Arras*, trans. Lewis Galantière (Harmondsworth: Penguin, 1961), 67.

[40] William James, *Psychology: Briefer Course* (New York: Macmillan, 1962), 291.

In a state of war, one is always waiting. We have become waiting-machines. For the moment it is food we are waiting for. Then it will be the post. But each in its turn. When we have done with dinner we will think about the letters. After that, we shall set ourselves to wait for something else.[41]

Preternatural clock-watchers, these men know that their food should take five hours to arrive from the dug-out where it is prepared and also know, precisely, when it takes 'seven hours forty-seven minutes'.[42]

Boredom became an operational issue in the Second World War when lapses in the concentration of RAF radar operators tasked with detecting the infrequently occurring signals of enemy submarines led the phenomenon to be referred for psychological study. The 'vigilance task' test devised by the Cambridge psychologist Norman F. Mackworth revealed a 'vigilance decrement' over time. Explanations for this included theories of inhibition ('a fatigue-like construct which is considered to build up with each non-reinforced occurrence of a conditioned response')[43] and habituation (the 'decrease in an innate response as a result of repetition of the stimulus').[44] Vigilance decrement – losing interest – is therefore a function both of the passage of time (which appears to move slowly) and of the repetitiveness of activities performed within that time. As noted above, Barbusse implies vigilance decrement on the part of the *poilus* in his suggestion that events are no longer 'heard' in the overwhelming stasis. But vigilance decrement is also induced in the *reader* in *Under Fire*. Chapter II of the work, 'In the Earth', describes a day's troglodytic existence. As the sky changes over the course of the chapter from 'pale' to 'dark-blue' and 'the day matures', the attacks of the great guns form a barely heeded backdrop.[45] In the

---

[41] Barbusse, *Under Fire*, 17–18.

[42] *Ibid.*, 18. Tim O'Brien describes the same phenomenon in Vietnam: 'Paul Berlin tilted his wristwatch to catch moonlight. Twelve twenty now – the incredible slowness with which time passed. Incredible, too, the tricks his fear did with time. He wound the watch as tight as it would go. Facing east, out to sea, he counted to sixty very slowly, breathing with each count, and when he was done he looked at the watch again. Still twelve twenty. He held it to his ear. The ticking was loud, brittle-sounding. The second hand made its endless sweep. Maybe it was the time of night that created the distortions' (*Going After Cacciato*, 52). Berlin goes on to attempt 'tricks' with time: 'Counting, that was one trick. Count the remaining days. Break the days into hours, and count the hours, then break the hours into minutes and count them one by one, and the minutes into seconds' (*ibid.*, 53). Using the technique of stretch and accumulating horological vocabulary, O'Brien conveys the time-obsessed element of boredom. As a character later remarks, 'Time goes faster when you don't know the time' (*ibid.*, 206).

[43] D. R. Davies and R. Parasuraman, *The Psychology of Vigilance* (London and New York: Academic Press, 1981), 10.

[44] Jane F. Mackworth, *Vigilance and Habituation: A Neuropsychological Approach* (Harmondsworth: Penguin, 1969), 14.

[45] Barbusse, *Under Fire*, 5, 45, 24.

foreground are the men's everyday concerns: eating, smoking, conversing, reading their mail. Activities are minimal: 'Mesnil Joseph drowses; Blaire yawns; Marthereau smokes, "eyes front." Lamuse scratches himself like a gorilla, and Eudore like a marmoset. Volpatte coughs.'[46] The accumulation of minor incidents, free of suspense, climax or denouement is chronos – time without meaning: 'To hell with time . . . it doesn't matter to me any more what time it is', claims Volpatte.[47] The reader also begins to habituate, lulled into lowering guard.

Habit-forming activities, as Bryony Randall points out, produce a psychological state in which 'the external has come to dominate over the internal': what Freud called a 'protective shield' and Bergson a 'crust'.[48] In war texts, imagery of automata, animality and encrustation work to convey a sense of habituation and hence of time as a 'rigid continual present'.[49] Aldington's 'human robots', their feelings 'eliminated', have already been mentioned. Barbusse's *poilus* are 'huge and misshapen lumps, bear-like, that flounder and growl' (6), 'simple men further simplified' (44), have 'an outer crust of coarseness and concealment' (39).[50] This crusting-over of inner life resembles the 'numbing of general responsiveness' that is one of the diagnostic elements of post-traumatic stress disorder (PTSD) listed in DSM-IV (1994), the American Psychiatric Association's latest *Diagnostic and Statistical Manual of Mental Disorders*.[51] Kirtland C. Peterson *et al.* characterise psychic numbing as a 'retreat to mental foxholes' and 'impacted grief'; the search for 'inner peace' gained through the maintenance of a 'dead space within'.[52] This numbed state is often articulated as

---

[46] *Ibid.*, 14.

[47] *Ibid.*, 55. '– J'me fous d'l'heure, dit Volpatte. L'temps qui passe, ça n'a pus rien à faire avec moi' (Barbusse, *Le Feu*, 70).

[48] Bryony Randall, *Modernism, Daily Time and Everyday Life* (Cambridge: Cambridge University Press, 2007), 44. In war, such a mechanism may not be without its uses – the psychologist Jane F. Mackworth argues that organisms have 'developed an ability to suppress responses to a repetitive event in order to be able to show maximum sensitivity and responsiveness to a new and unfamiliar event' (Mackworth, *Vigilance and Habituation*, 185).

[49] Stephen Spender, 'In No Man's Land' (1938), *New Collected Poems*, ed. Michael Brett (London: Faber, 2004), 79.

[50] Barbusse, *Under Fire*, 6, 44, 39. This numbed, habituated state is not solely a phenomenon of mass, industrialised warfare: 'A Soldier of the Seventy-First', who fought with the 71st Highlanders in the Peninsular War, found, after a long march in Spain, that 'my mind became unfit for any minute observation. I only marked what I myself was forced to encounter' ('A Soldier of the Seventy-First', *The Journal of a Soldier in the Peninsular War*, ed. Christopher Hibbert (Moreton-in-Marsh: The Windrush Press, 1997), 30).

[51] Tabulated in William Yule, Ruth Williams and Stephen Joseph, *Post-Traumatic Stress Disorders: Concepts and Therapy*, ed. William Yule (Chichester: John Wiley, 1999), 6. (DSM-V is in preparation at the time of writing: see Heidi Ledford, 'Psychiatry Manual Revisions', *Nature* 460 (23 July 2009), 445.)

[52] Kirtland C. Peterson, Maurice F. Prout and Robert A. Schwarz, *Post-Traumatic Stress Disorder: A Clinician's Guide* (New York and London: Plenum Press, 1991), 22–3.

the loss or exiting of linear temporal sequencing: Volpatte's 'To hell with time . . . it doesn't matter to me any more what time it is.'[53] This version of time distortion forms the narrative structure of de Saint-Exupéry's *Flight to Arras*. In the early chapters, anticipation of the deadly Arras mission casts an inhibiting shadow, sending the narrator into a trance-like state in which death seems absurd.[54] The flight itself is extended over seventeen chapters (4–21), 'stretched' by the narrator's reveries. Literally outside earth-time, flight-time is ductile, both condensed ('An hour of life spent at thirty-three thousand feet is equivalent to what? To a week? three weeks? a month of organic life, of the work of the heart, the lungs, the arteries?') and dis-tended ('My semi-swoonings have added centuries to me', 'I have aged so much that all I was is left behind me').[55] There is an overwhelming sense of time in abeyance:

I thought of clocks out of order. All the clocks of France – out of order. Clocks in their church steeples. Clocks on railway stations. Chimney clocks in empty houses. A charnel-house of clocks. 'The war,' I said to myself, 'is that thing in which clocks are no longer wound up.'[56]

When clocks are out of order or no longer wound up, time is unmeasured: there exists only now – what Saint-Exupéry called 'the timelessness of suspense'.[57] Sagon, who has crawled out of his burning plane to lie on a wing, floats 'in a sort of infinite leisure . . . a creature flung out of the dimension of time'.[58] A temporal vacuum is suggested, in which the timeless float like the weightless in space.

Exiting linear temporality causes a cessation of the ability to act, or stasis. Emmanuel Lévinas characterises this phenomenon in terms of 'indolence' and 'fatigue': both of these are withdrawals from (or, in Terr's terms, a foreshortening of) the future, the former 'an impossibility of beginning', the latter 'an impossibility of following through'.[59] Here, for example, is Harold Nicolson writing in his diary on 15 June 1940:

Then there is another state of mind which I notice. I am able almost entirely to dismiss from my thoughts any consideration of the future. I do not even have such pangs about the past as I had when the situation was less catastrophic. My reason tells me that it will now be almost impossible to beat the Germans, and that the probability is that France will surrender and that we shall be bombed and

---

[53] Cf. The protagonist of Aldington's *Death of a Hero*, who finds battle 'a timeless confusion, a chaos of noise, fatigue, anxiety, and horror. He did not know how many days and nights it lasted, lost completely the sequence of events, found great gaps in his conscious memory' (250).

[54] De Saint-Exupéry, *Flight to Arras*, 8.   [55] *Ibid.*, 48, 69.

[56] *Ibid.*, 9.   [57] *Ibid.*, 114.   [58] *Ibid.*, 45.

[59] Emmanuel Lévinas, *Existence and Existents*, trans. Alphonso Lingis (Dordrecht: Kluwer Academic Publishers, 1988), 26, 30.

invaded. I am quite lucidly aware that in three weeks from now Sissinghurst may be a waste and Vita and I both dead. Yet these probabilities do not fill me with despair. I seem to be impervious both to pleasure and pain. For the moment we are all anaesthetised.[60]

Nicolson describes the deleterious mental effect of a truncated future: a state of inertia. Asked in April 1945 to fill in a form specifying where he would live, what job he would do and what training he would like to have, Henry Treece displayed the same symptom:

I really haven't a clue. I wrote 'Not known,' 'Nil,' etc, to nearly all my questions. I don't want to be taught anything. I'm not even sure I want to do anything ever again! For four years the R. A. F. has taught me to do a certain job in a certain way, and I don't feel now that I have the interest or energy left to start anything new.[61]

In other cases, there is a reining-in of expectations. 'I try not to think of the future', wrote Gladys Brett-James to her soldier son Antony on 2 June 1940,[62] signalling a kind of self-imposed and apotropaeic negative capability. This has further political implications since attitudes to the unknown future are an important consideration in maintaining morale during conflict – itself part of the war effort.

Terr's final traumatised temporal distortion is retrospective presifting. Wartime, refusing the possibility of future retrospect, creates in its place its temporal mirror image. Though the area is still under investigation,[63] psychological studies have shown that the misperceptions of duration and sequencing which are 'common' distortions of temporal sense after trauma include 'omen formation' or the construction of 'retrospectively formed warnings'.[64] Terr writes:

---

[60] Harold Nicolson, *Diaries and Letters 1939–45*, ed. Nigel Nicolson, 3 vols. (London: Collins, 1967), vol. II, 96.

[61] Stefan Schimanski and Henry Treece, eds., *Leaves in the Storm: A Book of Diaries* (London: Lindsay Drummond, 1947), 284.

[62] Quoted in Tamasin Day-Lewis, ed., *Last Letters Home* (Macmillan, 1995), 39.

[63] See Lenore C. Terr, 'Time and Trauma', *Psychoanalytic Study of the Child* 39 (1984), 633–65, and Micah D. Lueck, 'Anxiety Levels: Do They Influence the Perception of Time?', *UW-L Journal of Undergraduate Research* 10 (2007), 1–5. DSM-IV includes in the criteria for PTSD a 'sense of foreshortened future' (Yule *et al.*, *Post-Traumatic Stress Disorders*, 6). The psychiatrist Jonathan Shay expands traumatic symptoms to include the feeling that past and future have been obliterated and there obtains only an endless present, a consequent shrinkage of the temporal horizon and a suppression of the will (Jonathan Shay, *Achilles in Vietnam: Combat Trauma and the Undoing of Character* (New York and London: Simon & Schuster Touchstone, 1995), 176, 190–1).

[64] Terr, 'Time Sense Following Psychic Trauma', 253. Temporally and structurally, the phenomenon of retrospective omen formation resembles Freud's *Nachträglichkeit* (deferral), insofar as it constitutes a later recognition of traumatic origin. Jean-François Lyotard describes the process as 'the setting into diachrony of what takes place in a time that is not diachronic since what happened earlier is given at

In order to search for an omen, the individual must feel utterly unable to cope with the present. Potential actions, defenses, thoughts, and plans are experienced as ineffective. In this helpless state, the victim grasps for an opportunity to control some portion of time in the past. Was there a sign? Was there a turning point? Did the individual have a choice somewhere further back in time? . . . Omen formation requires that the individual relinquish a sense of the inevitable forward movement of time, and turn back to earlier times for a chance at effective action.[65]

In contrast to anticipated retrospect, omen formation is retrospective anticipation: *I remember that I foretold this* replaces *I foretell that I will remember this*. As Terr notes, this depends on a sense of the forward movement of time towards the future being relinquished. In his Second World War memoir, *The Last Enemy* (1942), Richard Hillary, whose plane was shot down from behind by a Messerschmitt, describes being anaesthetised so that his burnt hands can be operated on. Under the anaesthetic, he not only 'sees' the death of his friend, Peter Pease, in similar circumstances, but 'shouts out' to warn him of the approaching German plane: 'Peter, for God's sake look out behind!'.[66] Soon after he comes round from the operation, he receives news of Pease's actual death. Hillary's anaesthetised cries take on the character of a premonition – a premonition that occurs *after* the event and so distorts normal time sequencing (the distorted sequencing is dramatised in the anaesthetised vision in the fact that Hillary warns Pease to look behind him). To an extent, the reader of in-war writing sifts for omens, too, particularly when the writer is, like Hillary, known to have died before the termination of the conflict. Taking his or her cue from Hillary, the reader of *The Last Enemy* becomes sensitive to ironies created by apparent predictions of his death.

The thrust of all these examples is to show that war is felt as an immeasurable and directionless present, removed from temporal markers. At first glance, it might seem that wartime is phenomenological or subjective time, as opposed to cosmological or objective time. But rather than fitting the standard temporal categories – cosmological

a later date (in analysis, in writing), and since what is later in the symptom (the second blow) occurs "before" what happened earlier (the first blow)' (*Heidegger and "the jews"*, trans. Andreas Michel and Mark S. Roberts (Minneapolis: University of Minnesota Press, 1990), 16). Philip Weinstein notes that Freud conceptualises trauma as 'the wound to the psyche that makes it inhabit a temporality both then and now' (*Unknowing: the Work of Modernist Fiction* (Ithaca: Cornell University Press, 2005), 4). See also Michael Rothberg on Blanchot's 'noncontemporaneous désormais' (*Traumatic Realism*, 83).

[65] Terr, 'Time Sense Following Psychic Trauma', 253.

[66] Richard Hillary, *The Last Enemy* (London: Pimlico, 1997), 115.

versus phenomenological or A-series versus B-Series[67] – wartime arguably requires another oppositional set, with notable narratological consequences. Wartime is synchronic (or paradigmatic) as opposed to diachronic (or syntagmatic) time.[68] That is, it is not time conceptualised as linear, whether tensed or in a block – what David Crystal calls the 'Newtonian metaphor of time as a line along which we progress, which we segment into durational quantities, and which we use to schedule things'[69] – but a layered temporal experience in which two or more mutually incompatible outcomes hang simultaneously in the balance. What it feels like can be inferred from the following description by de Saint-Exupéry of waiting for a telegram that would announce to him either the death or recovery of a wounded friend:

> Time flows by unutilized and holds me in suspense. Time has ceased to be a stream that feeds me, nourishes me, adds growth to me as to a tree. The man I shall be when the news comes, dwells outside me: he is moving towards me like a ghost about to fuse with me. And for want of knowing who I am, I am suspended in anguish.[70]

The polarity of the possible outcomes of the telegram – life or death – offers two possible futures so unlike each other as to render what is to come unimaginable. As already discussed, the unimaginability of the future – the denial of future retrospect – paralyses the speaker in the present (de Saint-Exupéry also writes, 'I have stopped projecting myself into the

---

[67] 'A-series' time is a tensed theory of time comprising past, present and future. 'B-series' time is an untensed theory of time as a block in which events are seen as occurring earlier or later (Currie, *About Time*, 142).

[68] The use of 'synchronic', 'diachronic', 'paradigmatic' and 'syntagmatic' is derived from Saussure's application of these terms in linguistics. The synchronic lies on 'the axis of simultaneities . . . which stands for the relations of coexisting things *and from which the intervention of time is excluded*' (added emphasis), while the diachronic lies on 'the axis of successions . . . on which only one thing can be considered at a time' (Ferdinand de Saussure, *Course in General Linguistics*, trans. Wade Baskin, eds. Charles Bally and Albert Sechehaye (New York: McGraw-Hill, 1966), 80). Similarly, 'paradigms . . . are typical of associative groupings', while 'combinations supported by linearity are *syntagms*' (*ibid.*, 126, 123) (original emphasis). For further application of 'syntagmatic' and 'paradigmatic', see Jakobson, 'Two Aspects of Language and Two Types of Aphasic Disturbance', 53–82, and Lodge, *The Modes of Modern Writing*. Syntagmatic time can be conceptualised as located on the axis of combination, paradigmatic time on the axis of substitution – except that, in paradigmatic time, all possible substitutes are simultaneously there.

[69] David Crystal, 'Talking About Time', in *Time*, ed. Katinka Ridderbos (Cambridge: Cambridge University Press, 2002), 116.

[70] De Saint-Exupéry, *Flight to Arras*, 28. In the original: 'Tant que l'incertitude me tient en suspens, mes sentiments et mes attitudes ne sont plus qu'un déguisement provisoire. Le temps cesse de fonder, seconde par seconde, comme il bâtit l'arbre, le personage veritable qui m'habitera dans une heure. Ce moi inconnu marche à ma rencontre, de l'extérieure, comme un fantôme. Alors j'éprouve une sensation d'angoisse' (Antoine de Saint-Exupéry, *Pilote de guerre* (New York: Éditions de la Maison Française, 1942), 42).

future').[71] But the situation is also capable of a Heideggerian reading. As Currie points out, the Heideggerian 'future-oriented project of anticipatory resoluteness creates a split in the self and produces a temporal distance between the reflective consciousness and the consciousness reflected on'.[72] In de Saint-Exupéry's case, this autoscopic project has failed: the putative reflective consciousness – 'the man I shall be' ('ce moi inconnu') – is insubstantial, merely a ghost. As this indicates, the appearance of the ghostly in war texts can be as much a sign of structural failure (the unavailability of a point to look back from) as of psychic unrest. In Henri Barbusse's *Under Fire*, for example, the men enter a wood 'so strangely full of obstructing shadows that the deep darkness of the forest itself might by some magic have overflowed upon it'.[73] It is in this enchanted setting that the narrator encounters, 'in a fleeting vision', 'Eudoxie, the fairy woman',[74] tantalising yet unreachable:

[S]he is truly enticing in the sunshine, this woman crowned with gold, and one's glance is impelled and astonished by the moon-like purity of her skin. Her eyes sparkle; her teeth, too, glisten white in the living wound of her half-open mouth, red as her heart.[75]

Like the end of the war, Eudoxie is both idealised and unavailable. Though she falls at last into the arms of Lamuse, who has desired her ('the woman I could never go near before . . . that I only saw a long way off and couldn't ever touch, same as diamonds'), the embrace is grotesque: 'the face, all stove in and mouldy, the neck pulped, and all the lot dead for a month perhaps'.[76] The corpse's putrid kiss is an horrific parody of a home-coming embrace: Eudoxie's long-deadness figures the shrivelling of prospect and future retrospect.

Eudoxie and 'the man I shall be' are also significant from a Derridean perspective. Currie takes Derrida's phrase from 'The Law of Genre' – 'an internal pocket larger than the whole'[77] – as 'a useful way of describing the fictional representation of time, since fiction is capable of temporal distortion which cannot be reproduced in lived experience'.[78] Eudoxie's

[71] De Saint-Exupéry, *Flight to Arras*, 28.

[72] Currie, *About Time*, 57; Martin Heidegger, *Being and Time*, trans. John Macquarrie and Edward Robinson (Oxford: Blackwell, 1978), 377f.

[73] Barbusse, *Under Fire*, 59.

[74] *Ibid.*, 65. The French original is 'femme-biche' ('doe-woman') (Barbusse, *Le Feu*, 82), suggesting an ambiguous state between human and animal.

[75] Barbusse, *Under Fire*, 79.   [76] *Ibid.*, 197.

[77] Jacques Derrida, 'The Law of Genre', in *Acts of Literature*, ed. Derek Attridge (London and New York: Routledge, 1992), 228.

[78] Currie, *About Time*, 85.

remains have been putrifying in a disused trench and are only discovered
when the men begin digging out a sap.[79] This 'internal pocket', far from
opening out time, is a space of decomposition. 'The man I shall be' similarly
reduces the Derridean prolapse: he 'dwells outside me' but 'he is moving
towards me' and is 'about to fuse with me' ('le personnage veritable qui
m'habitera . . . [c]e moi inconnu march à ma rencontre, de l'extérieure').
As temporal prolepsis, this future time is a burst balloon.

But if war renders future, diachronic time unavailable, synchronic time
still exists in abundance. As de Saint-Exupéry's wait for the telegram
demonstrates, synchronic time involves the maintenance of two or more
incompatible outcomes. Though this might suggest the holding out of
future prospects, the incompatibility of the outcomes denies the possibility
of retrospect to come – the future is once again foreclosed. Instead of a
broken circle, shrivelled pocket or deflated balloon, a more appropriate
analogy for this state of affairs can be drawn from quantum physics: that
of *superposition*. Superposition is the combination of all possible states of a
system. In Erwin Schrödinger's famous thought experiment demonstrating
what this means[80] – and the bizarreness of its consequences (Schrödinger
himself described the case as 'quite ridiculous')[81] – a cat is shut into a
steel chamber with a Geiger counter and a small amount of radioactive
substance which has a 50–50 chance of emitting a particle in the course of
an hour. If a particle is emitted, a hammer will break a flask of acid, killing
the cat. During the hour that the box remains closed, the cat, according
to quantum mechanics, is in a quantum superposition of *both* dead and
alive states: 'The psi-function [the function describing the probability of
a system being in a certain state] of the entire system would express this
by having in it the living and dead cat (pardon the expression) mixed or
smeared out in equal parts', wrote Schrödinger.[82] According to the so-
called 'Copenhagen interpretation', advanced by Niels Bohr in a lecture of
1927, the superposition collapses into a definite state only at the moment
of quantum measurement. That is, it is only when the box is opened and
the cat is observed to be alive or dead that it actually *is* alive or dead. For
other people – reporters waiting outside the room to be told the results of
the experiment, say – the superposition nevertheless persists until they, too,

[79] Barbusse, *Under Fire*, 197.
[80] First published as 'Die Gegenwärtige Situation in der Quantenmechanik', in *Naturwissenschaften* (November 1935), 807–12, 23, 44–9. John D. Trimmer's translation is quoted from here.
[81] John D. Trimmer, 'The Present Situation in Quantum Mechanics: A Translation of Schrödinger's "Cat Paradox" Paper', *Proceedings of the American Philosophical Society* 124.5 (1980), 328.
[82] *Ibid.*, 328.

are informed of the definitive outcome. The superposition, in other words, describes the state of mind of the observer: 'the strangest thing about the standard Copenhagen interpretation of the quantum world is that it is the act of observing a system that forces it to select one of its options, which then becomes real'.[83] The plethora of potentialities existing in the super-position before it is collapsed into a definitive state have therefore been described as 'ghost realities, ghost *worlds* that only exist when we are not looking at them ... a myriad array of ghost realities corresponding to all the myriad ways every quantum system in the entire universe could "choose to jump"':[84] de Saint-Exupéry's phantasmal 'the man I shall be' is a case in point. Such notions, writes John Gribbin, 'strike at the roots of sanity, let alone our concept of reality'.[85] Analogously, the superpositions thrown up by war produce surreal effects in narrative structure on every level. Super-position plays havoc with temporal expressions as standard tenses prove unequal to expressing alternative possible future retrospective statements about events yet to come at the time of writing. The subgenre of in-war writing in which this phenomenon can best be observed is that of the letter written to a loved one to be opened in the event of the writer's death.

Letters such as this were written by Sergeant Ted Baker and Submariner Glyn Williams during the Second World War. Their families were informed that they were missing but then had to wait a significant period before their deaths were confirmed: a year in Baker's case, four and a half years in Williams's. During the interim between notification of their being missing and confirmation of their deaths, Baker and Williams were, as far as their families were concerned, effectively both alive and dead (in Schrödinger's model, the notification of their deaths would be the act of observation which collapsed the superposition). This state of affairs did not cause problems in terms of classical physics but did – does – have radical con-sequences for temporal representation. In a letter to his wife Ruby, Baker wrote: 'If anything happens to me be brave and proud of me and remember I wasn't afraid of death and also that I hate tears.'[86] This looks forward to a retrospect (albeit one that the writer will be unable to share), but the polar possibilities of that retrospect create an insupportable pressure and the envisaged anticipation collapses. The past perfect ('I wasn't afraid') cannot be maintained and the inexorable present ('I hate') reasserts itself. Baker also wrote a letter for his young daughter, Pat, to open when she was grown up. With even more layers of time to encompass, the epistolary

[83] John Gribbin, *In Search of Schrödinger's Cat* (London: Wildwood House, 1984), 172.
[84] *Ibid.*, 176.   [85] *Ibid.*, 162.   [86] Quoted in Day-Lewis, ed., *Last Letters Home*, 11.

voice wobbles between the present tense of an envisaged future and the present tense of the time of writing:

I am writing this assuming you are now grown up, as you will not receive this till then. I can picture you a lovely girl, very happy with lots of boyfriends. I am finding it very hard to write this as I may never see you at this stage . . . Always loving you.[87]

This is wholesale diachronic failure. 'Now' and 'then' refer, impossibly, to the same time. It is unclear whether 'I can' is set in the writer's present or in an imagined future (the latter would require Baker to 'picture' his daughter from the grave). The first three occurrences of 'this' refer to the letter but the last 'this' suggests a future already arrived; 'that stage' would make better sense. The grammatical difficulties are a direct result of the superposition of states: Baker is both dead (the condition that must be fulfilled for the letter to be opened) and living (speaking both in his own present and in the present of his daughter's adulthood). Indeed, Pat Baker commented: 'The letter is as if he is still alive.'[88]

In similar vein, Gwyn Williams wrote to his girlfriend Betty Kelly:

I expect by now my sister has informed you that I have died in fighting for our and other countries, but I may say darling that my last thoughts were of my family and you, and I love you while there is a breath in my body.[89]

'I expect' projects the speaker into a future which is the present for his girlfriend ('now') but refers to events of different degrees of pastness ('has informed you', 'I have died'). Williams simultaneously refers to his own death in the present perfect tense ('I have died'), speaks in the present tense ('I love you') and utters his pre-death thoughts in the simple past tense ('my last thoughts were of my family and you'). Like Baker, Williams is both dead (the condition that must obtain for the letter to be opened) and alive (making utterances in the present): a demonstration of how the logical impossibility of the superposition ripples across language. 'It is very difficult to write now of future things in the past tense, so I am returning to the present', acknowledged the writer of another 'open in the event of my death' letter.[90]

Like the Baker and Williams families, the poet Henry Vaughan had to wait an unconscionable interval before learning the fate of an individual in conflict. It was a year before Vaughan discovered that his friend, Mr. R. W., had died at the battle of Rowton Heath, a Civil War battle which took place on 24 September 1645, resulting in a Parliamentary victory. The

[87] *Ibid.*, 13.   [88] *Ibid.*, 16.   [89] *Ibid.*, 92.   [90] *Ibid.*, 19.

dead/alive superposition governs Vaughan's 'An Elegie on the Death of Mr. R. W. slain in the Late Unfortunate Differences at Routon Heath, near Chester, 1645', wrinkling the poem's fabric. The title and first three words of the poem – 'I am confirmed'[91] – appear to collapse the superposition and produce a definitive state (R. W. is dead), but it is immediately resurrected again in the lines that follow, in which Vaughan recreates the experience of attempting to hold his grief, like the outcome, in abeyance:

> A full year's grief I struggled with, and stood
> Still on my sandy hopes' uncertain good,
> So loath was I to yield, to all those fears
> I still opposed thee, and denied my tears.[92]

'Sandy hopes', with its faint allusion to Matthew 7.24–7, suggests the precariousness of the superposition: R. W.'s dead/alive state teeters throughout the poem. The speaker notes that he still does not know 'whether that day thy breath / Suffered a *civil* or the *common* death' – that is, whether R. W. was stripped of his civil status[93] or (as the poet thinks more likely (line 69)) met a soldier's death in battle. Questioning R. W.'s corporeal whereabouts and lamenting the fact that the speaker did not actually witness his fate,[94] the elegy therefore functions as a kind of poetic *habeas corpus*, but, no body

---

[91] Henry Vaughan, *The Complete Poems*, ed. Alan Rudrum (New Haven: Yale University Press, 1976), 81. Alan Rudrum identifies the poem as 'an anniversary elegy', noting that, at the time that Vaughan was writing, a year was the conventional period of mourning, 'after which one could commemorate without expressing grief' ('Henry Vaughan's Poems of Mourning', in *Of Paradise and Light: Essays on Henry Vaughan and John Milton in Honor of Alan Rudrum*, ed. Donald R. Dickson and Holly Faith Nelson (Newark: University of Delaware Press, 2004), 326n, 312). It seems more likely (especially as the poem does express grief) that the writing of the poem marks the receipt of definitive news of R. W.'s death, after a year during which the poet was unaware of his fate (this view is shared by Stevie Davies in *Henry Vaughan* (Bridgend: Seren, 1995) and Philip West in *Henry Vaughan's Silex Scintillans: Scripture Uses* (Oxford: Oxford University Press, 2001)). This reading is supported by the first six-and-a-half-lines and, in particular, the opening three words – 'I am confirmed' ('to confirm' has the contemporary meaning of to make firm or strengthen in an opinion (*OED* 6)). The doubt introduced into the reliability of the information by the reference to civil death is discussed below.

[92] Vaughan, *The Complete Poems*, 81.

[93] The legal process known as *civiliter mortuus*. The reference to civil death suggests that line 64, 'hurled thee prisoner to some distant sky', refers to the possibility of R. W.'s having been taken prisoner and removed to a remote part of the country rather than, figuratively, to his having been killed. Alan Rudrum glosses '*civil*' as 'non-military' and '*common*' as the ordinary death of wartime (*ibid.*, 484), and the terms might also be read as 'legally deemed dead' and 'a matter of general knowledge', respectively. Whichever meaning is preferred, a superposition obtains.

[94] The poem's envoy quotes *Aeneid* 6.507–8: 'Nomen & arma locum servant, te, amice, nequivi / Conspicere' (*ibid.*, 84) ('The name and arms guard the place; thee, my friend, I could not see'). These words are addressed by Aeneas to the mutilated ghost of his former comrade, Deiphobus. Unable to find Deiphobus' corpse, Aeneas erected an empty tomb for him. Through this allusion, Vaughan refers both to the fact that R. W.'s body is missing and to the fact that he did not actually see what happened to him in the battle.

being forthcoming, the superposition shakily endures. The final lines of the poem, in a standard deployment of the '*aere perennius* trope – the desire for poetry to be a memorial "more lasting than bronze"',[95] seek to place R. W. in an eternal doubling of life and death: dead in battle, immortalised (redeemed or bought back) through words:

> It [the poem] may redeem thee to a fairer date;
> As some blind dial, when the day is done,
> Can tell us at mid-night, *There was a Sun.*[96]

This final, horological image recapitulates the superposition and all its ambivalences in miniature. At twelve o'clock, either the brightness of noon or the darkness of midnight may be indicated: that the dial or watch is 'blind' to which it may be allows both possibilities – and, by extension, the possibilities that R. W. is alive (light midday) and that he is dead (dark midnight) – to exist in synchronous tandem.

The concept of superposition is figured in the poem by an unstable image of two trees. In line 10, Vaughan invokes 'A well-built *Elme* or stately *Cedar*', going on to suggest that R. W.'s premature death resembles the crashing to ground of such mighty trees in strong wind (the allusion is to Virgil's twin oaks[97] or to his description of the felling of an ash).[98] But six lines later, Vaughan has turned the 'elm *or* cedar' into '*Shady twins*': in Stevie Davies's words, '[t]he unconscious and unrevised slip turns the singular 'R. W.' into a plural "twins"'.[99] Davies's diagnosis is that Vaughan hence 'records the threat to his own identity incurred by self-projection',[100] but it is just as likely that the shady twins point to the dual states of R. W. as alive and dead: an astigmatic vision in which a single tree splits in two.

In the rest of the poem, temporal compressions accumulate. R. W. has died 'untimely'; before his time 'immaturely Death / Stifled his able heart and active breath'.[101] His years 'could not be summed (alas!) / To a full score' but in less than twenty years – 'so short a span' – 'His riper thoughts had purchased more of man / Than all those worthless livers, which yet quick, / Have quite outgone their own *arithmetic*'.[102] Wise beyond his years, that is, R. W. had accomplished more ('purchased') than his elders, an instance of action condensed into time mirrored in a later image of 'those *lost youths* of the stage / Who only flourished for the *play's* short

---

[95] William N. West, 'Less Well-Wrought Urns: Henry Vaughan and the Decay of the Poetic Monument', *English Literary History* 75.1 (Spring 2008), 199.
[96] Vaughan, *The Complete Poems*, 84.   [97] *Aeneid* 9.679–82.   [98] *Aeneid* 2.626–31.
[99] Davies, *Henry Vaughan*, 77.   [100] Ibid., 77.
[101] Vaughan, *The Complete Poems*, 81, 82.   [102] Ibid., 82.

age / And then retired'.[103] In another image of foreshortened time, Vaughan
notes:

> how soon the nimble *eye*
> Brings the *object* to *conceit*, and doth so vie
> Performance with the *soul*, that you would swear
> The *act* and *apprehension* both lodged there.[104]

In this contraction of perception and comprehension ('conceit') into a
single instant, Vaughan provides a figure that not only captures the fleet-
ingness of his friend's brief life but also, like the other temporal compressions, suggests a timeless present, devoid of future retrospect. The necessary
conditions for a superposition are therefore in place: what is striking are
the instabilities and ambiguities which its existence cause in the poetic
texture.

Ted Baker and Glyn Williams wrote their letters during the Second
World War; Henry Vaughan composed his elegy while the English Civil
War was still in process. Representation of wartime has a further temporal
dimension: that governing the act of writing itself. In this dimension, texts
of war are affected by factors such as the time taken to 'work through' the
experience of writing about it, publishing exigencies and various deadlines.
The temporal lapse between wartime and war text renders the latter vulnerable to the kind of anachronism that Michael André Bernstein attacks in
Foregone Conclusions: Against Apocalyptic History (1994). Specifically writing about the Holocaust, Bernstein argues against 'backshadowing', which
he defines as a kind of 'retroactive foreshadowing' in which 'shared knowledge of the outcome of events by narrator and reader is used to judge
participants in those events as though they should have known what was
to come'.[105] In particular, Bernstein recommends, readers should be wary
of predictions in historical novels that are really instances of narratorial
back-shadowing.[106] Bernstein is right to call attention to the ethical issues
inherent in narratorial devices such as backshadowing and foreshadowing, but if synchronic wartime is to be recreated in post-war writing, the
question is, how? Bernstein is in favour of what he terms 'sideshadowing':
allowing the proliferation of 'multiple contingencies', including the 'wildly
improbable'.[107] What he is recommending is artificial perpetuation of the
superposition.

---

[103] *Ibid.* [104] *Ibid.*, 83.
[105] Michael André Bernstein, *Foregone Conclusion: Against Apocalyptic History* (Berkeley: University of
California Press, 1994), 16.
[106] *Ibid.*, 30. [107] *Ibid.*, 2, 16, 14, 12.

Perpetuation of the superposition is a radical narrative approach equally likely to stimulate and discontent the reader. Its effects can be observed in two apparently very different novels about the Second World War, Kurt Vonnegut's wayward and futuristic narrative, *Slaughterhouse-Five*, and Ian McEwan's more traditionally realist *Atonement*, both of which experiment with the representation of synchronic time. *Slaughterhouse-Five* is non-sequential: its hops in time are so many pullings on an emergency escape lever, adding up to an adynatic statement on a grand scale to the effect that its professed subject – the bombing of Dresden – can barely be approached, let alone represented ('there is nothing intelligent to say about a massacre').[108] As Jerome Klinkowitz remarks, the spatial displacements draw on the techniques of science fiction, 'but they also draw on the activities of daydreaming, fantasizing and the methods of self-distraction we use to face horror with'[109] (though 'self-distraction' is surely a means of avoiding horror, rather than facing it).

The novel must therefore offer a new philosophy of time and it does so in the temporal understanding of the Trafalmadorians (Trafalmadorian aesthetics are espoused when the narrator draws lines like the stars' trajectories to illustrate events).[110] The Trafalmadorians 'can see where each star has been and where it is going, so that the heavens are filled with rarefied, luminous spaghetti' and perceive human beings as 'great millipedes – "with babies' legs at one end and old people's legs at the other"'.[111] Ostensibly linear (spaghetti and millipedes), this temporal philosophy is synchronic insofar as all states are simultaneously and perpetually present and capable of being experienced. In other words, they exist in superposition: 'many marvellous moments seen all at one time'.[112] This underlies the Trafalmadorians' sanguine view of death:

> When a person dies he only *appears* to die. He is still very much alive in the past, so it is very silly for people to cry at his funeral. All moments, past, present, and future always have existed, always will exist. The Trafalmadorians can look at all the different moments just the way we can look at a stretch of the Rocky Mountains, for instance. They can see how permanent all the moments are, and they can look at any moment that interests them. It is just an illusion we have here on Earth that one moment follows another one, like beads on a string, and that once a moment is gone it is gone forever.[113]

Explicitly remarking that people are simultaneously dead and alive ('He *is* still very much alive in the past'), this outlook recreates the very bizarreness

---

[108] Vonnegut, *Slaughterhouse-Five*, 14.
[109] Jerome Klinkowitz, *Kurt Vonnegut* (London and New York: Methuen, 1982), 66.
[110] Vonnegut, *Slaughterhouse-Five*, 4.   [111] *Ibid.*, 63.   [112] *Ibid.*, 64.   [113] *Ibid.*, 19–20.

exposed by Schrödinger's thought experiment. It is not so much fatalism that permits the Trafalmadorian 'so it goes' attitude to death or even the uselessness of protest in the face of mass slaughter, but rather the notion that all moments are permanent and viewable; existing, even if in mutual contradiction, simultaneously.

Can Vonnegut recreate this simultaneity in his novel? Not literally ('the "earthling" cannot read or write the scenes or symbols of the novel simultaneously'),[114] but he does what he can: placing moments from different periods in swift succession (now Billy is in 1944, now 1958, now 1961), dispensing with scene-shifting preliminaries and insisting through narratorial comment on the fact that they are all contemporaneously and perpetually available. Time is shown to behave peculiarly: stalling ('the time would not pass'), accelerating ('The second hand on my watch would twitch once, and a year would pass') and reversing (the description of the movie running backwards[115] inspired the entire narrative structure of Martin Amis's *Time's Arrow* (1991)).[116]

What is missing from *Slaughterhouse-Five* is any collapse of the superposition, the 'traumatic intervention'[117] of measurement that converts the simultaneous existence of possible outcomes into a single definitive outcome. The song 'My Name is Yon Yonson' provides a narratological model for this in its refusal to terminate, its return in an inescapable loop to its opening lines: 'And so on to infinity'.[118] Though the reader is told how the novel ends – 'It ends like this: *Poo-tee-weet?*'[119] – the questioning tweet of a bird is not an ending in the sense of providing any resolution or closure. Similarly, though the reader knows that Dresden is bombed, that the war ends, that Billy dies (and how and when) and even that the universe ends, blown up by the Trafalmadorians experimenting with new fuels for their flying saucers, the concept that all moments exist simultaneously and forever ensures that no outcome is authoritative. Time is structured so that

[114] Catherine Burgass, 'A Brief Story of Postmodern Plot', *The Yearbook of English Studies* 30 (2000), 182.

[115] Vonnegut, *Slaughterhouse-Five*, 15, 53–4.

[116] Mark Currie, *Postmodern Narrative Theory* (Basingstoke: Macmillan, 1998), 68. The same technique is used in Carol-Ann Duffy's 'Last Post' (2009). As Gertrude Stein noted in *Wars I Have Seen* (1945), 'war makes things go backward as well as forward' (*Wars I Have Seen* (London: Brilliance Books, 1984), 5).

[117] J. C. Polkinghorne, *The Quantum World* (London: Penguin, 1984), 31.

[118] Vonnegut, *Slaughterhouse-Five*, 2. Cf. the army marching song, sung to the tune of *Auld Lang Syne*, quoted by Vera Brittain in *Testament of Youth* (289): '*We're here because / We're here because / We're here because / We're here* ...'

[119] Vonnegut, *Slaughterhouse-Five*, 16.

all that happens always has happened and always will happen – and this functions to keep mutually incompatible states forever in play.

In *Atonement*, the principal superposition is [Robbie and Cecilia died in 1940] / [Robbie and Cecilia survived the war and had a life together] (a subsidiary, related superposition is [Robbie raped Lola] / [Paul Marshall raped Lola]). In the narrator, Briony, McEwan creates a Mistress of Ceremonies, a director and writer whose 'controlling demon' is the 'desire to have the world just so'.[120] Briony's act of atonement (at-one-ment suggests her desire to produce a definitive outcome) to those whose actions she has, so the fiction goes, wrongly, and catastrophically, interpreted is to rewrite history (her novel has been drafted eight times in fifty-nine years) and impose a merciful ending. In other words, she attempts to 're-collapse' the superposition. Afflicted with vascular dementia – a slow form of forgetting – Briony reflects on the process of fictionalisation and conveys a strong sense of writerly control: 'I merged [the hospitals] in my description to concentrate all my experiences into one place.'[121] Her final soliloquy addresses the question of superposition and the post-war novelist:

It is only in this last version that my lovers end well, standing side by side on a South London pavement as I walk away. All the preceding drafts were pitiless. But now I can no longer think what purpose would be served if, say, I tried to persuade my reader, by direct or indirect means, that Robbie Turner died of septicaemia at Bray Dunes on 1 June 1940, or that Cecilia was killed in September of the same year by the bomb that destroyed Balham Underground station.

. . . How could that constitute an ending? What sense of hope or satisfaction could a reader draw from such an account? . . . I face an incoming tide of forgetting, and then oblivion . . . I know there's always a certain kind of reader who will be compelled to ask, But what *really* happened? The answer is simple: the lovers survive and flourish . . .

The problem these fifty-nine years has been this: how can a novelist achieve atonement when, with her absolute power of deciding outcomes, she is also God? There is no one, no entity or higher form that she can appeal to, or be reconciled with, or that can forgive her. There is nothing outside her. In her imagination she has set the limits and the terms.[122]

The assumptions underlying this are that the writer *can* collapse or re-collapse the superposition; that writing, like quantum measurement, brings about a definitive state. But, though her narrative describes the lovers here in the present tense (they 'survive and flourish'), Briony's attempt to re-collapse the superposition in a particular direction fails. By having his

---

[120] Ian McEwan, *Atonement* (London: Vintage, 2002), 5, 4.   [121] *Ibid.*, 356.   [122] *Ibid.*, 370–1.

narrator refer to literary conventions – knowing that he or she is being offered 'comfort', 'the reader' is unsure whether to accept it or not and hence definitive conclusion is avoided – McEwan keeps both outcomes in play, fulfilling Briony's prediction (a rehearsal of the *aere perennius* trope) that 'as long as there is a single copy, a solitary typescript of my final draft, then my spontaneous, fortuitous sister and her medical prince survive'.[123] What has been referred to, earlier in the novel, as 'the unchangeable past' in fact turns out to be an inability – or an unwillingness – to bring about the 'tidy finish' that Briony aspired to.[124] Less controlling than his narrator, McEwan, in rejecting her view of the novelist as God, deftly recreates the agnosticism that characterises the temporal experience of wartime.

Is wartime *sui generis*? One initial objection to claims for its distinctiveness is that many modernist and post-modernist texts display the same open-endedness. Plot is long since passé and the narratology of *Atonement* may owe more to early twenty-first-century ideas of metafiction than to the temporality of conflict. Indeed, the 'unknowing' induced by the loss of 'linear/progressive time' has been claimed as the hallmark of modernist epistemology: 'one enters, as it were, a state of fibrillation; purposive behavior ceases'.[125] To this, it can be replied that even modernist works still 'carry the reader forward by way of plotted narrative elements', avant-garde anti-narratives 'still depend for effect on the presupposition of the traditional narrative line of choice'.[126] The dead end of deliberately withheld closure does have a different feel from the bewildering, truly unknowable nature of in-war endinglessness. Wishing to impose completion on this chaos is understandable – 'there is evidence that the public wishes to understand more of what has happened to the victims of famines, wars and disasters after the crisis is over', notes Jean Seaton[127] (a desire as likely to be sympathetic as prurient) – and even morally desirable (as Simone Weil argues, the fact that war effaces the notion of being brought to an end makes it look as though intolerable sufferings are easy to bear).[128] Nonetheless, the expectation that war and wartime will unfold in logical succession is ever ripe for challenge. Emplotting war risks giving meaning, and hence accommodation, to the atrocity, and, as Bernstein argues, risks unfair judgement of those who knew less at the time.

[123] *Ibid.*, 371. [124] *Ibid.*, 348, 353. [125] Weinstein, *Unknowing*, 2, 128.

[126] Chatman, *Story and Discourse*, 57. See also Paul Ricoeur, *Time and Narrative*, trans. Kathleen McLaughlin and David Pellauer, 3 vols. (Chicago: University of Chicago Press, 1985), vol. II, 23–5.

[127] Seaton, *Carnage and the Media*, 245. [128] Weil, *War and The Iliad*, 23.

The challenge for texts of war, therefore, is to end without ending. The ends of wars themselves are problematic. It has been pointed out that war does not end: 'war is not an occasional interruption of a normality called peace; it is a climate in which we live', writes Samuel Hynes.[129] There are apocryphal stories of isolated soldiers continuing to fight individual wars long after they are over:[130] non-apocryphally, sixty years after the official end of the Second World War, the United States still maintains military bases in many of the countries it fought in and continues to incur significant 'war expenses' in relation to it.[131] Wartime ends – or fails to end ('everybody talked about the war ending / And always it would be the last week of the war')[132] – as messily as it begins. Accordingly, the language of endings has a hollow ring. 'The last battle', 'the war to end all wars' are eschatological concepts that offer the false hope of perpetual peace, or at least a return to order and the possibility of a redemptive fresh start.[133]

In contrast to this is the wearisome winding-down of hostilities, a debilitating phase marked by the same inertia as anticipation of its start. Barbara Herrnstein Smith writes on poetic closure:

We tend to speak of conclusions when a sequence of events has a relatively high degree of structure, when, in other words, we can perceive these events as related to one another by some principle of organization or design that implies the existence of a definite termination point. Under these circumstances, the occurrence of the terminal event is a confirmation of expectations that have been established by the structure of the sequence and is usually distinctly gratifying. The sense of stable conclusiveness, finality, or 'clinch' which we experience at that point is what is referred to here as *closure*.[134]

Structure, organisation, design, conclusiveness, finality, 'clinch': the nature of wartime is to withhold any such indicators of ending. In place of conclusion is, to paraphrase Herrnstein Smith, a simple lack of expectation of continuation.[135] It is not the case that 'we feel we know all there is to know'; the idea of closure as 'a modification of structure that makes *stasis*, or the absence of further continuation, the most probable succeeding event'

---

[129] Hynes, *A War Imagined*, xii.
[130] Clemence Dane's *The Arrogant History of White Ben* (1939) and Haruki Murakami's *Kafka on the Shore* (2002), among others, exploit this phenomenon.
[131] Oliver Boyd-Barrett, 'Understanding: The Second Casualty', in *Reporting War*, ed. Allan and Zelizer, 34.
[132] Michael Longley, 'The War Poets' (1979), *Poems 1963–1983* (Edinburgh and Dublin: Salamander Press / Gallery Press, 1985), 168.
[133] See John Kerrigan, *Revenge Tragedy: Aeschylus to Armageddon* (Oxford: Oxford University Press, 1996), 314, and Jay Winter, *Sites of Memory, Sites of Mourning: The Great War in European Culture* (Cambridge: Cambridge University Press, 1995), 200.
[134] Herrnstein Smith, *Poetic Closure*, 2.   [135] *Ibid.*, 44.

has no purchase when stasis is the prevailing temporal experience.[136] Henry Treece wrote on 13 April 1945:

It's no fun, waiting for the war to end. A year ago, these days would have seemed like the anteroom to Paradise! Now each day bring more confusions, more anxieties – and no relief.[137]

The pacifist Frances Partridge described the 'fag-end' of the Second World War as an 'uneasy waiting state . . . The pressure has let off, the prison bars are being raised, but we don't know how to get used to freedom'.[138] The end, if and when it does come, often has more of the nature of a cessation than of a culmination. 'When the sound of victorious guns burst over London at 11 a.m. on November 11th, 1918,' noted Vera Brittain, 'the men and women who looked incredulously into each other's faces did not cry jubilantly: "We've won the War!" They only said: "The War is over".'[139] On 1 May 1945, hearing of the German surrender in Italy, Spike Milligan thought only, '31,000 Allied troops had died – a city of the dead. Is a war ever really over?'[140] Violet Bonham Carter noted in her diary on 3 May 1945 that the German surrender brought 'no wild excitement, no exhilaration or kick – no desire to throw one's hat into the air'.[141] For Bao Ninh, the end of the Vietnam War resembled 'the deflation of an entire landscape, with fields, mountains and rivers collapsing in on themselves'.[142] The texts explored in this chapter reach equally tentative halting-places. *Flight to Arras* finishes with the observation that 'There was nothing to say'.[143] The last word of Vaughan's 'Elegie' is 'end' but the Virgilian envoy re-resurrects a shade and an empty tomb. Barbusse's *Under Fire* concludes with a soldier venturing, 'with lowered voice', 'If the present war has advanced progress by one step, its miseries and slaughter will count for little.'[144] Briony's intention to sleep forms the last words of *Atonement*; *Slaughterhouse-Five* finishes in the tweet of a bird. These terminus points are anti-eschatological: denying finality, expressions of stopping rather than ending.

No grand finales then: the ambiguous easing into peace seems to bring only exhaustion, sorrow over what has occurred and fear for the future. Peter Brooks argues that the beginning and end of a narrative 'stand in metaphorical relation in the sense that the latter is the same as the former,

---

[136] *Ibid.*, 120, 34.   [137] Schimanski and Treece, eds., *Leaves in the Storm*, 283.
[138] Frances Partridge, *A Pacifist's War* (London: The Hogarth Press, 1978), 210.
[139] Brittain, *Testament of Youth*, 399.   [140] Milligan, *Milligan's War*, 293.
[141] Violet Bonham Carter, *Champion Redoubtable: The Diaries and Letters of Violet Bonham Carter 1914–1945*, ed. Mark Pottle (London: Phoenix, 1999), 342.
[142] Ninh, *The Sorrow of War*, 98.   [143] De Saint-Exupéry, *Flight to Arras*, 168.
[144] Barbusse, *Under Fire*, 344.

but different'.[145] Wartime rejects even this near-symmetry. In similarly refusing easy conclusions – or any conclusions at all – war texts can convey what the temporality of conflict feels like, so providing a structural response to both formal and ethical challenges.

[145] Peter Brooks, *Reading for the Plot: Design and Intention in Narrative* (Cambridge, MA: Harvard University Press, 1996), 27.

CHAPTER 5

Diversions

In Book 2 of the *Iliad*, Homer protests that describing the Greek forces is beyond him:

The multitude I could not tell or name, not even if ten tongues were mine and ten mouths and a voice unwearying, and the heart within me were of bronze, unless the Muses of Olympus, daughters of Zeus who bears the aegis, call to my mind all those who came beneath Ilios.[1]

The actual problem is one of scale, but this disclaimer, an instance of the adynaton or *impossibilia* trope (discussed in more detail later in this chapter), phrases the challenge in terms of the poet's inability to 'tell or name' the rank and file.[2] His capacity to enunciate is simply not up to the task. Similar linguistic disclaimers proliferate in war writing, from the most exquisitely wrought masterpieces to the hastiest scribbles home.[3]

---

[1] 2.488–92. For further discussion of these lines, see Bruce Heiden, 'Common People and Leaders in Iliad Book 2: The Invocation of the Muses and the Catalogue of Ships', *Transactions of the American Philological Association* 138.1 (Spring 2008), 127–54.

[2] The first verb is μυθήσομαι (to tell, speak of), the second ὀνομήνω (to name individually or taliation nominatim, as discussed in Chapter 2) (see *ibid.*, 130).

[3] For example, Henry James commented in 1915: 'The war [i.e. the First World War] has used up words; they have weakened, they have deteriorated like motor car tyres; they have, like millions of other things, been more overstrained and knocked about . . . during the last six months than in all the long ages before, and we are now confronted with a depreciation of all our terms' (Preston Lockwood, 'Henry James' First interview', *New York Times* 21 March 1915, 4). Here, language has become war-weary. An associated notion, that war has reversed words' meanings, is also often found. 'The ordinary acceptation of words in their relation to things was changed as men thought fit', noted Thucydides of the Peloponnesian War (3.82.4f). Two-and-a-half millennia later, Hemingway had Frederic Henry voice Thucydidean sentiments: 'I was always embarrassed by the words sacred, glorious, and sacrifice and the expression in vain . . . I had seen nothing sacred, and the things that were glorious had no glory and the sacrifices were like the stockyards of Chicago if nothing was done with the meat except to bury it. There were many words that you could not stand to hear and finally only the names of places had dignity . . . Abstract words such as glory, honor, courage, or hallow were obscene beside the concrete names of villages' (*A Farewell to Arms* (London: Vintage, 1999), 165). Similarly, Cecil Day Lewis wrote in 'The Stand-To' (1940): 'Destiny, History, Duty, Fortitude, Honour – all / The words of the politicians seem too big or too small / For the ragtag fighters of lane and shadow, the love that has grown / Familiar as working-clothes, faithful as bone to bone'

Though the difficulties may strictly inhere in the subject matter or arise
from deficiencies on the part of the reader, what are indicted are authorial
debility and insufficiency of language (emphases vary between the inability
of the writer to find words and the unavailability of words for the writer to
find). 'Hard would it be for me, as though I were a god, to tell the tale of
all these things', despairs Homer later in his epic (12.176–7), exposing the
limitations of (even divine) linguistic resourcefulness. 'As for me, I went to
see, and not to write, and as little thought then of these Memoirs, as I ill
furnished myself to write them', confesses Defoe's narrator in *Memoirs of a
Cavalier*, apologising for his lapses as a writer of war.[4] In Joseph Addison's
'The Campaign', a petition to the Muse casts doubt on whether poetic
discourse will be adequate to the task of describing battle: 'But O, my
Muse, what numbers wilt thou find / To sing the furious troops in battle
join'd!' (lines 278–9). The *Der Spiegel* journalist Carolin Emcke, returning
from the 1999 war in Albania and Kosovo, is reduced to inarticulacy as
words which will both convey the experience and not alienate the listeners
prove elusive:

At first there was only speechlessness.
   After spending a month and a half in Albania and Kosovo during the war, I
returned to Berlin in the summer of 1999 and did not know what to tell my friends.
How to convey my experiences in words that would not disturb them? How to
describe this encounter with death and destruction? How to explain that war and
violence inscribe themselves on your soul and continue to live with you?
   My friends did not know how to ask, and I did not know how to respond.[5]

This chapter considers the specific challenge of finding adequate language to represent war. This challenge is, as it were, a meta-challenge: the
sense that words are insufficient or unavailable might arise as a reaction
to the difficulties already discussed in this book – credibility, scale, space
and time – or, indeed, as a reaction to a whole range of representational
obstacles. But the crucial feature of the disclaimers cited is that, whatever
the cause of the difficulty, the obstacle is characterised as being that of

---

(*The Complete Poems*, 334). Storm Jameson, writing in 1941 and lamenting the end of a European
culture in which ideas could 'cross and re-cross without being held up at frontiers', remarked that
'[w]ords no longer mean the same thing to men of equal intelligence in different nations – or to two
men of the same nation. The word for justice, the word for pity, the word for truth has a different
meaning according as it is spoken by a Russian or a German or a Frenchman' (*The Writer's Situation
and Other Essays* (London: Macmillan, 1950), 37). The thought is not so much that war creates a
new semantic system as eviscerates the existing one: 'Language, coral island / accrued from human
comprehensions, / human dreams, / you are eroded as war erodes us', wrote Denise Levertov on
Vietnam ('Prologue: An Interim' (1971), *Poems 1968–1972* (New York: New Directions, 1987), 130–1).
[4] Defoe, *Memoirs* (1974), 33.   [5] Emcke, *Echoes of Violence*, xi.

an author's linguistic resources. A common and understandable response to the problem has simply been silence. George Steiner, in 'Silence and the Poet' (1966), an early and still influential essay concerning silence as a literary reaction to the Holocaust, is specific about the inception of 'the most honest temptation to silence in contemporary feeling': the date he gives is '*c*.1914'.[6] Silence in the face of war is indeed powerful, not least when experienced as the ritual refraining-from-sound observed in many parts of the world on martial anniversaries. *The Times* reported on what, in 1920, was only the second time the two-minute Great Silence had been kept on Armistice Day in Britain: 'Time and space were obliterated, and the thoughts of men and women encircled the world . . . The tension was almost too great. When seconds seemed to halt people held their breath lest they should be heard in the stillness.'[7] It is beyond the scope of this chapter to explore the complex ethico-aesthetic considerations inherent in silence as a reaction to disaster.[8] Here, the issues under consideration are formal. If silence is a meaningful representation of war (as distinct from a memorial response to it), how can it be staged as a *textual* event? As the *Times* piece eloquently illustrates, silence requires words to record and even interpret it. 'When the words in the city are full of savagery and lies, nothing speaks louder than the unwritten poem', states Steiner,[9] but how can such unwritten poems actually be heard? Again, Maurice Blanchot asserts that 'not writing is among the effects of writing',[10] but how might such an effect be registered and known by others?

In response to these questions, a body of theoretical work has arisen, much of it devoted to the specific problems involved in the representation of the Holocaust. On the one hand, a kind of 'underwriting' has been called for: an underwriting that, in its eschewal of literary ornament, acts as a sparse and serious surety for what it relates. This is the kind of writing endorsed by Berel Lang in *Act and Idea in the Nazi Genocide* (1990), where he argues that 'the most significant and compelling – the

---

[6] George Steiner, *Language and Silence* (Harmondsworth: Penguin, 1969), 70, 71.

[7] 'In the Abbey. The Warrior Laid to Rest', *The Times*, 12 November 1920, sec. Supplement, ii.

[8] See, for example, Theodor Adorno, *Negative Dialectics*, trans. E. B. Ashton (London: Routledge & Kegan Paul, 1973); Adorno, 'Commitment', in *Aesthetics and Politics*, ed. Ernest Bloch *et al.* (London: NLB, 1977), 177–95; Adorno, *Prisms*, ed. Samuel Weber and Shierry Weber (Cambridge: MIT Press, 1981); Klaus Hofmann, 'Poetry After Auschwitz – Adorno's Dictum', *German Life and Letters* 58.2 (April 2005), 182–94; Friedlander, 'Introduction'; Irving Howe, 'Writing and the Holocaust', in *Writing and the Holocaust*, ed. Berel Lang (New York: Holmes & Meier, 1988), 179–99; Berel Lang, *Act and Idea in the Nazi Genocide* (Chicago: University of Chicago Press, 1990), esp. 124–7; Rothberg, *Traumatic Realism*, 36; and Thomas Trezise, 'Unspeakable', *The Yale Journal of Criticism* 14.1 (2001), 39–66.

[9] Steiner, *Language and Silence*, 76.   [10] Blanchot, *The Writing of the Disaster*, 11.

most valuable – writings about the Nazi genocide appear in the forms of historical discourse, not in those of fictional prose or drama or poetry'.[11] Aprosodic and annalistic, the writing Lang advocates is writing at its most diminished:[12] a nondescript writing that is barely there. A contrasting approach is somehow to refer to what is beyond conception by conveying an absence that is elsewhere: this is, to use Jorge Semprun's coinage, text as 'alibi'.[13] Distinguishing between 'actuality' (events that literally occurred) and 'reality' ('the attempts of the mind to absorb such events into a literary harmony or to compose a new dissonance that will make them endurable and meaningful to the imaginative "ear"'), Lawrence L. Langer posited in 1975 an 'irrealism': 'a complex amalgamation of reality and unreality' that is 'discontinuous and dislocated'.[14] Rather than constituting a not-writing because of its deliberate impoverishment, irrealism cultivates techniques that convey absence: dissonance, discontinuity, dislocation and distortion. Twenty-five years after Langer, Michael Rothberg proposed something very like, if not identical to, irrealism in the phenomenon he terms 'traumatic realism'. Like irrealism, traumatic realism entails the 'survival of claims of realisms into discourses that could be considered modernist, even post-modernist'.[15] Again, this epistemological mélange comprises not-writing in the sense that it 'evokes the real as a "felt lack"': the traumatic realist detail, unlike the standard realist detail, points to a 'necessary absence'.[16] The necessary absence achieves the avoidance of what Eric L. Santner has called 'narrative fetishism':[17] 'the construction and deployment of a narrative consciously or unconsciously designed to expunge the traces of the trauma or loss that called that narrative into being in the first place'.[18] The non-fetishist alibi narrative, by contrast, constantly recalls the 'site and origin of loss'.[19] But the question remains: in formal, literary terms, exactly how is the necessary absence to be rendered legible? How is the hole to be seen?

The literary response explored in this chapter is a paradoxical one: not silence but, rather, a mode of writing that is a 'not-writing'. Worked out

---

[11] Lang, *Act and Idea in the Nazi Genocide*, 123.
[12] As Thomas Trezise points out, 'in his emphasis on the moral superiority of literal or historical discourse, Lang elides the historicity of that discourse itself (Trezise, 'Unspeakable', 49).
[13] Jorge Semprun, *Literature or Life*, trans. Linda Coverdale (New York: Viking, 1997), 13.
[14] Lawrence L. Langer, *The Holocaust and the Literary Imagination* (New Haven: Yale University Press, 1975), 92, 45, 47, 33.
[15] Rothberg, *Traumatic Realism*, 99.   [16] *Ibid.*, 104.   [17] See *ibid.*, 139.
[18] Eric Santner, 'History Beyond the Pleasure Principle: Some Thoughts on the Representation of Trauma', in *Probing the Limits of Representation*, ed. Friedlander, 144.
[19] *Ibid.*, 144.

in literature over centuries, the means of not-writing range from topoi to topic-matter, pushing linguistic resources to their limits in the project of *not* telling, with the result that the problem of words' inadequacy becomes, in the end, its own solution. The trick – simply put – is that not-writing functions analogously to military diversion tactics: attention is diverted away from the main action, but with the inevitable result that the true target eventually becomes clear. It should be emphasised that such tactics are means of *deliberately* circumventing the direct depiction of conflict, as opposed to the failure to discuss war even while an attempt is being made to do so, artistic aloofness or the surrender to the temptation to look away from horror. These are literary means of intentional avoidance.

This chapter investigates a range of diversionary tactics in action in four works: Charles Wolfe's 'The Burial of Sir John Moore after Corunna' (1816), Wilfred Owen's 'Anthem for Doomed Youth' (1917), Dylan Thomas's 'A Refusal to Mourn the Death, By Fire, of a Child in London' (1944) and Ernest Hemingway's 'On the Quai at Smyrna' (written *c*.1926–7). These texts indicate, if not a non-writing tradition (no intertextual influence is asserted), at least the possibility of a common practice – a possibility strengthened by the fact that they exemplify both poetry and prose. Such tactics traced, the adynaton trope – the most significant of the evasion techniques – is then considered in detail, before a discussion of the theoretical implications of not-writing, with particular reference to the role of the sublime.

Charles Wolfe's poem on the burial of the Scottish general Sir John Moore (1761–1809), commander of the British Army during the Peninsular War from 1808 to 1809, contains only a couple of oblique references to the military encounter in which he died. The battle took place on 16 January 1809, at A Coruña, north-west Spain, as, under pressure from French forces headed by Marshal Soult, Moore led the British in retreat to the coast, intending to sail for home. Though Moore was killed, the battle was a British victory and the majority of his troops were able to embark safely, albeit still in retreat.[20] Describing Moore's interment from the point of view of a member or members (the first person plural is used) of the burial party, the poem remarks that the general is laid down 'From the field of his fame fresh and gory'.[21] This allusion to the recentness and bloodiness of Moore's injuries scarcely does justice to the historical event: according to a

---

[20] Charles Esdaile, *The Peninsular War: A New History* (London: Penguin, 2003), 141–55.
[21] Charles Wolfe, 'The Burial of Sir John Moore After Corunna', in *The Oxford Book of War Poetry*, ed. Stallworthy, 84.

contemporary report, an enemy cannon-shot threw him from his horse and 'carried away his left shoulder and part of the collar-bone, leaving the arm hanging by the flesh'.[22] Nonetheless, the cursory reference is an example of what, after the semiotics of C. S. Peirce, may be termed an 'indexical' account of war. What is being described is not battle itself but the physical signs of battle's effects: in Peircean semiotics, the gore on Moore's dead body signifies war in the same way that smoke signifies fire.[23] Privileging the indexical over the iconic, Wolfe is effectively constructing a text with a battle-shaped hole at its heart.

The depiction of the injured or dead body is part of a distinct sub-genre of war writing: a concentration on the 'outskirts' of armed conflict (at least when combat is located as the central experience). Circumvent-ing Whitman's 'red business' of actual fighting,[24] this subgenre deals in such phenomena as eve-of-battle scenes, preparation, waiting and recov-ery, aftermath. It may aptly be termed 'parapolemics':[25] the discourse of the temporal and spatial borders of war (it is traditionally the field to which those without combat experience, particularly women, are confined). With the word 'distant' – 'the distant and random gun / That the foe was sullenly firing' – Wolfe matches the parapolemical subject matter of his poem with its *mise-en-scène*.

Within the poem, there are further distancing effects. Wolfe deploys euphemism, favouring words with pleasant or positive connotations over harsher or more offensive terms that would more precisely designate what is intended. In instances of the rhetorical down-sizing device of meiosis (allied to litotes), Moore's grave becomes a 'bed', the earth his head will lie on becomes a 'smoothed down... pillow' and death becomes 'sleep'. Euphemisms – as in this case – are often also clichés. According to Anne Carson, '[w]e resort to cliché because it's easier than trying to make up something new. Implicit in it is the question, Don't we already know what we think about this? Don't we have a formula we use for this?'[26] The deployment of cliché and euphemism – widespread in war writing – 'throws white paint' (Carson's metaphor) over its subject, concealing it from view rather than illuminating it.

---

[22] James Carrick Moore, *A Narrative of the Campaign of the British Army in Spain: Commanded by His Excellency Sir John Moore... Authenticated by Official Papers and Original Letters* (London: J. Johnson, 1809), 359. Carrick Moore quotes a letter from a Captain H. Hardinge.

[23] Peirce, 'From "On the Algebra of Logic"', 226–8.

[24] Whitman, *Complete Poetry and Selected Prose*, 417.   [25] McLoughlin, *Martha Gellhorn*, 105.

[26] Anne Carson, 'Variations on the Right to Remain Silent', *A Public Space* 7 (2008), 179–87: 178.

Further strategies are used to distance the poem from war. The predominant structural unit is negative. Wolfe concentrates not on what did occur or what was present, but on what did not or was not: 'Not a drum was heard', 'not a funeral note', 'Not a soldier discharged his farewell shot', 'No useless coffin enclosed his breast', 'Not in sheet or in shroud we wound him', 'Few and short were the prayers', 'not a word of sorrow', 'We carved not a line, and we raised not a stone'. But the reality of Moore's interment was rather different. In *A Narrative of the Campaign of the British Army in Spain*, the dedication of which is dated 4 July 1809, James Carrick Moore described how six soldiers carried his brother in a blanket from the field of fighting outside the town – slowly, so as not to cause him pain by jostling his wounds – to his lodgings in Corunna, where he died some hours later, aware of the British victory.[27] Rather than 'hurrying' his corpse out for burial, Moore's military colleagues then deliberated over how to inter it with 'peculiar respect' and 'unfelt honours'.[28] Carrick Moore continues his account:

At twelve o'clock at night the remains of Sir John Moore were accordingly carried to the Citadel . . . A grave was dug by a party of the 9th Regiment, the Aides-de-Camp attending by turns. No coffin could be procured, and the body was never undressed, but wrapt up by the Officers of his Staff in a military cloak and blankets.

Towards eight o'clock in the morning some firing was heard. It was then resolved to finish the interment, lest a serious attack should be made; on which the Officers would be ordered away, and not suffered to pay the last duties to their General.

The officers of his family bore the body to the grave; the funeral service was read by the Chaplain, and the corpse was covered with earth.[29]

Now, an account of Moore's death very similar to this appeared in the *Edinburgh Annual Register* for 1808, published on 21 July 2010 and written by Robert Southey.[30] It follows James Carrick Moore's version, with the

---

[27] Moore, *A Narrative of the Campaign*, 358–65. Moore quotes letters from Captain Hardinge and a Colonel P. Anderson.

[28] *Ibid.*, 366.   [29] *Ibid.*, 366–7.

[30] See Harold A. Small, *The Field of His Fame: A Ramble in the Curious History of Charles Wolfe's Poem 'The Burial of Sir John Moore'* (Berkeley: University of California Press, 1953), 1; Robert Southey, *New Letters of Robert Southey*, ed. Kenneth Curry, 2 vols. (Cambridge: Cambridge University Press, 1965), vol. I, 515. The present writer has not found evidence to corroborate the hypothesis that Southey read James Carrick Moore, but the resemblances between the accounts are remarkable. Southey drew on his historical contributions (covering the years 1808–11) to the *Edinburgh Annual Register* in writing his *History of the Peninsular War* (1823–32). The account of Moore's burial in this *History* also contains the word 'hastened' (*History of the Peninsular War*, 3 vols. (London: J. Murray, 1823), vol. I, 805). The critical view of Moore's competence that Southey expressed in the *History* angered Sir William Napier, prompting him to write his rival *History of the War in the Peninsula and in the*

addition of a single salient detail. This is that the interment was 'hastened' when the enemy firing was heard.[31] It was the *Register's* version, read to him by a fellow-student at Trinity College, Dublin, that would inspire Wolfe to compose his verses.[32] Far from believing that 'not a funeral note' and 'not a word of sorrow' were heard, Wolfe would have been aware that Moore had received the full rites of burial, including the funeral service read by the Chaplain and the 'last duties' of his fellow-officers. No coffin or shroud was available, but the funeral ritual was not hurried halfway through ('But half of our heavy task was done') and the interment was not completed 'darkly at dead of night . . . / By the struggling moonbeam's misty light / And the lanthorn dimly burning' but was still in process early in the morning and brought to a conclusion so that the officers could pay their last duties. The final couplet 'We carved not a line, and we raised not a stone, / But we left him alone with his glory' is an ironic written testament to non-writing (the literary monument cancels out the lack of lapidary monument), but it also ignores significant subsequent memorialising of which Wolfe would also presumably have been aware: a vote of thanks proposed to Moore in the House of Lords on 25 January 1809;[33] James Carrick Moore's *A Narrative of the Campaign* published in July 1809, with twenty pages of eulogies from various military dignitaries to his brother; a monument erected by the Spanish at Corunna over Moore's grave, later made permanent by the British; the marking of the precise spot where he fell; the erection in 1809 of a public monument in St Paul's Cathedral, London, on the orders of the British government.[34] Indeed, the final stanza itself, with its reference to the field of his 'fame', confusingly suggests that Moore's conduct in his last battle was already renowned. What, then, motivated Wolfe to claim the opposite of these things, to insist – ten negatives in the poem – on the absence or lack of due obsequies?

South of France from the Year 1807 to the Year 1814 (1828–40) (W. A. Speck, *Robert Southey: Entire Man of Letters* (New Haven and London: Yale University Press, 2006), 191–2) – but Southey is not the only commentator to have cast aspersions on Moore's command. Small, for example, enquires, 'Might he not have beat the French, and not merely beat them off, if he had sent for reinforcements instead of empty transports?' (*The Field of his Fame*, 1). A negative view of Moore's achievements as a military commander would produce a different reading of Wolfe's poem, but there is not enough evidence to speculate here as to whether Wolfe shared Southey's negative opinion.

[31] 'Chapter XXIII', *Edinburgh Annual Register* 1 (1 January 1808), 458–9.
[32] C. Litton Falkiner, 'Introductory Memoir', in *The Burial of Sir John Moore and Other Poems by Charles Wolfe* (London: Sidgwick & Jackson, 1909), xxv–xxviii.
[33] See Hansard HL Deb 25 January 1809 vol. 12 cc133–8, 'Vote of Thanks – Battle of Corunna'.
[34] John Sweetman, 'Moore, Sir John (1761–1809)', in *Oxford Dictionary of National Biography*, ed. H. C. G. Matthew and Brian Harrison, 60 vols. (Oxford: Oxford University Press, 2004), vol. XXXVIII, 979.

Likely, his motivation was his recognition of the power of indirection. The device Wolfe uses is a species of paralipsis (also known as cataphasis): the rhetorical trope of stating and drawing attention to something in the very act of appearing to pass it over. The trick of this trope depends upon the power of the absent referent: conjuring up what is not there by naming it *in absentia*. Every element listed in Wolfe's lines is felt as something missing and therefore summoned into virtual being. Hence the rudimentary burial evokes the respect due to the great warrior, the lack of ceremony evokes the famous victory (and, in passing, Wolfe comments on the vanity of all earthly glory). Aided by a balladic form more suited to bruiting martial exploits than elegising the fallen, the poem points beyond its ostensible subject matter of a modest burial to trace the contours of a bloody battle.

A century later, another poem was written about what was not available by way of obsequies to those killed in armed conflict. Wilfred Owen had served at the front in the First World War for some eighteen months before he was posted, suffering from shellshock, to Craiglockhart Hydropathic Hospital outside Edinburgh, where, with some help from Siegfried Sassoon, he composed 'Anthem for Doomed Youth'.[35] 'Anthem' begins with what seems like a rhetorical question – 'What passing-bells for these who die as cattle?',[36] though Jon Stallworthy suggests that this may in fact be in the manner of a response, prompted by the anonymous prefatory note to *Poems of Today: An Anthology* (1916), of which Owen possessed the December 1916 reprint: 'there is no arbitrary isolation of one theme from another; they mingle and interpenetrate throughout, to the music of Pan's flute, and of Love's viol, and the bugle-call of Endeavour, and the passing-bells of Death'.[37] Owen's opening interrogatory is therefore orphaned of its antedecent. The reply – '– Only the monstrous anger of the guns' – is also somehow wanting, an incomplete sentence that forms a laconic riposte. In his first draft, Owen followed this with 'Let the majestic insults of their mouths / Be as the priest-words of their burials'.[38] As Dominic Hibberd points out, this could be interpreted as 'a statement in support of the British war effort': 'the only possible response to the slaughter (of British troops) is that "our" guns should hurl angry "insults" at the

[35] Jon Stallworthy, *Wilfred Owen* (London: Oxford University Press and Chatto and Windus, 1974), 188.

[36] Wilfred Owen, *The Complete Poems and Fragments*, vol. I: *The Poems*, ed. Jon Stallworthy (London: Chatto and Windus, The Hogarth Press, Oxford University Press, 1983), 99–100.

[37] *Ibid.*, 99n.

[38] Wilfred Owen, *The Complete Poems and Fragments*, vol. II: *The Manuscripts of the Poems and Fragments*, ed. Jon Stallworthy (London: Chatto and Windus, The Hogarth Press and Oxford University Press, 1983), 250.

enemy'.[39] But the original wording makes a further suggestion: that interment is a possibility. In no subsequent draft did Owen again make the
mistake of mentioning 'burials': lack of interment and disinterment were
the norm in the trenches of France and Belgium during the First World
War, where corpses were routinely used to prop up dug-outs, form parapets,
and line trenches and where half the British dead left no identifiable body.[40]
Later versions of the poem concentrated on the absent or the insufficient,
moving from the inappropriate replacements of the battlefield in the octave
to the pathetic stand-ins of the home front in the sestet.[41] Words such as
'only' (repeated) and 'save' emphasise the inadequacy of the substitutes,
an inadequacy reinforced by the Keatsian allusion – the 'choirs of wailing
shells' recall the 'wailful choir' in which small gnats mourn in 'To Autumn'.
As Hibberd points out, the allusion 'is meant to be noticed, revealing the
battlefield as a demented parody of the Romantic landscape'[42] – a further
sense in which something is wanting.

There are a few inconsistencies in the series of negatives. The pleonasm
of 'orisons' and 'prayers' suggests a doubly felt lack, and there is not even an
unsatisfactory substitute for the missing 'bells'. 'And bugles calling for them
from sad shires' is the last line of the octave, the last in the series of battlefield
stand-ins for funeral elements. Specifically, alongside the noise of shells,
the bugles must do the work of 'voices of mourning'. The oddity is that
the bugles, which in this case call from sad shires rather than sound on the
battlefield,[43] more properly belong with the home substitutes of the sestet:
shining eyes, pale brows, lowering of blinds. It is possible to read the line as
an articulation in the middle of the sonnet – the joint between octave and
sestet – but there is also a sense in which the natural division between the
two parts has torn off an extra line, giving the poem a ragged edge at its very
centre. The most jarring inconsistency is 'No mockeries now for them'. At

[39] Dominic Hibberd, *Owen the Poet* (Basingstoke: Macmillan, 1986), 110.
[40] Trudi Tate, *Modernism, History and the First World War* (Manchester: Manchester University Press,
1998), 66, 65.
[41] This list of substitutes for what is *not* there recalls a strand of Christian imagery in which Christ's
attributes are substituted for wordly attributes. An example is Robert Southwell's 'New Heaven,
New War' (published ?1602): 'His naked breast stands for a shield; / His battering shot are babish
cries, / His arrows looks of weeping eyes, / His martial ensigns cold and need / And feeble flesh
his warrior's steed' (*Chapters Into Verse*, eds. Robert Atwan and Laurance Wieder, 2 vols. (Oxford:
Oxford University Press, 1993), vol. II, 32).
[42] Hibberd, *Owen the Poet*, 110.
[43] 'Spring Offensive' (1918) suggests, again paraliptically, that bugles belong on the battlefield ('No
alarms / Of bugles' (Owen, *The Complete Poems and Fragments*, vol. II, 192)). Fragments of 1917,
'I know the music' and 'But I was looking at the perement stars', place them in England (see *ibid.*,
100n).

odds with the structure of gap-and-unsatisfactory-substitute, the absence of 'mockeries' suggests that the dead are now (happily) beyond insult (a suggestion in line with Hibberd's reading of the first draft of the poem). The antithesis to the overall thesis that the dead are let down or dishonoured by the missing obsequies, the line opens the way for synthesis – but there is none. Rather, a further implication is made, that Hibberd picks up in his analysis: that 'the domestic funeral rites may be as much a parody of true religious observance as the rites on the battlefield'.[44] Given the tenderness with which the other funerary elements are written, it seems unlikely that Owen viewed them as parodic. Nonetheless, 'No mockeries now for them' is a rogue entry in the catalogue of absences, another perforation in the poem's fabric.

Like Wolfe, then, Owen exploits the power of both parapolemics and paralipsis to regret what is AWOL or what has never been there. The trope of the inadequate substitute extends even to the poem's title. It was Sassoon who suggested 'Anthem' (initially 'for Dead Youth'), but Owen declared it 'just what I meant it to be'.[45] Yet, just as the rifles' rattles are no orisons and the pallor of girls' brows no palls, the 'Anthem' is no anthem, at least not in the *OED* definition of 'a song, as of praise or gladness'. Reproachful and sorrowing rather than praiseful or glad, Owen's sonnet is a dirge, a non-anthem or anti-anthem for bodies missing anyway; a hole where an anthem should be. (Owen himself remarked that his poems were 'elegies . . . in no sense consolatory',[46] again suggesting an emptying-out of genre.)[47] George Steiner, writing on efforts in modern art to access what is anterior to language or outside it, notes the proliferation of titles which are 'often . . . ironic mystification[s]' and a tendency within the works to 'seek to establish reference only to themselves'.[48] In its own (mis-)naming, Owen's 'Anthem' is a trope on a large scale whose turn is inwards – away from the war. The poem turns only to collapse in on itself by failing to fulfil its own self-description.

If Owen's sonnet is an anthem that is not an anthem, Dylan Thomas's 'A Refusal to Mourn the Death, By Fire, of a Child in London' is an elegy that

---

[44] Hibberd, *Owen the Poet*, 112.
[45] Wilfred Owen, *Collected Letters*, ed. Harold Owen and John Bell (Oxford: Oxford University Press, 1967), 496.
[46] Owen, *The Complete Poems and Fragments*, vol. I, 535.
[47] In another approach, Jahan Ramazani posits a complex, twentieth-century anti-elegy movement of which 'Anthem for Doomed Youth' would be an instance (*Poetry of Mourning: The Modern Elegy from Hardy to Heaney* (Chicago: University of Chicago Press, 1994), 2–4, 41–6, 70–3). See also Gilbert, 'Rats' Alley', esp. 188.
[48] Steiner, *Language and Silence*, 42.

is not an elegy. Again, the subject matter is worth a preliminary remark. Though Thomas lived in London for part of the Second World War, he wrote the poem in New Quay on the Cardiganshire coast.[49] A word in the poem – 'Zion' – is the common name of a Welsh chapel; indeed, there was a Mount Zion in Thomas's childhood city of Swansea which was damaged in the Blitz.[50] As Barbara Hardy notes, though Swansea was extensively bombed, Thomas 'wrote his blitz poems about deaths and destructions in London', not Wales.[51] Aside from the tiny, puncture-like allusion to 'Zion' – and the linking of this to a Welsh chapel is speculative – the poem can be read as a diversion tactic on a considerable scale. In writing about the Blitz in distant London, Thomas not-writes about the war in Wales.

Like Owen's 'Anthem', this poem also contradicts its own title: in attempting to give a child's death in the Blitz due deference and meaning, Thomas arguably shows a willingness, rather than a refusal, to mourn. This is a species of paralipsis, a trope that is exploited extensively in the poem. The first thirteen lines out of twenty-four – a long sentence which invades the third stanza, breaking up the poem's form – are an extended statement of what the speaker will not do and when he will not do it:

> Never until the mankind making
> Bird beast and flower
> Fathering and all humbling darkness
> Tells with silence the last light breaking
> And the still hour
> Is come of the sea tumbling in harness
> And I must enter again the round
> Zion of the water bead
> And the synagogue of the ear of corn
> Shall I let pray the shadow of a sound
> Or sow my salt seed
> In the least valley of sackcloth to mourn
> The majesty and burning of the child's death.[52]

In these lines, mourning, weeping, the wearing of sackcloth are mentioned paraliptically, as are, later, words by the grave (one meaning of 'grave truth') and 'elegy'. Paralipsis has a ghostly effect: what is petitioned in the negative is summoned into being, but not full being, haunting the lines as mere potential. That the potential is tenuous indeed is indicated by further

---

[49] Paul Ferris, *Dylan Thomas* (London: Hodder & Stoughton, 1977), 22.
[50] Barbara Hardy, *Dylan Thomas: An Original Language* (Athens: University of Georgia Press, 2000), 22.
[51] *Ibid.*, 21.   [52] Dylan Thomas, *Collected Poems 1934–1952* (London: J. M. Dent, 1952), 101.

qualifications: the hypothetical prayer will only be 'the shadow of a sound' and tears will only fall 'in the least valley of sackcloth'. But the speaker of the poem is not 'unmourning' in the same way as the 'water / Of the riding Thames': the river may rush by, unconcerned, but the speaker protests too much so that his 'refusal' begins to suggest its opposite.

The poem is also rich in periphrasis or circumlocutio ('salt seed' for tears, the multiple-epithet-bearing darkness) and tends towards abstraction (as in the reference to 'the synagogue of the ear of corn'), bypassing the bombardment to the point of baffling readers. 'On the poem *A Refusal to Mourn* Mr. Holbrook grumbles that it is not clear why the poet says he won't say things', wrote William Empson waspishly, 'the poem is about the German bombing of London, and the poet erected not writing propaganda into a point of honour. There is no great credit in not understanding this.'[53] Like euphemism and cliché, periphrasis and abstraction throw white paint at the red business, redirecting the discourse from the apparent matter in hand.

But the first thirteen lines of 'A Refusal to Mourn the Death, By Fire, of a Child in London' go further than mystical-sounding abstraction. Thomas sets a number of conditions that must be fulfilled before he will mourn. To paraphrase: before grieving can take place, the darkness must signal the last day, the sea must be still, and the speaker himself must have returned in death to the elements, his atoms re-entering the promised land that is the drop of water and the holy place that is the ear of corn. To satisfy such conditions is obviously impossible, not least because the speaker's own death would prevent his mourning anyway (this is an example of the adynaton topos, explored in detail below). Establishing insuperable criteria serves to postpone mourning indefinitely. Therefore also in play in the poem is the rhetorical figure of praeteritio.[54] Though this term can be used loosely to describe the strategy of drawing attention to something by professing to omit it (the function of paralipsis or cataphasis mentioned above), it more strictly refers to a temporal act of passing over. Praeteritio says, 'I will speak of this, but not yet'; in Thomas's case, the claim is 'I will mourn, but not yet'. Deferring the expression of grief, 'A Refusal to Mourn the Death, By Fire, of a Child in London' is an elegiac raincheck.

A twenty-four-line postponement of mourning may seem a counter-intuitive way to mark the London Blitz (let alone the Swansea Blitz). Yet,

---

[53] William Empson, 'Dylan Thomas', *Essays in Criticism* 13.2 (1963), 205.

[54] See H. A. Kelly, '*Occupatio* as Negative Narration: A Mistake for Occultatio/Praeteritio', *Modern Philology* 74.3 (February 1977), 311–15.

arguably, Thomas is not so much ignoring or diminishing the catastrophe as drawing back from it. Steiner writes: 'language does have its frontiers . . . it borders on three other modes of statement – light, music, and silence', and when the poet enters the last of these, 'the word borders not on radiance or music, but on night'.[55] In its apocalyptic and sacred-sounding imagery, 'A Refusal to Mourn the Death, By Fire, of a Child in London' borders light and silence/darkness, invoking 'the last light breaking' and the stillness of the sea. But while Steiner is concerned with the evocation of the ineffable 'transcendent presence in the fabric of the world',[56] the unsayable in Thomas's case is the pain and loss inflicted by a bombing campaign of the Second World War. In what amounts to a 'private notation'[57] of abstract images, combined with the metonymy of the death of a single child ('After the first death, there is no other'), Thomas conveys the scale of the trauma even as he deliberately refuses to acknowledge it.

If Thomas's circumlocutions obscure through their richness, the opposite is true of Hemingway's 'On the Quai at Smyrna', a short story that is not a short story, a piece of journalism that is not a piece of journalism, an essay that is not an essay. For Steiner, the Hemingway style is a 'thin medium', but he also calls it 'a powerful lyric, shorthand'.[58] 'On the Quai at Smyrna' was first published as 'Introduction by the Author' in the 1930 Scribner's edition of *In Our Time*, but it is likely to have been written around 1926–7.[59] As is sometimes the case with Hemingway's war writing, it concerns an event which he did not witness directly. When the fire started in Smyrna (now Turkish Izmir) on 13 September 1922, Hemingway was at home in Paris, though he did set out soon after for Anatolia to cover the Graeco-Turkish War for the *Toronto Daily Star*. According to Michael Reynolds, he did not see the evacuation which is the subject of 'On the Quai', but 'either heard or read the detailed stories [in the newspapers], remembering them five years later with great clarity'.[60] The subject matter of the piece is, therefore, doubly absent: a non-witnessing of an event that was itself parapolemical – an evacuation or emptying-out.

The notable laconicism of 'On the Quai' can be attributed to a number of factors. Still in the process of honing his pared-down, declarative sentences, Hemingway had already happened upon his favourite 'iceberg

---

[55] Steiner, *Language and Silence*, 60, 69.   [56] *Ibid.*, 60.   [57] *Ibid.*, 48.   [58] *Ibid.*, 51.
[59] See Michael Reynolds, 'Hemingway's *In Our Time*: The Biography of a Book', in *Modern American Short Story Sequences: Composite Fictions and Fictive Communities*, ed. J. Gerald Kennedy (Cambridge: Cambridge University Press, 1995), 44–5. Though it is analysed here as a stand-alone piece, it is also possible to read 'On the Quai' in conjunction with the other vignettes in *In our time* which treat the Graeco-Turkish War – a reading in which further lacunae accumulate.
[60] *Ibid.*, 76.

principle'[61] – the idea that revealing only the small part of a whole max-imised communication: essentially the principle that 'less is more'. He had learned concision during his journalistic apprenticeship on the *Kansas City Star* and the *Toronto Daily Star*. 'Use short first paragraphs. Use vig-orous English. Be positive, not negative', ran the *Kansas City Star* house style-sheet.[62] Plain speaking was anyway in the stylistic air, and in the piece Hemingway is trying to reproduce the clipped discourse of a British officer. But even when these factors are taken into consideration, 'On the Quai at Smyrna' still constitutes a notably oblique account of an incident – or the aftermath of an incident – in the Graeco-Turkish War.

The piece is distinctive for the gaps in its information (incidentally demonstrating that the tactics of indirection go beyond poetic obliquity). With no prior knowledge, the reader may wonder who exactly is speaking; who 'they' are who are screaming; who the women with the dead babies are and why the babies are dead; who or what has to be cleared off the pier; what is meant by 'it wasn't at all like an earthquake or that sort of thing because they never knew about the Turk'; who ordered whom 'not to come in to take off any more'.[63] It is possible to read critical explanations which furnish enough historical details to make all these puzzles clear,[64] but to supplement Hemingway's text with information in this way is arguably to miss the point of the speaker's failure to be forthcoming. Horror has been witnessed – 'That was the only time in my life I got so I dreamed about things' – and is simultaneously being tentatively revisited and strenuously avoided. In the words of Cathy Caruth, 'the historical power of the trauma is not just that the experience is repeated after its forgetting, but that it is only in and through its inherent forgetting that it is first experienced at all'.[65]

The traumatised voice of 'On the Quai' attempts to approach the atrocity but various lacunae render this a lacerated narrative. The beginning *in media res* denies the reader the sense-making assistance of a context. The 'welter of antecedentless pronouns'[66] makes it difficult to identify the

---

[61] 'The dignity of movement of an ice-berg is due to only one-eighth of it being above water . . . If a writer of prose knows enough about what he is writing about he may omit things that he knows and the reader, if the writer is writing truly enough, will have a feeling of those things as strongly as though the writer had stated them' (Ernest Hemingway, *Death in the Afternoon* (New York: Scribner's, 1932), 192).

[62] Quoted in Ronald Weber, *Hemingway's Art of Non-Fiction* (Basingstoke: Macmillan, 1990), 6.

[63] Ernest Hemingway, *In Our Time* (New York: Scribner's, 2003), 11–12.

[64] An excellent guide is Matthew Stewart, '"It Was All a Pleasant Business": The Historical Context of "On the Quai at Smyrna"', *The Hemingway Review* 23.1 (Fall 2003), 58–70.

[65] Cathy Caruth, *Unclaimed Experience: Trauma, Narrative, and History* (Baltimore: The Johns Hopkins University Press, 1996), 17.

[66] Stewart, 'It Was All a Pleasant Business', 59.

voice(s) of the piece. The references to information which is presumed
already to be known to the interlocutor ('You remember when they ordered
us not to come in to take off any more?', 'You remember the harbor') but
which is not in the public domain and so is unavailable to the reader creates
confusion. Irony adds to the sense that the piece's prima facie meaning is
not reliable and the inclusion of 'non-stories' induces perplexity.

The irony in 'On the Quai' consists of straight semantic reversals. 'Great
friends we were', 'plenty of nice things floating around in it', 'nice chaps'
and 'a most pleasant business' all signify the opposite of their ostensible
meanings. The 'non-stories' are three. The narrator relates that a Turkish
officer complained to him 'because one of our sailors had been most
insulting to him' and pointed out as the offender a 'most inoffensive chap':

I called him over and said, 'And just in case you should have spoken to any Turkish
officers.'
  'I haven't spoken to any of them, sir.'
  'I'm quite sure of it,' I said, 'but you'd best go on board ship and not come
ashore again for the rest of the day.'
  Then I told the Turk that the man was being sent on board ship and would
be most severely dealt with. Oh most rigorously. He felt topping about it. Great
friends we were.

Taking up about a quarter of the short piece, this is an account that is at least
second-hand of an incident that most likely did not take place, followed by
a 'punishment' that is not a punishment. In the course of the description of
these non-events is an odd non-utterance: 'And just in case you should have
spoken to any Turkish officers'. This, an incomplete sentence desperate for
a main clause, recapitulates in miniature the elliptical quality of the whole
account. The second 'non-story' concerns the death of an old woman on
the pier. The narrator relates: 'Just then she died and went absolutely stiff.
Her legs drew up and she drew up from the waist and went quite rigid.'
Performing what Caruth calls the 'determined repetition' of trauma,[67] the
narrator reveals that he has articulated this experience before – to a doctor
who told him he 'was lying' and that what he described 'was impossible'.
The doctor's scepticism is stated twice by the narrator, as though his
failure to be believed were itself traumatic. The reader is left pondering
the ontological status of an event said to be a medical impossibility, while
the repetition contributes a tautological emptiness. The third 'non-story'
in the piece concerns an attempt by the narrator to bring his ship in close
to the pier and shell the Turkish quarter of the town. Though not stated

[67] Caruth, *Unclaimed Experience*, 63.

explicitly, it is apparent that this manouevre was aborted. The event is placed in the realm of the hypothetical: 'It would have been a hell of a mess.'

'On the Quai at Smyrna' adds ironies, ellipses and omissions; ontologically problematic incidents and unwarranted assumptions; lack of context and orphaned pronouns to the diversionary tactics already illustrated in this chapter: indexical signs, parapolemics, euphemism, cliché, meiosis/litotes, paralipsis/cataphasis, rhetorical questions, self-referentiality, abstraction, negativity, periphrasis/circumlocutio, praeteritio, lacunae, inconsistencies, contradictions and repetition.[68] Examples of meta-writing, these tactics do not function primarily to pose questions about the epistemological status of the discourses in which they feature (the definition of 'metafiction' offered by both Patricia Waugh and Mark Currie),[69] but to puncture the textual weave of those discourses. Essentially, they are feints. Feigned or false attacks, feints aim at a part other than that truly intended, diverting defences and uncovering flanks. Deriving from the Latin *fingere* (to mould, form) and cognate with 'fiction', 'fashion' and 'figment', they possess fictitious, pretentious and pretending qualities which the tropes of diversion also share. Obviously, such qualities are also to be found in literature concerned with subjects other than war. The point to be made here is that they are particularly apposite responses to the representation-resistant phenomenon that is armed conflict.

All these techniques so far described adumbrate catastrophe without articulating it. But beyond them, at the far end of the spectrum of diversionary tactics, lies explicit acknowledgement of the fact of adumbration. Examples of such acknowledgements – explicit statements (as opposed to

---

[68] Other avoidance tropes pointed out by critics include elision, apostrophe and apophasis ('rhetorical forms of structured silence' which 'ground the said in the unsaid' (Peter Haidu, 'The Dialectics of Unspeakability: Language, Silence, and the Narratives of Desubjectification', in *Probing the Limits of Representation*, ed. Friedlander, 278–9)); metaphor ('only metaphor, the figure of speech that asserts something contrary to fact, can convey what must incredibly be known' (John Felstiner, 'Translating Paul Celan's "Todesfuge": Rhythm and Repetition as Metaphor', in *ibid.*, 243)); and allusion ('with its hidden allusion [to *Kubla Khan*], "Melancholy" proves the lengths to which [Edward] Thomas will sometimes go to write war poems which avoid all overt reference to war' (Tim Kendall, *Modern English War Poetry* (Oxford: Oxford University Press, 2006), 74)). Antony Rowland lists in his 'taxonomy of awkward poetics', 'metrical tension, the anti-elegiac, self-questioning, embarrassed rhetoric, anti-rhetoric, juxtaposition, incongruity, self-declared inadequacies, paradox, minimalism, non-catharsis, heightened tone, hermeneutics, the anti-redemptive, archaisms, anti-objectivism and "stylistic eccentricities"' (*Holocaust Poetry: Awkward Poetics in the Work of Sylvia Plath, Geoffrey Hill, Tony Harrison and Ted Hughes* (Edinburgh: Edinburgh University Press, 2005), 12).

[69] Patricia Waugh, *Metafiction: The Theory and Practice of Self-Conscious Fiction* (London: Routledge, 2003), 2; Mark Currie, 'Introduction', in *Metafiction*, ed. Mark Currie (London and New York: Longman, 1995), 2.

implications) that war cannot be, and is not being, written about – were quoted at the beginning of this chapter in the form of authorial disclaimers and excuses. The rhetorical term for such disclaimers – adynaton – has already been cited. Ἀδύνατον is a cognate of ἀδυναμία (adynamia): want of strength or lack of dynamism; its Latin isotrope, *impossibilia*, also contains the etymological suggestion of powerlessness. Though strictly applied to the stating of unfulfillable conditions (as observed in the long opening sentence of Thomas's 'A Refusal to Mourn the Death, By Fire, of a Child in London'), adynaton has also been defined in rhetorical handbooks as the expression of 'the impossibility of addressing oneself adequately to the topic'.[70] Homer's disclaimer quoted at the beginning of this chapter reveals the crucial connection: the insuperable criteria figure irremediable authorial inadequacy.

The mother of all diversionary tactics, adynaton not-writes about war by making not-writing its very subject. Pervasive in literature about conflict, the phenomenon has not gone unnoticed by critics,[71] but its precise functioning is still to be theorised. Circumspection is required. Confusingly, the posited representational failure tends to be articulated clearly and at length; these disclaimers and excuses proliferate in apparently *successful* depictions of war. Homer's self-deprecating protestation occurs in the early stages of the greatest ever tale of war, an epic during which the poet appears to demonstrate every competence in depicting, not only the Greek forces, but the very experience of the battlefield itself. The 480 lines of Addison's 'The Campaign' suggest no ultimate difficulty in finding 'numbers . . . / To sing the furious troops in battle join'd!' Despite Carolin Emcke's concerns, *Echoes of Violence* was named German political book of the year in 2005 and was a finalist for the international Lettre-Ulysses award for the art of reportage: evidence that she did indeed succeed in conveying her experiences in Albania and Kosovo in a way meaningful to others.

So what motivates these immediately belied disclaimers, these wordy disavowals of words? Some instances may be no more than conventional protestations of false modesty, decorous commonplaces of self-deprecation.

---

[70] Brian Vickers, *In Defence of Rhetoric* (Oxford: Oxford University Press, 1988), 491. For further information on adynaton, see H. V. Canter, 'The Figure Adunaton in Greek and Latin Poetry', *American Journal of Philology* 51.1 (1930), 32–41, and Ernst Robert Curtius, *European Literature and the Latin Middle Ages*, trans. Willard R. Trask (London: Routledge & Kegan Paul, 1953), 94ff.

[71] See, for example, Dawes, *The Language of War*, 6, 10–11, 17; Norris, *Writing War in the Twentieth Century*, 2; Longley, 'The Great War, History, and the English Lyric', 66.

The self-censorship implied in the topos might also be viewed as a form of sensationalism. Hypocrisy lurks in the idea of rhetoricians repudiating rhetoric, polemicists putting down polemics. The hyperbole-disguised-as-inadequacy of adynaton might justly be regarded as a form of linguistic posturing, even dissembling. Paul Fussell, writing about the First World War, saw no problem with linguistic resources but rather located the difficulty in the relationship between the subject matter of the communication and the sensibilities of the recipient:

One of the cruxes of the [First World] war . . . is the collision between events and the language available – or thought appropriate – to describe them . . . Logically there is no reason why the English language could not perfectly well render the actuality of trench warfare: it is rich in terms like *blood, terror, agony, madness, shit, cruelty, murder, sell-out, pain* and *hoax*, as well as phrases like *legs blown off, intestines gushing out over his hands, screaming all night, bleeding to death from the rectum*, and the like. Logically . . . there's no reason why a language devised by man should be inadequate to describe any of man's works. The problem was less one of 'language' than of gentility and optimism; it was less a problem of 'linguistics' than of rhetoric . . . The real reason is that soldiers have discovered that no one is very interested in the bad news they have to report. What listener wants to be torn and shaken when he doesn't have to be? We have made *unspeakable* mean indescribable: it really means *nasty*.[72]

But care must be taken to distinguish between genuine problems and protestations. The linguistic disclaimers that Fussell rightly notes to be 'one of the motifs of all who write about war',[73] may not be functioning at the literal level but on a more complex plane of communication.

The suggestion of this chapter so far has been that diversions are apophatic: like the sculptor's mould or the artist's depiction of negative space, they represent war, as it were, in relief. But it is possible to be more precise about what is happening when a writer states or implies that he or she cannot or will not write about war. When, for example, Carolin Emcke comments, '[e]verything is clear and yet it is impossible to transform it into an adequate and intelligible narrative',[74] her anguished perception that something is wanting must be taken seriously, even if her narrative may seem supremely adequate and intelligible. This sense of something wanting points to the presence, in war, of certain qualities of excessiveness and ineffability. Such qualities are well-known elements in discourses concerning another literary concept of ancient standing: the sublime. Appreciation of

---

[72] Fussell, *The Great War and Modern Memory*, 169–70.   [73] *Ibid.*, 170.
[74] Emcke, *Echoes of Violence*, 3.

the workings of the sublime – long integrated into theories of representing the Holocaust[75] – sheds light on the representational functioning of diversionary tactics. To elucidate, this chapter now concentrates on adynaton, but the applicability of the argument to the other avoidance strategies is also borne in mind.

What has the sublime to do with warfare? For Longinus, whose first-century CE work *Peri hupsos* was influential in translation in the eighteenth century, the sublime 'always pleases'.[76] This might seem to remove armed conflict from its aegis, but other theorists, including John Dennis, Joseph Addison and Immanuel Kant, did include the warlike in their lists of sublime phenomena.[77] Edmund Burke, in his *Philosophical Enquiry into the Origins of Our Ideas of the Sublime and the Beautiful* (1757), argued, like Addison, that the sublime depends upon a feeling of terror:

> Whatever is fitted in any sort to excite the ideas of pain, and danger, that is to say, whatever is in any sort terrible, or is conversant about terrible objects, or operates in a manner analogous to terror, is a source of the *sublime*.[78]

Having cited terror as both source and 'ruling principle' of the sublime,[79] Burke then suggests how it can be evoked. One means is a 'richness and profusion' of images:[80] by way of example he (mis)quotes Shakespeare's description of the king's army in *1 Henry IV*:

---

[75] See, for example, Michael Bernard-Donals and Richard Glejzer, *Between Witness and Testimony: The Holocaust and the Limits of Representation* (Albany: State University of New York Press, 2001); Felstiner, 'Translating Paul Celan's "Todesfuge"'; Friedlander, 'Introduction'; Haidu, 'The Dialectics of Unspeakability'; Geoffrey H. Hartman, 'The Book of the Destruction', in *Probing the Limits of Representation*, ed. Friedlander, 318–34; Lang, 'The Representation of Limits', in *ibid.*, 300–17; Felman and Laub, *Testimony*; LaCapra, *History and Memory After Auschwitz*; LaCapra, *Writing History, Writing Trauma* (Baltimore: The Johns Hopkins University Press, 2003); Lawrence L. Langer, *Holocaust Testimonies: The Ruins of Memory* (New Haven and London: Yale University Press, 1991); and Trezise, 'Unspeakable', as well as the other works discussed in this chapter.

[76] Dionysus Longinus, *Dionysius Longinus on the Sublime. Translated from the Greek, with Notes and Observations; and some Account of the Life, Writings, and Character of the Author*, trans. William Smith, 5th edn (Dublin: William Sleater, 1792), 55.

[77] John Dennis, 'From *The Grounds of Criticism in Poetry*', in *The Sublime: A Reader in British Eighteenth-Century Aesthetic Theory*, ed. Andrew Ashfield and Peter de Bolla (Cambridge: Cambridge University Press, 1996), 37; Joseph Addison, 'From *The Spectator*', in *ibid.*, 68; Kant, *Critique*, 146. Kant's remark is: 'Even war, if it is conducted with order and reverence for the rights of civilians, has something sublime about it.'

[78] Burke, *A Philosophical Enquiry*, 36. See also Ferguson, 'The Sublime and the Subliminal', 10. Ferguson is concerned with sublimity in relation to the experience of combat rather than in relation to its representation.

[79] Burke, *A Philosophical Enquiry*, 54.   [80] *Ibid.*, 72.

> All furnished, all in arms,
> All plumed like ostriches that with the wind
> Baited like eagles having lately bathed:
> As full of spirit as the month of May,
> And gorgeous as the sun in Midsummer,
> Wanton as youthful goats, wild as young bulls.[81]

The ostriches, eagles, goats and bulls, vying with the month of May and sun in Midsummer, dazzle the mind, inducing the reaction, which Burke conflates with terror, of astonishment: 'that state of the soul, in which all its motions are suspended, with some degree of horror'.[82] The reader or audience-member is thunderstruck or, it might be said, given the nature of the subject matter, shell-shocked. Burke, incidentally anticipating the basis on which many of today's anxiety-relieving treatments, such as cognitive behavioural therapy, are founded, continues with an even more apposite description of how terror may be induced:

To make anything very terrible, obscurity seems in general to be necessary . . . When we know the full extent of any danger, when we can accustom our eyes to it, a great deal of the apprehension vanishes.[83]

Alluding to the scale of the catastrophe without explicitly delineating it, adynaton functions in precisely this way.

More insight into this functioning is provided by Kant's 'Analytic of the Sublime', contained in his *Critique of the Power of Judgment* (1790). Kant encapsulates his theory thus:

What is properly sublime cannot be contained in any sensible form, but concerns only ideas of reason, which, though no presentation adequate to them is possible, are provoked and called to mind precisely by this inadequacy, which does allow of sensible presentation.[84]

To expand this: the sublime brings with itself 'the idea of its infinity' and causes the recipient a feeling of 'displeasure' at the inability of the imagination to apprehend it.[85] (In the case of the 'mathematically sublime', the imagination cannot apprehend Nature's magnitude; in the case of the 'dynamically sublime', it falters in the face of 'a power that has no dominion over us'.)[86] A feeling of 'submission, dejection, and . . . complete powerlessness'[87] is experienced. But the failure of the imagination 'makes

---

[81] 4.1.97–104. Burke quotes to line 109 but omits line 105: 'His cuishes on his thighs, gallantly armed'.
[82] Burke, *A Philosophical Enquiry*, 53.   [83] *Ibid.*, 54.   [84] Kant, *Critique*, 129.
[85] *Ibid.*, 138, 141.   [86] *Ibid.*, 131–43, 143.   [87] *Ibid.*, 146.

intuitable the superiority of the rational vocation of our cognitive faculty'
and this, in turn, evokes a feeling of 'pleasure'.[88] In a complex power-play
between the faculties, the Kantian sublime renders the despair of an initial
failure of imaginative apprehension the precondition of joyful aesthetic
judgement. This aesthetic judgement is exercised by the imagination, but
the latter now functions as 'an instrument of reason'.[89]

Adynaton resonates at various junctures with Kant's 'Analytic'. When
Homer professes himself unable to describe the battlefield before going on
to do precisely that or Emcke labels what seems to be an adequate and
intelligible narrative of horror inadequate and unintelligible, the reader
must pause to revise preconceptions and recalibrate his or her apprehension of the atrocities. In this sense, the trope is hyperbolic: not just in its
extravagant claims to inadequacy, but in that it opens up limitless scope
for imaginative aesthetic judgement.[90] The suggestive power of the absent
referent is well documented; direct representation curtails the power to
envisage. The rhetorical trick of communication-by-implication is that
absence conjures up presence: a reader informed that a battle is too shocking to be described is likely to envisage horrors exceeding anything that
straightforward description could invoke. As Derrida writes, 'the feeling of
the colossal [a Kantian word] . . . is the experience of an inadequation of
presentation to itself, or rather, since every presentation is adequate to itself,
of an inadequation of the presenter to the presented of presentation'.[91]

As these remarks suggest – 'an inadequation of the presenter to the presented of presentation' – the successful execution of this rhetorical trick
necessitates a curious disempowerment. Harold Bloom thought the sublime reliant 'upon the trope of hyperbole, the overthrowing (or overtaking,
or overreaching) that is closer to simplification through intensity than it is
to exaggeration'.[92] Adynaton works in a more complex way. As a linguistic disclaimer, it makes hyperbolic claims, but they are, paradoxically, big
claims to inadequacy and diminution, large-scale confessions of smallness
and ineptitude, of being unequal to the task. These disclaimers correspond

---

[88] *Ibid.*, 141.
[89] Kant's use of the terms 'reason', 'imagination' and 'judgment' is complicated. In his 'General remark
on the exposition of aesthetic reflective judgments', he brings imagination under the auspices of
reason by writing, 'in the aesthetic judgment of the sublime this dominion [of reason over sensibility]
is represented as being exercised by the imagination itself, as an instrument of reason' (*ibid.*, 151).
[90] Kant's word for the imagination at this point is 'unbounded' (*unbegrenzt*) (*ibid.*, 156).
[91] Jacques Derrida, *The Truth in Painting*, trans. Geoff Bennington and Ian McLeod (Chicago:
University of Chicago Press, 1987), 132.
[92] Harold Bloom, 'Introduction', in *Poets of Sensibility and the Sublime*, ed. Harold Bloom (New York:
Chelsea House, 1986), 1.

to the point, identified by Kant, during which the 'momentary inhibition of the vital powers' in the face of the colossal occurs:[93] the instant at which the adynatic evokes an a-dynamic response. Moments of self-effacement, withdrawal, mortification, defeat, each deployment of adynaton is a miniature may-day, a distress-flare declaring a representational state of emergency. And each such declaration represents a gesture towards death on the part of the writer, even a death itself.

But an instant later comes Kant's 'vital outpouring':[94] the point at which aesthetic judgement apprehends what reason considered to be beyond its limits. In this sense, each occurrence of adynaton is also a cause for celebration, marking the moment when representative possibilities are released and aesthetic judgement is given free rein. Hence, the trope figures the beginning, as well as the end, of communication, which makes its presence in successful war representations more comprehensible. Indeed, 'success' is twofold, since the ensuing depiction comprises both all that the writer can convey and all that the reader can apprehend. Understood in this way, adynata can be seen to function as *parerga*, defined by Derrida, after Kant, in the following terms:

A parergon comes against, beside, and in addition to the *ergon* [the work] . . . but it does not fall to one side, it touches and cooperates within the operation, from a certain outside. Neither simply outside nor simply inside.[95]

Examples of parerga or *hors-d'oeuvres* are columns around buildings, frames for paintings, clothing on statues that obscures certain parts for reasons of modesty – and is not adynaton, too, a protestation of modesty that functions as a cover-up? Adynata are 'accessories'[96] to the main work: linguistic bosses; opuscules that function on the one hand as sites of self-sacrifice (on the part of the writer) and sites of mourning (for the writer, for the task) and, on the other, as sites of joy (on the part of both writer and reader, for the task).

These effects, while concentrated in the adynaton topos, permeate war writing in the form of the avoidance tactics explored in this chapter. While adynatic opuscules are the purest instances of the sublime, all the rhetorical diversions noted keep open possibilities and license the imagination to perform aesthetic judgement. Lessing, writing on the *Iliad* in *Laocoön: An Essay Upon the Limits of Painting and Poetry* (1766), noticed precisely this effect:

[93] Kant, *Critique*, 128–9.   [94] *Ibid.*   [95] Derrida, *The Truth in Painting*, 54.   [96] *Ibid.*

When, for instance, the gods who take different sides in the Trojan war come at last to actual blows, the contest goes on in the poem unseen [21.385]. This invisibility leaves the imagination free play to enlarge the scene at will, and picture the gods and their movements on a scale far grander than the measure of common humanity.[97]

Similarly, Wolfe's parapolemical account of Sir John Moore's burial keeps the Battle of Corunna off-stage, but his insistence on the paltriness of the funeral obsequies establishes the sense of an unknown comparator. The reader is led to ponder what enormity of fighting might render the hastiness of the interment so remarkable. Owen, asking 'What passing-bells for these who die as cattle?', immediately invokes loss on a scale that defies commemorative marking; by concentrating on memorialising substitutes, he licenses the reader to fathom the possible scale. Thomas's refusal to give meaning to the death of a child by bombing – 'I shall not murder the mankind of her going with a grave truth' – leaves open a space in which the reader is drawn to ponder the mass casualties of the Blitz. Hemingway's fitful, fragmentary account of the scene at Smyrna is a mesh cordoning off the horrific consequences of the fire. Allowed only glimpses through the mesh, the reader is free to enlarge the significance of incomplete information.

All these cases involve a *transcendent* sublime that invokes something that is elsewhere: in Gareth Reeves's useful phrase, they 'reif[y] absence'.[98] It is this version of the sublime which is posited by Holocaust theorists such as Langer and Rothberg. As they point out, there is a further irony to the absent elsewhere glimpsed through punctured texts: what is absent, being ungraspable, was in a sense never actually there. In Lyotard's words, '[t]he Forgotten is not to be remembered by what it has been and what it is, because it has not been anything and is nothing'.[99]

What not-writing about war can achieve, therefore, is, by diverting attention, to disclose the transcendent sublime, allowing and encouraging the reader to engage with the directly unrepresentable. At this point, a comment is required on the notion of 'combat gnosticism' (already encountered in Chapters 1 and 3). Treating war as sublime or ineffable arguably perpetuates this ideology. However, the ascription demands caution. Of the four

[97] Gotthold Ephraim Lessing, *Laocoön: An Essay Upon the Limits of Painting and Poetry*, trans. Ellen Frothingham (Boston: Roberts Brothers, 1880), 78. I am grateful to Brad Prager for drawing my attention to this passage.
[98] Gareth Reeves, '"This is Plenty: This is More than Enough": Poetry and the Memory of the Second World War', in *The Oxford Handbook of British and Irish War Poetry*, ed. Kendall, 579–91: 589.
[99] Lyotard, *Heidegger and 'the jews'*, 3.

authors discussed in this chapter, only Wilfred Owen had what might be called full combat experience of the subject matter of his text (a curious non-experience, it has to be said, of things that were not there). Rev. Charles Wolfe had no military experience, let alone in the Peninsular War. Dylan Thomas did experience the Blitz but was exempted from military service on medical grounds. Hemingway served as a volunteer ambulance-driver in Italy in the First World War but would not have witnessed refugee scenes comparable to the one described in 'On the Quai at Smyrna'. The gnosis, or insight, of the works considered derives from imagination, rather than from experience; hence the texts themselves are, in Steiner's words, 'acts not primarily of *communication* but of *initiation* into a private mystery'.[100]

But the specific context of armed conflict gives rise to other, more problematic issues with respect to how the sublime functions. Kant's original analysis related to natural phenomena, including natural disasters. When his theories are applied to man-made disasters such as war, and their representation, certain unignorable consequences arise.[101] The Kantian position is that of the edified but unscathed bystander. The astonishment induced in the spectator by natural grandeur 'is, in view of the safety in which he knows himself to be, not actual fear but only an attempt to involve ourselves in it by means of the imagination, in order to feel the power of that very faculty, to combine the movement of the mind thereby aroused with its calmness, and so to be superior to nature within us, and thus also that outside us'.[102] When the object of scrutiny is armed conflict, this position of serene aloofness can come to connote negative qualities ranging from uncaringness to voyeurism.[103] The *locus classicus* of the phenomenon is Pierre Bezuhov climbing onto a knoll at Tatarinova to view a 'huge panorama' stretching

---

[100] Steiner, *Language and Silence*, 48.

[101] For further discussion, see Zachary Braiterman, 'Against Holocaust-Sublime: Naive Reference and the Generation of Memory', *History and Memory* 12.2 (Fall 2000), 7–28. I am grateful to Brad Prager for drawing my attention to this article.

[102] Kant, *Critique*, 152.

[103] Are even darker motives involved? The figure of the unharmed spectator or reader of war, terrorised but joyful, potentially embodies what David Bromwich terms 'the non-moral theory of art' (*Skeptical Music: Essays on Modern Poetry* (Chicago: University of Chicago Press, 2001), 234) in relation to the literature of armed conflict, but delighted diversion is distinct from the deployment and reception of diversionary tactics. Bromwich draws attention to the pleasure that can be taken in the representation of suffering and destruction, relating it to Burke's concept of sympathy occasioned by the sublime. This Burkean sympathy has nothing to do with 'beneficent mutual sensitivity and vulnerability'; rather, it is 'the state of being held to attention by helpless feelings *about* someone else, who at the moment is visibly suffering' (*ibid.*, 237). But the joyfulness experienced by the serene reader is not the same as this kind of pleasure. The (Kantian) joyfulness is that occasioned by a sense of the limitless power of the imagination, under the auspices of reason, to apprehend what initially seemed to the reason to be ungraspable: the transcendent sublime. The pleasure described by Burke and Bromwich is induced by another 'modalit[y]' (LaCapra, *History and Memory After*

'like an amphitheatre before him', 'bathed in brilliant light'.[104] As Gene
Ray remarks, '[t]o be able to find pleasure in avalanches and fissured glacier
fields sets English nobles and bourgeois travelers on the Grand Tour apart
from Swiss peasants for whom such natural features are a despised daily
danger'.[105] What is true of Alpine hikers is also true of the non-belligerent
like Bezuhov diverted by watching or reading about men at war. Rather
than combat gnosticism, non-combatant agnosticism becomes valorised –
and the non-combatant agnostic, like Bezuhov, is apt to be found an
interfering nuisance and directed from the field.

In addition to permitting aloofness, the Kantian sublime creates a sense
of being 'superior to nature within us, and thus also that outside us'. Kant
posits the elevation of reason or the power 'to assert our independence in
the face of the influences of nature, to diminish the value of what is great
according to these, and so to place what is absolutely great only in its (the
subject's) own vocation'.[106] Indeed, for him, apprehension of the sublime
becomes a moral exercise in which aesthetic judgement, performed by the
imagination as an instrument of reason, is asserted over the senses.[107] But
the excesses of man-made conflict undermine any claims to the superiority
of human reason. As Ray writes:

In the twentieth century, the genocidal catastrophes of human making displaced
the natural disaster as the source of sublime feeling and effects – but with a
crucial difference. In bourgeois aesthetics, exemplified by Kant's 1790 *Critique of
Judgment*, the pain of imagination's failure before the power or size of raw nature
was compensated for by reason's reflection on its own supersensible dignity and
destination. Nature's threat to dominate the human was contained by human
capacities for self-admiration. In the wake of Auschwitz and Hiroshima, however,

---

Auschwitz, 32n) of the sublime: the 'immanent' or 'spectacularized'. LaCapra writes, '[w]hat would
seem most prominent in the Nazi phenomenon is the role of an immanent or desublimated sublime related to a certain kind of carnivalization as well as to sacrificialism, regenerative violence,
and victimization or scapegoating' (*ibid.*, 33n). Notably, Kant states that the transcendent sublime
itself can evoke 'enthusiasm', which is 'aesthetically sublime, because it is a stretching of the powers
through ideas, which give the mind a momentum that acts far more powerfully and persistently
than the impetus given by sensory representations' (*Critique*, 154). But when Lyotard describes
Kantian enthusiasm as being 'on the edge of dementia', a 'pathological outburst' that 'as such
has no ethical validity', he is explicitly referring to '[h]istorical-political enthusiasm', such as that
experienced by the spectators of the French Revolution (*The Differend: Phrases in Dispute*, trans.
Georges Van Den Abbeele (Manchester: Manchester University Press, 1988), 166). While Kant's
spectator may rub his or her hands in glee at the war poem or novel, it is because the text has
unleashed his or her aesthetic judgement rather than brought him or her 'close to a scene of risk'
(Bromwich, *Skeptical Music*, 234).

[104] Tolstoy, *War and Peace*, 904.
[105] Gene Ray, 'Reading the Lisbon Earthquake: Adorno, Lyotard, and the Contemporary Sublime',
Yale Journal of Criticism 17.1 (2004), 7.
[106] Kant, *Critique*, 152.   [107] *Ibid.*, 151.

the ruined dignity and destiny of human reason and its moral law can offer no compensatory pleasure. The terror of the sublime becomes a permanent, ghastly latency, compounded by the anguish of shame.[108]

But a questionable sense of superiority is not the only troubling aspect of Kantian reason in the face of the sublime. Kant writes, in his 'General remark on the exposition of aesthetic reflective judgments':

[I]f someone calls the sight of the starry heavens sublime, he must not ground such a judging of it on concepts of worlds inhabited by rational beings, taking the bright points with which we see the space above us to be filled as their suns, about which they move in their purposively appointed orbits, but must take it, as we see it, merely as a broad, all-embracing vault; and it must be merely under this representation that we posit the sublimity that a pure aesthetic judgment attributes to this object.[109]

Purposive reflection, in other words, must not intrude upon reason's instrument, the imagination, exercising aesthetic judgement. What the *Critique of the Power of Judgment* appears to endorse is a reason at once self-congratulatory and *unthinking*. If the former quality overlooks the victims of conflict, the latter occludes the causes and consequences of battle. To spell out the significance of this in literary terms: when Emcke's reader, having been told that '[e]verything is clear and yet it is impossible to transform it into an adequate and intelligible narrative'[110] and having therefore despaired at the prospect of apprehending the horror in Albania and Kosovo, subsequently rejoices at his or her ability to grasp it imaginatively, there is a risk that the joyfulness be unattended by any thought of what led to the wars in the first place or of the ramifications for the victims.

These difficulties arising, it is unsurprising that the Kantian sublime has been critiqued in the light of the mass, man-made disasters of the twentieth century (and, given that the crucial factor is not scale but human intervention, there is every reason to extend the critics' arguments to wars of preceding ages). Adorno's commendation of the poetics of Paul Celan – he likely had in mind the dying cadences of 'Die Todesfuge' – praised the emulation of a language 'that lies below the helpless prattle of human beings – even below the level of organic life as such . . . the language of dead matter, of stones and stars'.[111] This is, again, a nondescript language,

---

[108] Gene Ray, *Terror and the Sublime in Art and Critical Theory: From Auschwitz to Hiroshima to September 11* (Basingstoke and New York: Palgrave Macmillan, 2005), 5.

[109] Kant, *Critique*, 152.   [110] Emcke, *Echoes of Violence*, 3.

[111] Theodor Adorno, *Aesthetic Theory*, trans. C. Lenhardt, ed. Gretel Adorno and Rolf Tiedemann (London: Routledge & Kegan Paul, 1984), 444.

sublime in its indirection but tending towards a louring of the spirits rather than towards delight. To such literary (self-)chastening, Adorno added the requisite that apprehending the disaster be accompanied not only by thought, but by self-critical thought:

> If negative dialectics calls for the self-regulation of thinking, the tangible implication is that if thinking is to be true – if it is to be true today, in any case – it must also be a thinking against itself. If thought is not measured by the extremity that eludes the concept, it is from the outset in the nature of the musical accompaniment with which the SS liked to drown out the screams of its victims.[112]

What Adorno located as 'after Auschwitz' is the possibility that haunts all war writing: that the freedom permitted to the imagination by the sublime is unaccompanied by reflective responsibility.

But what might neutralise this risk? If a kind of socialist realism in war representation appears to be called for, it is quickly dismissed by the thought that realism, whether socialist or not, is, as has been demonstrated throughout this book, extremely problematic as a representational response to conflict. Difficulties also inhere in Adorno's demand for 'thought against thought': what has happened is unthinkable and, as Lyotard pointed out, thought is itself anyway in ruins:

> Adorno's thought knows . . . that metaphysics, and even the critique that tries to overcome it by revealing the lure that polarizes it (to represent what one cannot represent) – that even the Kantian, Marxian, Frankfurtian critique of metaphysics as thought and as reality fails to find the 'reason' for the disaster. And this is simply because the critique builds an architectonics of reasons, but it is impossible to build anything whatsoever from or on this debris.[113]

What is left is a logical impasse or, rather, a number of impasses. Simply put, the sublime (incarnated in the various diversionary tactics explored in this chapter) drives out reason. This is unacceptable in the face of war: reason must be reintroduced. But the very subject is beyond reason. Hence those who would convey war are driven back to sublime or indirect representations and the whole circular argument starts again. Indeed, the task of the war writer resembles that of Sisyphus (a figure who will be encountered in the next chapter), forced constantly to roll the representational boulder uphill, watch it fall and descend to retrieve it again.

The sublime of the humanly wrought disaster – the sublime of war – is not a matter, finally, of delight, but of despair. It is therefore the negative of Kant's sublime or, rather, to Kant's two-stage dismay-joy it adds a third stage

---

[112] Adorno, *Negative Dialectics*, 365.   [113] Lyotard, *Heidegger and 'the jews'*, 43.

that is a return to dismay. At this point, this tertiary stage of despair must remain somewhat nebulous: all that is known is that it incorporates both the dismay that arises when the causes and consequences of war are thought through and the dismay induced by the realisation of the limitations of any such through-thinking. In the next chapter, a phenomenon is discussed which further illuminates this complicated tertiary stage. Ray notes that the word into which Adorno 'chose to condense the ruination of the Kantian sublime in the face of contemporary history' was *Erschütterung*: 'the tremor or shudder of what is beyond imagination and conventionalized experience – the shock waves of traumatic experience'.[114] Adorno himself expounded the concept as follows:

Erschütterung, starkly opposed to the normal conception of experience [*Erlebnisbegriff*], is no particular satisfaction for the ego, which, shaken to the core [*als erschüttertes*], becomes aware of its own limitedness and finitude.[115]

Ray notes the aptness of the word in the context of the Lisbon earthquake of 1755, which Kant refers to in the *Critique of the Power of Judgment*.[116] *Erschütterung* has etymological affinities with injury and adversity (*der Schaden*), as well as tremoring, trembling, shuddering and shaking. The last of these might refer, in addition to earthquakes, to another phenomenon: a kind of bodily quaking, a physical upheaval.[117] This phenomenon is also referred to by Kant in *Critique of the Power of Judgment*, in his analysis of the incongruous.[118] It is a phenomenon that, despite initial appearances, marks the ego's awareness, not only of its own limitedness, but of the finitude of human reason. As the next and final chapter argues, the literary representation of war has the potential to induce what lies beyond the unleashing of aesthetic judgement: mirthless, senseless, side-splitting laughter.

---

[114] Ray, 'Reading the Lisbon Earthquake', 13.
[115] Adorno, *Aesthetic Theory*, 245: translation from Ray, 'Reading the Lisbon Earthquake', 13.
[116] *Ibid.*, 10.
[117] Samuel Weber draws attention to Freud's use of the word *überrumpelt* in 'Wit and Its Relation to the Unconscious' (1905) to characterise what happens to the attention of someone listening to a joke just before he or she breaks into laughter: '*rumpeln* signifies, onomatopoeically, a rumbling, rattling noise' (Samuel Weber, 'Laughing in the Meanwhile', *MLN* 102.4 (September 1987), 702).
[118] Kant, *Critique*, 209f.

CHAPTER 6

Laughter

In Trevor Griffiths's play *Comedians* (1975), Eddie Waters, an ageing stand-up comedian, recalls visiting a Nazi death camp. Waters, who toured Germany with the Entertainments National Service Association a year or two after the Second World War, relates that, at the end of the day in which the entertainers visited the camp, he was in the audience as a fellow-comedian told 'this joke about a Jew' and notes that 'people laughed, not inordinately, just... easily... And I sat there. And I didn't laugh.'[1] The twin realisations come to Waters that some places are or should be unvisited by laughter and that laughter itself can be lethal: 'I discovered... there were no jokes left. Every joke was a little pellet, a... final solution.'[2]

Waters's failure to join in the laughter expresses an intuitive understanding of the ethics of humour. Laughter, as Philip Glenn points out, is indexical: 'it is heard as referring to something and hearers will seek out its referent'.[3] But seeking laughter's referent – 'the laughable'[4] – in the war zone uncovers death on a mass scale, appalling injury, incalculable loss. Now, laughter and its causes are culturally specific[5] and its appropriateness, as has been widely discussed, varies according to such factors as historical moment, subject,[6] social setting, situation[7] and genre.[8] Nonetheless, laughter's universality has also been asserted[9] and, whatever the cultural and historical variables, it is hard to imagine finding war's potential 'laughable'

---

[1] Trevor Griffiths, *Comedians* (London: Faber, 1979), 64.   [2] *Ibid.*, 64.
[3] Philip Glenn, *Laughter in Interaction* (Cambridge: Cambridge University Press, 2003), 48.
[4] *Ibid.*, 49.
[5] See R. D. V. Glasgow, *Madness, Masks, and Laughter: An Essay on Comedy* (London and Toronto: Associated University Presses, 1995), 15.
[6] See Steve Lipman, *Laughter in Hell: The Use of Humor During the Holocaust* (Northvale and London: Jason Aronson, 1993), 7.
[7] Cf. Shakespeare's 'Why dost thou laugh? It fits not with this hour' (*Titus Andronicus* 3.1.1406).
[8] See, for example, Bakhtin, *Rabelais and His World*, 66, 67; Nicholas Brooke, *Horrid Laughter in Jacobean Tragedy* (London: Open Books, 1979).
[9] See Glenn, *Laughter in Interaction*, 13; Jerry Palmer, *Taking Humour Seriously* (London: Routledge, 1994), 58.

anything other than very unamusing indeed. Prima facie, war is agelastic. 'Outside the hospital there was still nothing funny going on', writes Joseph Heller early in *Catch-22*:

The only thing going on was a war . . . strangers he [Yossarian] didn't know shot at him with cannons every time he flew up in the air to drop bombs on them, and it wasn't funny at all. And if that wasn't funny, there were lots of things that weren't even funnier.[10]

Conflict is a matter of deadly seriousness, a fact which has prompted representation in the same vein: plainspoken realism; sombreness of tone; conservatism of style and structure – all these adding up to a decorum of war writing. Humour has been noted for its 'apparent unsuitability as a discourse as a basis for practical action',[11] an unsuitability particularly devastating in conflict, where swift and effective responses are a requisite. References to laughter in the war zone strike a jarring note. When Dorothy Mackay opens her Second World War memoir *Laughter in Khaki* (1987) with the statement 'I had a most amusing and interesting six years of war. This may sound callous, but would any of us have survived mentally if we had not had a lot of laughs?',[12] it may sound not only callous, but inhuman, puerile and even in bad taste. Humour, as Jerry Palmer points out, 'must not only be *recognised* as such, but also *permitted*'.[13] The jolly japes which make up Mackay's war reminiscences are beyond a joke.

But, as Waters discovers, people do laugh in and about war.[14] They even laugh at genocide. 'Some things aren't funny', wrote Kurt Vonnegut, 'I can't imagine a humorous book or skit about Auschwitz, for instance.'[15] Terrence Des Pres, debating this in a 1988 essay titled 'Holocaust Laughter', concluded:

Most of us would agree that humor heals. Even so, can laughter be restorative in a case as extreme as the Holocaust? That something so light should alleviate the burden of something so gigantic might, on the face of it, be a joke in itself. But then, humor counts most in precisely those situations where more decisive remedies fail.[16]

---

[10] Heller, *Catch-22*, 25–6.

[11] Michael Mulkay, *On Humour: Its Nature and Its Place in Modern Society* (Cambridge: Polity Press, 1988), 218.

[12] Dorothy Mackay, *Laughter in Khaki* (Edinburgh: Pentland Press, 1987), 1.

[13] Palmer, *Taking Humour Seriously*, 12 (emphasis original).

[14] The military is an established humorous category, as evidenced by the *Reader's Digest* long-standing column 'Humour in Uniform' and the popularity of television programmes such as *Hogan's Heroes* (CBS, 1965–71), *M*A*S*H* (CBS, 1972–83), *Dad's Army* (BBC, 1968–77) and *Blackadder Goes Forth* (BBC, 1989).

[15] Kurt Vonnegut, *A Man Without A Country*, ed. Daniel Simon (London: Bloomsbury, 2006), 2–3.

[16] Terrence Des Pres, 'Holocaust Laughter?', in *Writing and the Holocaust*, ed. Lang, 217–18.

Des Pres here specifically links laughter with humour and relief but, arguably, other kinds of laughter might also be fitting, even with regards to an unthinkable event like the Holocaust.[17] Two separate points should be made. The first is that laughter is not necessarily incompatible with high seriousness and in some historical periods has been its natural accompaniment.[18] The second is that, although laughter in and about conflict is often associated with humour, this is not always the case.

Indeed, the audience's reaction to the joke about the Jew which Waters observes may be explained by a multitude of gelastic theories: in addition to an appreciation of the funny, the audience's laughter might be expressing superiority,[19] relief,[20] a recognition of incongruity,[21] hostility and aggression, embarrassment, pleasure, anxiety, murderous violence ('pellets' will appear again, in the form of Zyklon-B), subversion, camaraderie, sympathy, moral seriousness, sentimentality, absent-mindedness or radical criticism.[22] The joke might have constituted an attempt at persuasion or social control, functioned as a form of therapy[23] or played a phatic role.[24] None of these, it should be noted, has induced Waters to laugh. But Waters also mentions another kind of laughter, in another place. It is the laughter – or almost laughter – that he is moved to in the death camp itself:

They'd cleaned it up, it was like a museum, each room with its separate, special collection. In one of 'em . . . the showers . . . there was a box of cyanide pellets on the table. 'Ciankali' the label said, just that. A block away, the incinerators, with a big proud maker's label moulded on its middle, someone in Hamburg . . . And then this extraordinary thing. (*Longish pause.*) In this hell-place, a special block, 'Der Straf-bloc', 'Punishment Block'. It took a minute to register, I almost laughed, it seemed so ludicrous.[25]

[17] See Lipman, *Laughter in Hell* and Alan Dundes and Thomas Hauschild, 'Auschwitz Jokes', *Western Folklore* 42.4 (October 1983), 249–60.

[18] See Palmer, *Taking Humour Seriously*, 131.

[19] See Thomas Hobbes, *Leviathan*, ed. Richard Tuck (Cambridge: Cambridge University Press, 1991), 43.

[20] See Sigmund Freud, *Wit and Its Relation to the Unconscious*, trans. A. A. Brill. (London: Kegan Paul, Trench, Trübner, 1922), 180f.

[21] See Kant, *Critique*, 208–10; Arthur Schopenhauer, *The World as Will and Idea*, trans. R. B. Haldane and J. Kemp, 3rd edn, 3 vols. (London: Kegan Paul, Trench, Trübner, 1891), vol. I, 76f.

[22] See Manfred Pfister, 'Beckett, Barker, and Other Grim Laughers', in *A History of English Laughter from Beowulf to Beckett and Beyond*, ed. Manfred Pfister (Amsterdam and New York: Rodopi, 2005), 19, 186.

[23] See Dundes and Hauschild, 'Auschwitz Jokes'. This is a form of therapy which Rosaline orders Berowne to carry out on 'the speechless sick' at the end of *Love's Labour's Lost*. Berowne is dubious: 'To move wild laughter in the throat of death? / It cannot be; it is impossible; / Mirth cannot move a soul in agony' (5.2.843–5).

[24] Robert R. Provine, *Laughter: A Scientific Investigation* (London: Faber, 2000), 47.

[25] Griffiths, *Comedians*, 64.

What is distinctive about this (almost) laughter? The same theories – bloodlust (Waters confesses that the camp also gave him an erection – 'Something ... (*He touches his stomach.*) ... loved it too'),[26] Hobbes's 'sudden glory',[27] Kantian/Schopenhauerian incongruity and Freudian relief – may all play a part in it. But Waters diagnoses his urge to laugh more acutely: 'Then I saw it. It was a world like any other. It was the logic of our world ... extended.'[28] His almost laughter is a response to the 'extended' logic of conflict, the hyperlogic or hypologic that posits that the notion of punishment can exist in a death camp.

To couch the phenomenon in terms of representative challenge and literary responses, this species of laughter – depicted in and evoked by war writing – is the riposte to the impression that war makes no sense. This impression may be made both on a macro level (for example, when waging a particular war for particular ends seems to have no good political or military argument to support it) and on a micro level (for example, when commands are opaque, ammunition does not function, blunders are routinely made – all instances of 'chickenshit', as Paul Fussell reminds his readers).[29] To be clear: this chapter does not make the claim that no war ever makes sense, nor that military running of wars is always stupid. Rather, the argument is that the perceived senselessness of armed conflict (though it may derive from a number of sources, including the unfamiliar effects of scale, space and time already encountered) is primarily a result of the vast disparity between the military endeavour and the individual caught up in it. A metaphor for this can be drawn from the physics of fluid turbulence. The overall motion of a turbulent flow may be in one direction, but the flow is not smooth. Some elements of the flow, while part of the overall movement, travel more or less at random in other directions, causing friction. In the same way, the 'flow' of war, as directed by the military authorities, may seem to the individual soldier to be running in opposition to what makes sense; actions undertaken by the individual may seem to have little to do with any larger purpose; indeed, they may appear to be utterly random – minor whorls within the great currents carrying them along. Attempting to characterise the situation in *On War*, Clausewitz, in his chapter on friction, also turned to metaphors of fluidity:

---

[26] *Ibid.*, 65. [27] Hobbes, *Leviathan*, 43. [28] Griffiths, *Comedians*, 64.
[29] Paul Fussell, *Wartime: Understanding and Behaviour in the Second World War* (Oxford: Oxford University Press, 1989), 80.

Everything in war is very simple, but the simplest thing is difficult. The difficulties accumulate and end by producing a kind of friction that is inconceivable unless one has experienced war . . . Action in war is like movement in a resistant element. Just as the simplest and most natural of movements, walking, cannot easily be performed in water, so in war it is difficult for normal efforts to achieve even moderate results.[30]

Ultimately, the phenomenon derives from the differential in scale between the prosecution of a war at a strategic level ('Strategy, to be quite frank, you will have no hand in. / It is done by those up above and it merely refers to / The larger movements over which we have no control')[31] and the experiences of the individual at the tactical and sub-tactical level.

The perception of senselessness that this differential produces resembles the *Weltanschauung* of the philosophy and aesthetics of the Absurd, but while the Absurd posits a godless universe, the war zone has something worse. Its god is the war machine – the regimen of rules and requirements that runs apparently regardless of human needs and very often counter to them. The war machine ensures not only that the war zone makes no sense, but that it makes *more* no sense than does nonsense outside the zone. Accordingly, the laughter it finally evokes is not happy in the manner of Camus's Sisyphus accepting his destiny,[32] but mirthless and nihilistic.

It was argued in Chapter 3 that the war zone is a *sui generis* space: that space can now be further defined as one of incongruity or turbulence. The comic also has its own space – that 'nonsensical ontological no-man's-land'[33] in which anything may happen. The intention here is not to conflate the two spaces. The war zone is not governed by comic logic, nor by illogic (although illogicalities frequently occur in it). Rather, it is characterised either by a *failure* or *absence* of logic (hypologic) or by an *excess* of logic (hyperlogic). The turbulence caused by excessive logic is explored below in its portrayal and inducement in Spike Milligan's Second World War memoirs (collected as *Milligan's War* (1988)), Virginia Graham's undated Second World War poem 'It's All Very Well Now' and Joseph Heller's *Catch-22*. But first, turbulence due to the failure or absence of logic is illustrated with reference to the siege cantos (7 and 8, written in 1822) of Byron's *Don Juan* (1819–24): some 220 stanzas awash with images of

---

[30] Carl von Clausewitz, *On War*, trans. Michael Howard and Peter Paret (Princeton: Princeton University Press, 1976), 119–29.

[31] Reed, 'Movement of Bodies' (1950), *Collected Poems*, 52.

[32] Albert Camus, 'Le Mythe de Sisyphe', in *Essais*, ed. Roger Quilliot and Louis Faucon (Paris: Gallimard & Calman-Lévy, 1965), 197, 198.

[33] Glasgow, *Madness, Masks, and Laughter*, 161.

fluidity and flow. Along the way, consideration is given to the affinities between turbulence/incongruity and the carnivalesque, and to the figure of the *gelotopoios* or laughter-maker, as incarnated by Shakespeare's Falstaff, Jaroslav Hašek's Good Soldier Schweik, Heller's Yossarian, Spike Milligan as he appears in his memoirs and Tim O'Brien's Cacciato.

This chapter works towards the conclusion that, in depicting and evoking this ultimate brand of laughter (and depiction is a step towards evocation – the reader is shown how and when to laugh), writing makes a contribution to the representation of war of particular value. Shown others laughing, and joining in the laughter, the reader is, to an unprecedented extent, made to *feel* the experience of conflict. And this sensation is an extension of the sublime.

The 1818 Preface to the first two cantos of Byron's *Don Juan* requires the reader to imagine that the 'epic narrative' is related by a Spanish gentleman in a village on the road between Monasterio and Seville; 'not far off' is 'a knot of French prisoners', foremost among whom are 'a couple of hussars, one of whom has a bandage on his forehead, yet stained with the blood of a sabre cut', and 'a group of black-eyed peasantry . . . dancing to the sound of the flute' and creating 'musical hilarity'.[34] This combined reception of blood and cheer is given a further ingredient as Byron happily admits the 'utter impossibility of such a supposition'.[35] A thematic nexus is established which will inform the siege cantos: bleeding, hilarity, contingency.

Ostensibly, the poem presents the siege of Ottoman-ruled Ismail as a professional, organised affair. The appointment of Suwarrow (Byron's Anglicisation of Suvorov) (7.8.7) – a 'little, odd, old man', '[h]ero, buffoon, half-demon and half-dirt', 'the greatest chief / That ever peopled hell with heroes slain' (7.49.7, 7.55.5, 7.68.2–3) – to take the town 'at whatever price' evokes joy in the Russian troops (7.40.8, 7, 49.1), causing them to throw themselves into their preparations with new enthusiasm. Suwarrow even finds time to drill his men:

> Also he dressed up, for the nonce, fascines
> Like men with turbans, scimitars and dirks,
> And made them charge with bayonet these machines
> By way of lesson against actual Turks.   (7.53.1–4)

Suwarrow's charisma is irresistible, causing men to follow him '[a]s roll the waters to the breathing wind' (7.48.3). War itself is conveyed as a tremendous fluid force, sweeping up and carrying along the individual

---

[34] *Don Juan*, 38, 39.   [35] *Ibid.*, 39.

fighter in a 'sea of slaughter', an 'unebbing sea' of 'blood and tears', 'seas of gore'.[36] Early in canto 8, the Russian forces are characterised as a 'human Hydra' or sea-serpent; they liquefy, turning into an 'armed river', 'furious as the sweeping wave' (8.2.5, 7.86.5, 8.106.5). The elements merge into each other: 'one vast fire, air, earth and stream embraced . . . City, stream, and shore / Resounded "Allah!"' (8.7.5, 8.8.4–5) and the flame of the artillery across the sky is 'mirrored' and repeated in the water of the Danube. Canto 8, stanza 12 reports:

> Three hundred cannon threw up their emetic,
> And thirty thousand muskets flung their pills
> Like hail to make a bloody diuretic.   (8.12.1–3)

While the cannon induce vomiting and the muskets urinating, it also appears that the former *are* vomiting ('threw up') and the latter *are* urinating (the hail of pills itself is like urine). Elsewhere, the gun-fire is likened to 'lava' and rain: it 'poured as if all hell were raining'; it 'rained from bastion, battery, parapet' (8.16.3, 8.20.6, 8.37.2).

The fluid imagery figures the mighty force of warfare. But it is also apt to characterise the casualties of the torrent. The flow is impeded, congeals. Men sink and wallow in the 'bloody mire', the 'marsh of human blood' (8.20.1, 8.73.8). Their bodies and bodily effluents add to the volume and viscosity of the liquid ('[w]hose blood the puddle greatly did enrich' (8.71.3)). In one striking image, the defending Turks (who also have ships) are driven 'back into the water / Pell-mell' (7.31.7–8). In its military usage, the adverb has the sense of 'mêlée', which is etymologically related both to mixture and to conflict, quarrel or battle. This mélange of warring bodies is added to the water, creating, as it were, a kind of soup (Juan himself is described as 'a broth of a boy' (8.24.1) – the boiled-down essence of what a young man should be). But 'pell-mell' (also used in 8.109.4) also invokes Pall Mall (mentioned in 8.26.8), the street in London where the game pall-mall was played and the centre of the gambling clubs or 'hells'.[37] In this image, therefore, Byron associates a clogged flow with the vagaries of luck.

---

[36] *Ibid.*, 7.50.7, 8.122.8, 7.68.8, 8.3.8. There is not space to comment on all the references to fluidity and related matters in the siege cantos. In addition to those mentioned in the text, such references occur in 7.11.3, 7.80.7, 7.85.4–5, 7.87.8, 8.8.4, 8.24.3, 8.32.5, 8.82.7, 8.87.3.

[37] See *ibid.*, 8.26.7. For analysis of images of risk and financial calculation, gaming and hazard, auctioneering and sport in the siege cantos, see Jane Stabler, *Byron, Poetics and History* (Cambridge: Cambridge University Press, 2002), ch. 4.

Though drilling and other preparations have been carried out, it becomes clear that the individual soldier's experience of the siege is not of a carefully planned, professionally executed military exercise. Suwarrow might inspire men to follow him as the wind draws the waves, but his leadership is elsewhere likened to the treacherous lure of a will-o'-the-wisp:

> [L]ike a wisp along the marsh so damp,
> Which leads beholders on a boggy walk,
> He flitted to and fro a dancing light,
> Which all who saw it followed, wrong or right.
>
> (7.46.5–8)

The image is repeated in the next canto when, '[p]erceiving nor commander nor commanded / And left at large like a young heir to make / His way to – where he knew not – singlehanded', Juan is reduced to rushing to where the gun-fire is thickest, '[a]s travellers follow over bog and brake / An *ignis fatuus*' (8.32.4–5). Vainly attempting to follow a gaseous leader with a tendency to evaporate over damp, marshy, boggy ground, Juan literally loses his way in battle. Neither method nor logic are discernible in the fighting: Juan and Johnson fight 'not knowing / The way, which they had never trod before, / And still less guessing where they might be going' (8.19.2–4). Their situation is not helped by flaws in the Russians' planning and preparation. The batteries are a botched job, either 'because they were constructed in a hurry' or because of 'their engineer's stupidity / Their haste or waste' or because of 'some contractor's personal cupidity, / Saving his soul by cheating in the ware / Of homicide' (7.26.2, 7.27.1–2, 3–5). A 'sad miscalculation about distance' results in the fireships blowing up, mid-river, before they can be of assistance (7.28.1). The Cossack column 'blunder[s]' when trying to assail the city rampart (8.75.5). General Meknop falls because he has been 'badly seconded' (8.79.3). When things do go right, it is more the outcome of chance than of military foresight. The besieging forces can penetrate the city only because '[t]he Greek or Turkish Cohorn's ignorance / Had palisadoed in a way you'd wonder / To see in forts of Netherlands or France' (8.46.3–5). Were it not for the fortuitous arrival of 'stray troops', Koutousow 'might have lain / Where three parts of his column yet remain' (8.72.1, 7–8).

This is a realm of hypologic. Literally 'carried by the stream / To some spot where they lost their understanding', single soldiers are lost in the inexorable flow of the fighting (8.72.2–3). So much flotsam, Juan finds himself detached from his corps, stranded like a sailor, momentarily halted and leaderless (8.27, 8.32, 8.29, 8.31–3). It becomes apparent that the exigencies of the military endeavour are inimical to the individual ordinary soldier's needs and, indeed, chances of survival. This is made explicit in the description of Suwarrow's priorities:

> Suwarrow, who but saw things in the gross
> Being much too gross to see them in detail,
> Who calculated life as so much dross
> [. . .]
> And cared as little for his army's loss
> (So that their efforts should at length prevail)
> As wife and friends did for the boils of Job.
>
> (7.77.1–3, 5–7)

For Byron, the individual's fate in battle is the outcome of military ineptitude and blind chance ('[w]hat sages call chance, providence, or fate' (7.76.4)). 'You ask me for the plan of Donny Johnny', he wrote to his publisher, John Murray, on 12 August 1819: 'I *have* no plan – I *had* no plan.'[38] The poem's lack of planned direction matches what Jerome McGann calls the 'ad hoc' quality of its author's life, his 'covetousness for the unplanned and the circumstantial'.[39] Cantos 7 and 8 must be read as part of this outlook: Byron's conviction, expressed in a letter to Lady Blessington, 'that we are all creatures of circumstance', that 'the greater part of our errors are caused, if not excused, by events and situations over which we have had little control',[40] was not reserved for war. But incongruity – the discrepancy between the individual's lot and the large-scale unfolding of 'events and situations' – is particularly marked in the siege cantos. 'In a world where human resources are subject to such extreme limitations, both internal and external,' writes McGann, 'Byron proposes no quick solutions. Indeed, he insists that any systematic attempt to "make sense" of reality must be resisted.'[41]

'Sense-making' self-proscribed, Byron expresses in the siege cantos a *Weltanschauung* in many ways anticipative of Snowden's 'man is matter' secret in *Catch-22*. Canto 5, stanza 32 of *Don Juan* prepares the way for this:

---

[38] Byron, *The Works of Lord Byron: Letters and Journals*, ed. Rowland E. Prothero, 6 vols. (London: John Murray, 1898–1901), vol. IV, 342–3.

[39] Jerome J. McGann, *Don Juan in Context* (London: John Murray, 1976), 8.

[40] Ernest J. Lovell, Jr, ed., *Lady Blessington's Conversations of Lord Byron* (Princeton: Princeton University Press, 1969), 172.

[41] McGann, *Don Juan in Context*, 138.

> I think with Alexander that the act
> Of eating, with another act or two,
> Makes us feel our mortality in fact
> Redoubled. When a roast and a ragout,
> And fish, and soup, by some side dishes backed,
> Can give us either pain or pleasure, who
> Would pique himself on intellects, whose use
> Depends so much upon the gastric juice?
>
> (5.32.1–8)

Having subjugated the intellect to the fluid workings of the stomach, seven stanzas later Byron again speculates about the easy reduction of the body (and mind) to its elements, imagining blood that is formed not to flow but to fall:[42]

> Five bits of lead,
> Or three or two or one send very far!
> And is this blood then formed but to be shed?
> Can every element our elements mar?
> And air – earth – water – fire live – and we dead?
> We, whose minds comprehend all things?
>
> (5.39.2–7)

In the siege cantos, this outlook emerges in what McGann calls 'a pragmatic and functional attitude toward human affairs',[43] an attitude which posits a world ruled by chance rather than God, in which events are beyond individual understanding or control and man is no more than the contents of his stomach. And the proper response to 'the nothingness of life' is, Byron suggests, 'melancholy merriment' or laughter: 'I hope it is no crime / To laugh at all things, for I wish to know / What after all are all things – but a show?' (7.6.8, 8.89.5, 7.2.6–8).

The mock-heroic sentiment recalls the carnivalesque. Given the prima facie affinities of its world-view with that of the Absurd, it is worth pausing again to consider the possible functioning of the carnivalesque in the war zone.[44] Bakhtin has called laughter 'the basis of carnival',[45] thereby implicating it in all that that involves: licentious behaviour; the reversal of the normal social order; lustfulness and aggression; fertility, procreation,

---

[42] Cf. the 'whole mottled quarts of Snowden' that the flak draws out (Heller, 554).

[43] McGann, *Don Juan in Context*, 139.

[44] For further discussion of the carnivalesque potential of bodies and body parts and their roles as synecdoches, see Chapter 2.

[45] Bakhtin, *Rabelais and His World*, 8.

growth and abundance; grotesquerie and degradation; food and festivity; and the (gross and porous) body. In addition to accompanying carnival, laughter announces it, functioning as a licence or, in R. D. V. Glasgow's striking phrase, 'toothy metasignal', that inaugurates a 'play-context' in which 'actions do not signal what they would usually signal'.[46] War and the literature of war are filled with instances of horseplay and slapstick, role reversals, irreverent treatment of bodies and body parts,[47] practical jokes, ribaldry and uproar. Falstaff's 'pistol', for example, turns out to be a bottle of sack:

> FALSTAFF: There's that will sack a city.
> PRINCE: What, is it a time to jest and dally now?[48]

– a moment of pure carnival that unites death, urbicide, frivolity, drunkenness and excessive consumption. In *Catch-22*, after a Thanksgiving marked by 'wild, exultant shouts', 'people who were merry or sick', 'the recurring sound of retching and moaning, of laughter, greetings, threats and swearing' and 'dirty songs', Yossarian is the victim of a practical joke which almost kills him (some members of the company go to the recently installed machine gun emplacements and fire the guns). While Yossarian 'blaze[s] with hatred and wrath', his tormentors emit 'gloating laughter', 'rough laughter', 'taunting laughter', 'jeering laughter'.[49] Again, the essential elements of carnival are present: feasting is riotous and excessive; bodies gorge, vomit and moan; language turns 'dirty'; pranks are played (authority is in abeyance); individual life is held cheap. Above it all, rings the sound of laughter. Towards the end of the novel, revealing the manner of Snowden's death, Heller writes:

Man was matter, that was Snowden's secret. Drop him out of a window and he'll fall. Set fire to him and he'll burn. Bury him and he'll rot, like other kinds of garbage. The spirit gone, man is garbage. That was Snowden's secret. Ripeness was all.[50]

'Ripeness was all': the allusion to *King Lear*[51] invokes Edgar's remark that 'Men must endure / Their going hence, even as their coming hither'.[52] Together with Yossarian's 'Where are the Snowdens of yesteryear?',[53] an explicit reiteration ('*Où sont les Neigedens d'antan?*') of François Villon's

---

[46] Glasgow, *Madness, Masks, and Laughter*, 18; see also Glenn, *Laughter in Interaction*, 27.
[47] Bourke, *An Intimate History of Killing*, 15, 38.   [48] *1 Henry IV* 5.3.51–2.
[49] Heller, *Catch-22*, 456–7.   [50] *Ibid.*, 554.
[51] 5.2.11. There is also a possible echo of Shylock's 'If you prick us, do we not bleed?' speech in *The Merchant of Venice* (3.1.45–62).
[52] *King Lear* 5.2.9–10.   [53] Heller, *Catch-22*, 49.

ubi sunt lament, this creates a localised carnivalesque vision in accordance with the idea of man as matter, or as garbage. The reduction of Snowden to 'liver, lungs, kidneys, ribs, stomach and bits of the stewed tomatoes [he] had eaten that day for lunch'[54] – recalling Byron's prioritisation of the gastric juices over the intellect – is a particularly carnivalesque perception of the body as food and therefore potential waste.

Matter or garbage, the human body's ubiquity and importance in the war zone match its prominence and significance in carnival; Bakhtin identifies laughter and 'the material bodily element' as the 'degrading and regenerating principle' by which carnival is governed.[55] Laughter, carnival and war centre on the body – the body in a cycle of destruction and (if only in playful enactment) resurrection. In slapstick, the body becomes the fallguy of pretend violence. Spike Milligan recounts in his memoirs the antics of the 'Clubbers', a group of soldiers with a like sense of humour who amuse themselves by fashioning 'great gnarled clubs' from fallen branches and giving them names like 'Nurkes Nut Nourisher' and 'Instant Lumps'. The gang runs through the woods hitting trees and shouting 'Death to the Goons'. Ordered to destroy their weapons, they fill a truck on a small-gauge railway used to deliver rubbish to the bottom of a hill, soak them in petrol, set them alight and jump in:

The truck gathered momentum, flames built up, we were gathering speed and singing 'Round and round went the bloody great wheel', when suddenly it occurred to me that there was no method of braking. As we careered towards a mountain of old tins, crying with laughter, I shouted, 'Jump for it'. We all leaped clear, save Edgington, who seemed transfixed. At the very last minute he let out a strangled castrati scream and hurled himself sideways as the blazing truck buried itself into the mountain of tins with an ear splitting crash.[56]

Notable in this episode is the playful violence with the clubs – the nicknames reveal their actual potential to cause harm and pain – and the fact that, facing very real danger, the men cry with laughter, apparently unconcerned about their mortality. The etymology of 'slapstick' reveals that it is feigned violence (two pieces of flat wood clapped together to simulate the noise of slapping, a theatrical device introduced into England towards the end of the seventeenth century):[57] it therefore resembles the carnival tradition of licensed rough but non-lethal play. In this incident, the violence is

[54] *Ibid.*, 554.
[55] Bakhtin, *Rabelais and His World*; see also Glasgow, *Madness, Masks, and Laughter*, 14; Jim Holt, *Stop Me If You've Heard This: A History and Philosophy of Jokes* (London: Profile Books, 2008), 62; Ron Jenkins, *Subversive Laughter: The Liberating Power of Comedy* (New York: The Free Press, 1994), xii.
[56] Milligan, *Milligan's War*, 23.   [57] *OED* 1.

(albeit barely) authorised and is committed against trees. Milligan reveals that the episode performed exactly the same function as the carnivalesque: '[o]ccasions of insanity such as this stopped us all going mad'.[58]

Ultimately, however, the carnivalesque is more sanguine a vision than that available in the war zone; the military regimen permits not even such peace of mind as is offered by the man-is-matter world-view. Though it is tempting to characterise the war zone as the venue of carnival, the characterisation becomes too facile. Rather, as this chapter goes on to argue, though it does not match its outlook exactly, laughter in and about war has greater affinities with the Absurd.

Byron's battle zone is characterised by the *absence* or *failure* of logic that is randomness. But the zone can equally be governed by an *excess* of logic. This is the excessive logic of the military regime which, due to differences in scale between organisational and personal needs, comes to seem to the individual soldier who must bear the consequences of it a ruthless hyperlogic. Consisting of ordinary logic applied without appreciation of the ordinary, hyperlogic has no 'normal comparator' and therefore lacks a sense of its own ludicrousness.[59] Jonathan Shay lists some of the by-products of this hyperlogic: unfair distribution of risk; equipment failure; deconstruction of the familiar and safe; vitiation of the sense of 'what's right'; a sense of spiritual abandonment; friendly fire; fragging; suffering of the wounded; and civilian suffering;[60] to these could be added wrong-headed orders; failure to abort initiatives obviously destined to be fatal failures; and the myriad humiliations of regimental life.[61] Spike Milligan's account of being ordered to lay down a communications line one night while serving in Tunisia illuminates the phenomenon:

> [Sergeant] Dawson told us 'Silence is imperative.' We set off being imperatively silent which couldn't be heard because of the noise of the Bren Carrier. We walked behind with a cable drum that went clinkety-clank. Why? The 'hole' in the cable drum was *square* but the spindle was round. We all spoke in hysterical whispers. God knows why, to communicate we had to shout above the engine. As this

---

[58] Milligan, *Milligan's War*, 24.

[59] See Tzvetan Todorov, 'The Journey and Its Narratives', trans. Alyson Waters, in *Transports: Travel, Pleasure, and Imaginative Geography, 1600–1830*, ed. Chloe Chard and Helen Langdon (New Haven: Yale University Press, 1996), 168; Mark Weeks, 'Beyond a Joke: Nietzsche and the Birth of "Super-Laughter"', *Journal of Nietzsche Studies* 27 (Spring 2004), 2.

[60] Shay, *Achilles in Vietnam*, 12, 18, 35, 37, 75, 124–9.

[61] And the uniform application of military discipline, as in this passage from *Slaughterhouse-Five*: '"I think the climax of the book will be the execution of poor old Edgar Derby," I said. "The irony is *so* great. A whole city gets burned down, and thousands and thousands of people are killed. And then this one American foot soldier is arrested in the ruins for taking a teapot. And he's given a regular trial, and then he's shot by a firing squad"' (Vonnegut, *Slaughterhouse-Five*, 4).

charade went on, we started to giggle, then outright laughter. 'Stop the bloody Bren,' shouted Dawson, himself on the verge of laughter. There was a suppressed silence. Unable to stand it, we all burst out laughing again.

'Stop it at once!' said Dawson through his own laughter. We stopped. 'Now stop it, or I'll kill the bloody lot of you.'[62]

Orders which are logical in the grander military scheme of things (silence is imperative when carrying out a night operation in the vicinity of the enemy) become pointless in the local situation (the Bren Carrier is noisy and must be communicated over; faulty equipment also makes a noise) and attempting to obey them provokes contagious laughter. Though Milligan mentions 'giggling', the heart of this laughter is dark; it is bordering on the 'hysterical'.

More of the bizarre demands faced in wartime are listed in Virginia Graham's poem 'It's All Very Well Now': going to Waterloo station to meet two goats travelling from Camberley to Amberley; drinking port and lemon with a 'Church Army lady from Rye'; taking a vanload of corsets and molasses to 'already hopelessly confused Admirals at Trinity House'.[63] Graham interrogates these eccentric missions by couching their apparent rationales in the language of official propaganda – 'Did I really imagine it would lead us grimly forward to Victory / to share my smoked-salmon sandwiches with the Home Office cat?' – a macaronic of registers that permits the poem's double-edged ending: 'I shall nod my head and say, "Believe me, my children, / in my young days everybody was automatically quite insane".' Effectively exploiting the Clausewitzian distinction between strategy and tactics, Graham's poem illustrates that the point of the former can be quite lost when transferred into practical requirements on the level of the latter. Both Milligan and Graham convey situations in which a large-scale war effort has ceased to be perceptible or comprehensible to the individual adrift in it.

On a greater scale, *Catch-22* uses similar techniques in its completely realised recreation of the *Weltanschauung* of the war zone. By taking it literally at the local level, the novel traces war's relentless hyperlogic to its mad and destructive ends. Here, then, is the dead man in Yossarian's tent

---

[62] Milligan, *Milligan's War*, 68.

[63] Virginia Graham, 'It's All Very Well Now', in *Chaos of the Night*, ed. Reilly, 52. Cf. Aelfrida Tillyard's 'A Letter from Ealing Broadway Station' (1914). Cast as a letter from her brother, E. M. W. Tillyard, the poem creates ironic distance between the individual's duties and the collective war effort in the lines 'Well, if I serve the Belgian nation, / By guarding Ealing Broadway station, / I'll guard it gladly never fear' (Aelfrida Tillyard, 'A Letter from Ealing Broadway Station *(From E. M. W. T.)*', in *Scars Upon My Heart: Women's Poetry and Verse of the First World War*, ed. Catherine Reilly (London: Virago, 1981), 114).

('Yossarian didn't like him, even though he had never seen him'); Milo Minderbinder making a profit by buying eggs for 7¢ apiece and selling them for 5¢; Major Major who 'never sees anyone in his office while he's in his office'; Captain Black's retort to those complaining about the number of loyalty oaths that 'people who were loyal would not mind signing all the loyalty oaths they had to'; the psychiatrist's clinical opinion that Yossarian has 'a morbid aversion to dying. You probably resent the fact that you're at war and might get your head blown off any second';[64] Doc Daneeka being reported (and treated) as dead despite still being alive; Yossarian marching backwards to make sure no one is sneaking up on him from behind; and Corporal Whitcomb's psychological torment of the chaplain.[65] The war zone's world-view is most apparent in those dialogues in which language itself attempts to follow hyperlogic's mad spirals, resulting in utterances like Clevinger's 'I always didn't say you couldn't punish me, sir' and the fat colonel's Kafka-esque 'why would we be questioning you if you weren't guilty?'[66] Then there is Catch-22 itself. This merely specifies 'that a concern for one's own safety in the face of dangers that were real and immediate [is] the process of a rational mind'.[67] Supremely logical and wholly reasonable in general application, Catch-22 is also inexorably lethal and completely intractable to individual human needs.

Or to most human needs. The war zone's extended logic makes certain individuals thrive, even flourish. The function in war and war representation of the *gelotopoios* or laughter-maker[68] is to neutralise the pervading hyperlogic by matching or exceeding it. This figure – from Homer's Thersites[69] to Shakespeare's 'fool and jester' Falstaff[70] to Hašek's Schweik to Heller's Yossarian to Spike Milligan as he appears in his own memoirs to Tim O'Brien's Cacciato – is the (often self-appointed) creator and butt of jokes, described by Robert H. Bell (in the case of Thersites) as 'an avatar of comic energy that disrupts events, complicates issues, eludes closure, and generates inquiry'.[71] As Falstaff declares, '[t]he brain of this foolish-compounded clay, man, is not able to invent anything that intends

---

[64] Cf. Siegfried Sassoon's fictional counterpart laughing with his psychiatrist Rivers over the diagnosis that 'you appear to be suffering from an anti-war complex' (Siegfried Sassoon, *The Complete Memoirs of George Sherston* (London: Faber, 1972), 518).

[65] Heller, *Catch-22*, 33, 294, 139, 148, 384, 431f, 495, 262f.   [66] *Ibid.*, 102, 485.   [67] *Ibid.*, 62.

[68] Stephen Halliwell, *Greek Laughter: A Study of Cultural Psychology from Homer to Early Christianity* (Cambridge: Cambridge University Press, 2008), 75.

[69] *Iliad* 2.212f. See Robert H. Bell, 'Homer's Humor: Laughter in *The Iliad*', *Humanitas* 20.1/2 (2007), 96–116.

[70] *2 Henry IV* 5.5.48. On Falstaff as scapegoat or *pharmakos*, see Glasgow, *Madness, Masks, and Laughter*, 193–8.

[71] Bell, 'Homer's Humor', 106.

to laughter, more than I invent or is invented on me. I am not only witty in myself, but the cause that wit is in other men' (*2 Henry IV* 1.2.8), a formulation that echoes in Spike Milligan's description of himself as 'a morale-booster to the boys, organising dances and concerts, and always trying to keep a happy atmosphere'.[72] As a member of a band, Milligan assumed a quasi-professional role as entertainer and was also the author of innumerable practical jokes (sending a telegram to the War Office about an invasion fleet in the Channel and omitting the word 'Practice'; rising from a catafalque draped in black cloth; transforming a fellow-soldier's army bed into a magnificent four-poster complete with heraldic shield, a prank that leaves their officer 'choking with laughter').[73] Far from being crushed by war's inexorable logic, the *gelotopoios* prospers on, and even embodies, it, evincing an indestructibility best exemplified by the moment when Falstaff, whose dead body has just been mourned over, gets to his feet (*1 Henry IV* 5.4.102, 111) (another Falstaffian moment mirrored by Milligan in rising from the catafalque). And the figure permits a further parallel to be drawn with fluid dynamics: the *gelotopoios* can be likened to a particle introduced to a flow for the purposes of visualisation.

Laughter-makers are distinct from the Plautine *miles gloriosus* (with the exception of Falstaff's boastful account of Gad's Hill in *1 Henry IV* (2.4.151f.)) and also from the profiteer: their avatar is not Milo Minderbinder contracting with the enemy to bomb his own side but Yossarian rowing to Sweden. They are often the holy fools of war,[74] whose innocent folly, keeping pace with the war zone's folly, therefore fails to be destroyed by it. Standing in a comic tradition of such figures, which takes in Don Quixote, Tristram Shandy, Prince Myshkin, the Fat Boy and Sam Weller from *The Pickwick Papers* and Wodehouse's Bertie Wooster,[75] is Jaroslav Hašek's Good Soldier Schweik.[76] Schweik is ingenuous and literal-minded, variously described (and self-confirmed) as 'a congenital idiot', 'daft', 'barmy', 'radiating unconcern and innocence'; possessing 'simplicity and [an] honest countenance', 'good-natured, guileless... tenderness and complacency', 'gentleness'.[77] In the Czech Army during the First World

---

[72] Milligan, *Milligan's War*, 251.   [73] *Ibid.*, 29, 197, 322–3.

[74] On Falstaff as holy fool, see Roy Battenhouse, 'Falstaff as Parodist and Perhaps Holy Fool', *PMLA* 90.1 (January 1975), 32–52.

[75] J. P. Stern, 'War and the Comic Muse: *The Good Soldier Schweik* and *Catch-22*', *Comparative Literature* 20.3 (Summer 1968), 198–202.

[76] Byron's Don Juan does not belong in this list as he must contend with hypologic, rather than hyperlogic, in the battle zone.

[77] Jaroslav Hašek, *The Good Soldier Schweik*, trans. Paul Selver (Harmondsworth: Penguin, 1951), 213, 263, 296, 99, 117, 194, 213.

War (as would be the case in other armies in other wars), this mixture of honesty[78] and idiocy is a force of attrition, particularly to Lieutenant Lukash who, fate has determined (the chaplain Katz lost Schweik to Lukash in a game of cards), must suffer Schweik as his orderly. Like Falstaff and Milligan, Schweik is indestructible. Apparently shaken off, he always reappears, repeatedly sent back to Lukash by others who experience the painful results of his accident-provoking ingenuousness. A figure from folklore, the emanation of the people and as irresistible as the cycles of nature, Schweik is next-to-last seen leaving to walk by the stream where the forget-me-nots grow.[79] Rendered in turn furious, indifferent ('At the front, if the worst came to the worst, he would be killed and thus get away from this appalling world in which such monstrosities as Schweik were knocking about') and sadistic by his orderly's exploits, Lukash, the butt of Schweik's existence, is finally reduced to laughter: 'a kind of hysterical laughter which had an infectious influence'.[80]

Schweik's true heir is not Yossarian, whose literal-mindedness lacks vital innocence, nor Milligan, who is daft but not stupid, but the eponym of Tim O'Brien's *Going After Cacciato*. Cacciato's goodness and idiocy are underlined as Schweik's are: 'dumb as a bullet', 'dumb as a month-old oyster fart', 'dumb-dumb', 'a case of gross stupidity'.[81] On most of the occasions when he is observed, he is smiling. Cacciato's desertion draws the narrator, Paul Berlin, and others into a pursuit that, after a booby-trapped bomb is set off, rapidly turns fantastic, even featuring an Alice-down-the-rabbit-hole fall. In *Le Rire* (1899), Henri Bergson describes comic absurdity as 'of the same nature as that of dreams'[82] but, while O'Brien's characters' fugue certainly has an hallucinatory, dreamlike quality, its logic merely takes that of the normal world to its natural conclusions – in this case, to Paris. J. P. Stern argues that, in Hašek's case, the aim is to show that it is 'the outside world that becomes nonsensical, and it is the unexplored integrity of the hero that grows in assurance and strength'; further, that both *The Good Soldier Schweik* and *Catch-22* exhibit 'a peculiar logic which is at once a joke *and* an illumination of the logic of "ordinary"

---

[78] As J. P. Stern points out, Bertold Brecht failed to appreciate fully this aspect of Schweik ('War and the Comic Muse', 200): unlike Brecht's Schweyk, in *Schweyk in the Second World War* (1941–3), Hašek's Schweik would never be so politically aware (or suicidal) as to shout 'Hurrah for Beneš' in front of a sleeping SS man (trans. William Rowlinson, ed. John Willett and Ralph Manheim (London: Eyre Methuen, 1976), 76).

[79] Hašek, *The Good Soldier Schweik*, 442–3.   [80] *Ibid.*, 208, 322.

[81] O'Brien, *Going After Cacciato*, 10, 15.

[82] Henri Bergson, *Laughter: An Essay on the Meaning of the Comic*, trans. Cloudesley Brereton and Fred Rothwell (London: Macmillan, 1935), 186.

life'.[83] This can be refined: the hyperlogic of the war zone is the logic of ordinary life applied on a scale beyond the ordinary; the protagonists of *Schweik*, *Catch-22* and *Going After Cacciato* do not so much 'parry the assault of the military machine'[84] as match its literal-mindedness[85] (just as, in fluid dynamics, particles introduced to make visible the flow are passive, of the same density as the fluid). The machine will not be defeated, but neither will Schweik nor Cacciato.

The more vulnerable are crippled and crushed. For many of the psychiatrist Jonathan Shay's patients – Vietnam veterans with post-traumatic stress disorder – the military regime (in their parlance, REMF or rear-echelon motherfuckers) resembled a god: 'heartless, crooked, shallow, self-indulgent'.[86] Those trying to find relevance in the hyperlogic of the war zone for their own personal circumstances look for a central intelligence, so attempting a theology. Theodiceans are in short supply. In *Schweik*, Hašek writes:

The shambles of the World War would have been incomplete without the blessings of the clergy. The chaplains of all armies prayed and celebrated mass for the victory of the side whose bread they ate . . . Throughout Europe, men went to the shambles like cattle, whither they were driven by butchers, who included not only emperors, kings and other potentates, but also priests of all denominations.[87]

Yossarian's chaplain believes 'in the wisdom and justice of an immortal, omnipotent, omniscient, humane, universal, anthropomorphic, English-speaking, Anglo-Saxon, pro-American God', but his belief has 'begun to waver'.[88] Yossarian, walking through war-torn Rome, thinks he knows 'how Christ must have felt as he walked through the world, like a psychiatrist through a ward full of nuts, like a victim through a prison full of thieves'.[89] But no Christ has visited the world of *Catch-22*.

Insofar as it is godless, the war zone resembles the universe of the Absurd,[90] described by Albert Camus in 'The Myth of Sisyphus' (1942) as an inexplicable world without illusions or illuminations where humans feel themselves to be strangers and death is inevitable.[91] For Camus's Absurd hero, Sisyphus, the gods have decreed that there is no punishment more

---

[83] Stern, 'War and the Comic Muse', 202, 204. Cf. James Dawes's remark that '[o]rganizational rigidity in *Catch-22* is exaggerated to an absurd degree' (*The Language of War*, 178).

[84] Stern, 'War and the Comic Muse', 205.

[85] Stern also suggests this in his account of 'the peculiar logic of the self-contained activity' (*ibid.*, 209).

[86] Shay, *Achilles in Vietnam*, 154.   [87] Hašek, *The Good Soldier Schweik*, 123.

[88] Heller, *Catch-22*, 362.   [89] *Ibid.*, 523.

[90] See Martin Esslin, *The Theatre of the Absurd* (London: Eyre & Spottiswoode, 1962), 14; Halliwell, *Greek Laughter*, 334.

[91] Camus, 'Le Mythe de Sisyphe', 101, 109.

terrible than work without usefulness and without hope – a definition of work, it might be said, within which a great many of the activities performed in the war zone would fall. Camus's interest is in Sisyphus' descent to pick up his rock when it has fallen, as it will, yet again: his step is heavy but equal to the torment whose end he does not know. But this moment of descent is the moment when Sisyphus is stronger than his rock: knowing his destiny he is happy and his pronouncement 'all is well' 'chases from the world a god who had entered it with dissatisfaction and a taste for pointless suffering': 'All Sisyphus' silent joy is there. His destiny belongs to him. His rock is his.'[92] Absurdist laughter (and this has affinities with Zarathustra's laughing acceptance of 'eternal recurrence even for the smallest')[93] marks this knowledge.

But what is true for Camus's Sisyphus is not true for the inhabitant of the war zone, who is denied even the existential comfort of a godless, random universe. For the war zone does have a god and it is the hyperlogic-generating war machine.[94] The war machine is the military system of rules and regulations designed to make function a complex phenomenon and incapable of attending to that phenomenon's individual complexities: it is therefore seemingly independent of human creation, antithetical to human needs, literal-minded, endlessly repetitive and insane. Intended to facilitate strategy and tactics, it very often increases the risk of danger, injury and death and indulges in 'hellish merriment' at what it has wrought.[95] Its voice is heard in passages such as the following from *Catch-22*, in which the repetition of a word or phrase becomes increasingly unbearable:

Yossarian was in the hospital with a pain in his liver that fell just short of being jaundice. The doctors were puzzled by the fact that it wasn't quite jaundice. If it became jaundice they could treat it. If it didn't become jaundice and went away they could discharge him. But this being short of jaundice all the time confused them.[96]

Faced with this on the first page of the novel, the reader is taken aback by the intensity and insistence of the world he or she is about to enter.

---

[92] *Ibid.*, 196–7.

[93] Friedrich Nietzsche, *Thus Spoke Zarathustra* (Harmondsworth: Penguin, 1969), 236. See John Lippitt, 'Nietzsche, Zarathustra and the Status of Laughter', *British Journal of Aesthetics* 32.1 (January 1992), 39–49.

[94] Reference to the 'war machine' inevitably recalls Deleuze and Guattari's use of the same term. While the war machine posited here shares the self-governance and some of the nomadic qualities of Deleuze and Guattari's concept, it is not, like theirs, necessarily exterior to the state, and the two should not be assumed to be coincident. See *A Thousand Plateaus*, esp. 391, 397, 398, 419.

[95] Herbert Read, 'My Company' (1915), *Collected Poems* (London: Sinclair-Stevenson, 1966), 40.

[96] Heller, *Catch-22*, 13.

The repetitions – or substitutions – accumulate. The idea that one person can replace another (substitution) is essentially the idea that one person can *repeat* another: the reduction of human beings to cannon fodder is its ultimate application. *Catch-22* pursues this inhuman idea in the form letters sent to families ('*Dear Mrs., Mr., Miss, or Mr. and Mrs. Daneeka: Words cannot express the deep personal grief I experienced when your husband, son, father or brother was killed, wounded or reported missing in action*'); in the doctor's comment that 'one dying boy is just as good as any other'; in Yossarian taking the place of the dying Italian-American soldier; and in the recurring figure of the soldier in white.[97] The soldier in white is 'constructed entirely of gauze, plaster and a thermometer, and the thermometer was merely an adornment left balanced in the empty dark hole in the bandages over his mouth'.[98] His fellow-patients in the field hospital, not unreasonably, wonder whether 'he's even in there... whoever's supposed to be in all those bandages'.[99] Blackly humorous, the soldier in white demonstrates the human interchangeability imposed by the war zone, by reappearing after the 'original' has been taken away:

'It's the same one!' Dunbar shouted at him emphatically in a voice rising clearly above the raucous commotion. 'Don't you understand? It's the same one!'

[...]

It was, indeed, the same man. He had lost a few inches and added some weight, but Yossarian remembered him instantly by the two stiff arms and the two stiff, thick, useless legs all drawn upward perpendicularly by the taut ropes... and by the frayed black hole in the bandages over his mouth.[100]

The (re)apparition makes Dunbar 'scream and [go] to pieces',[101] his consternation due to the fact that the war machine will produce endless soldiers in white, no longer individuals but recurring substitutes.

Rigid in the formation, application and expression of its logic, the war machine fulfils Henri Bergson's criteria of the laughable in *Le Rire*: '[a]ny arrangement of acts and events is comic which gives us, in a single combination, the illusion of life and the distinct impression of a mechanical arrangement'.[102] This explains the laughter arising at military ceremonies ('the ceremonial side of social life must... always include a latent comic element');[103] at Falstaffian / Schweikian / Milliganian / al Cacciato indestructability (Bergson gives the example of Punch and Judy shows in which

---

[97] *Ibid.*, 436, 234.   [98] *Ibid.*, 214.   [99] *Ibid.*, 217.   [100] *Ibid.*, 461–2.   [101] *Ibid.*, 460.
[102] Bergson, *Laughter*, 69. Bergson stresses that repetition is machinic (*ibid.*, 72–3).
[103] *Ibid.*, 44.

the policeman bounces up repeatedly after being hit);[104] at dead and sundered bodies ('we laugh every time a person gives us the impression of being a thing'[105] – an additional explanation for the gelastic effect of the soldier in white); and even at mass death.[106] But above all, Bergson's machinic theory explains the laughter provoked when the true meaning of the logic of the war zone becomes apparent. It is a laughter, Bergson emphasises, from which feeling is absent[107] and, *pace* Aristotle, it lacks humanity.[108] Crucially, it signals a 'sudden realisation' after momentary deception or misconception.

A laughing matter, but there is nothing funny about it. When Wilfred Owen describes those who, their senses 'long since ironed', '[c]an laugh among the dying, unconcerned'[109] or Bao Ninh writes of the 'ghastly', 'crazed' and 'ghoulish' laughter of a comrade whose belly has been ripped open and arm torn off by a blast,[110] the laughter is, like Waters's almost laughter, mirthless. Is it therefore also pathological? 'Pathological laughter', writes Donald W. Black in *The Journal of Nervous and Mental Disease*, 'occurs when laughter is inappropriate, unrestrained (forced), uncontrollable, or dissociated from any stimulus'.[111] This kind of laughter is evident in Ernst Jünger's description of 'exalted, almost demoniacal lightness; often attended by fits of laughter I was unable to repress'.[112] The laughter provoked by hyperlogic and its carelessness of human needs is different. This laughter may be unrestrained (Waters does restrain his, of course) or uncontrollable, but it would not be correct to describe it as 'dissociated from any stimulus' or 'inappropriate'. The battlefield might seem an unlikely venue for risibility but certainly does not lack provocation for it. Nor is the laughter in question pathological in the sense of constituting a symptom of psychiatric or neurological trauma.[113]

---

[104] *Ibid.*, 70.   [105] *Ibid.*, 58.

[106] Bergson's comment that we laugh at the 'snowball effect' of toy soldiers tumbling down one after another (*ibid.*, 80) echoes in Siegfried Sassoon's 'Clockwork soldiers in a row' ('A Letter Home' (1916), *Collected Poems*, 41) and in George Winterbourne's musings in *Death of a Hero* (1929): "'They went down like a lot o' Charlie Chaplins," said the little ginger-haired sergeant of the Durhams. Like a lot of Charlie Chaplins. Marvellous metaphor! Can't you see them staggering on splayed-out feet and waving ineffective hands as they went down before the accurate machine-gun fire of the Durhams, sergeant?' (Aldington, *Death of a Hero*, 157–8).

[107] Bergson, *Laughter*, 4.

[108] That laughter is uniquely the property of humanity derives from Aristotle's observation that human beings are 'the only creatures that laugh' (*Parts of Animals*, 673a).

[109] Wilfred Owen, 'Insensibility' (1917–18), *The Complete Poems and Fragments*, vol. I, 145.

[110] Ninh, *The Sorrow of War*, 87.

[111] Donald W. Black, 'Pathological Laughter: A Review of the Literature', *The Journal of Nervous and Mental Disease* 170.2 (February 1982), 67.

[112] Jünger, *Storm of Steel*, 93.

[113] For examples, see Black, 'Pathological Laughter', 69; Josef Parvizi *et al.*, 'Pathological Laughing and Crying', *Brain* 124.9 (September 2001), 1708–9; Provine, *Laughter*, 157–75; Barbara Wild

The gelastic theory that most closely approaches this species of laughter is that of incongruity.[114] At its most basic level, this is the simple idea that inconsistencies, ambiguities, coincidences, unexpected twists of fate, bathos and sheer oddities can provoke laughter. War throws up any number of instances of these phenomena. But the incongruity theory has further-reaching philosophical implications. In *Critique of the Power of Judgment* (1790), Kant famously writes that 'laughter is an affect resulting from the sudden transformation of a heightened expectation into nothing'.[115] An obvious example would be a joke that sets up an incompatibility and then resolves the tension with a punch line. Kant himself offers the following 'joke':

An Indian, at the table of an Englishman in Surat, seeing a bottle of ale being opened, and all the beer, transformed into foam, spill out, displayed his great amazement with many exclamations, and in reply to the Englishman's question 'What is so amazing here?' answered, 'I'm not amazed that it's coming out, but by how you got it all in.'[116]

Though Kant insists that the 'hearty pleasure' afforded by this anecdote has nothing to do with superiority – we laugh 'not because we find ourselves cleverer than this ignorant person' – it is difficult now to resist the conclusion that some kind of colonialist one-upmanship is involved. But Kant's analysis is that our pleasure derives from the fact that a heightening of expectation is then dissipated: though he does not thoroughly unpick his own joke, it would seem that 'our expectation' refers to the reader's or listener's keenness to understand what lies behind the Indian's perplexing amazement. Kant continues:

It is noteworthy that in all such cases the joke must always contain something that can deceive for a moment: hence, when the illusion disappears into nothing, the mind looks back again in order to try it once more, and thus is hurried this way and that by rapidly succeeding increases and decreases of tension and set into oscillation, which . . . is bound to cause a movement of the mind and an internal bodily movement in harmony with it.[117]

Two things are important here: the 'nothing' which is ultimately reached after the mind has raked over its punctured expectations a few times and the

---

et al., 'Neural Correlates of Laughter and Humour', *Brain* 126.10 (October 2003), 2121–388. Notably, pathological laughter does NOT appear in the roster of symptoms for post-traumatic stress disorder in DSM-IV: see Yule *et al.*, 'Post-Traumatic Stress Disorder in Adults', 6–7.

[114] For accounts of the incongruity theory of laughter, see Glenn, *Laughter in Interaction*, 19; Mulkay, *On Humour*, 54; Palmer, *Taking Humour Seriously*, 96f.

[115] Kant, *Critique*, 209. Schopenhauer developed Kant's incongruity theory (see *The World as Will and Idea*, 76 (Book 1 §13), in particular), but there is not space to rehearse his arguments here.

[116] Kant, *Critique*, 209.

[117] *Ibid.*, 211.

physiological mechanisms which begin to thrum, as it were, in harmony with this oscillation. For Kant's argument is that the ultimate reaction to a joke is bodily:

For if one assumes that all of our thoughts are at the same time harmoniously combined with some kind of movement in the organs of the body, then one will have a fair grasp of how to that sudden shift of mind, first to one and then to another point of view for considering its object, there can correspond a reciprocal tensing and relaxing of the elastic parts of our viscera, which communicates itself to our diaphragm (like that which ticklish people feel), so that the lungs expel the air with rapidly succeeding pauses, and thus produce a movement that is conducive to health, which alone, and not what goes on in the mind, is the real cause of a gratification in a thought that at bottom represents nothing.[118]

The sudden evaporation of the cognitive moment of deception or misconception is, so to speak, the point at which the mind washes its hands of trying to make head or tail of the incongruity before it and the body takes over and starts to laugh.

Kant's theory of the incongruous can be compared and contrasted with his theory of the sublime. They are similar in that both involve a moment of 'misconception', a moment filled, in both cases, with mental oscillation. They differ in that the heightened expectation induced by the incongruous is transformed into 'nothing', whereas the displeasure in imaginative inadequacy occasioned by the sublime is quickly replaced by pleasure in 'the superiority of the rational vocation of our cognitive faculty'.[119] While the apprehension of a joke moves from mind to body, that is, apprehension of the sublime stays in the mind. Now, it was argued in Chapter 5 that diversionary tactics, particularly adynaton (linguistic/literary disclaimers of competence in relation to the subject matter of war), function as textual sites where the displeasure-followed-by-pleasure occasioned by the sublime is induced and enacted. Diversions can therefore be seen as having dual functions: marking both the limits of representative resourcefulness on the part of the writer and the boundless scope of aesthetic judgement on the part of the reader. But a third stage to the Kantian despair–joy dyad was hypothesised: a return to despair. The working of this tertiary stage can now be further illuminated through the mechanism of laughter, more pessimistic than the avoidance strategies. In contrast to the 'vital outpouring'[120] of joy that occurs when reason apprehends what it initially conceived to be beyond its capacities, the vital outpouring that is laughter commemorates

[118] *Ibid.*, 210.   [119] *Ibid.*, 141.   [120] *Ibid.*, 128–9.

the defeat of reason and the triumph of the body. As Kant writes: '[i]n the joke . . . the play begins with thoughts which, as a whole, insofar as they are to be expressed sensibly, also occupy the body; and . . . the understanding, in this presentation in which it does not find what was expected, suddenly relaxes'.[121]

Military hyperlogic dictates that parade grounds are weeded by hand; that guns are painted green and yellow and then stand out against the chalk white surroundings, needing to be draped with grey blankets ('"it would have been better if we'd painted the bloody rocks yellow and green," said crazed voices who had to wait all day to get their blankets back and then rise at dawn to give them up again'); that companies are sent forward into lethal and unwinnable situations; that one battery of engineers reels in an old telephone line only to find that another battery has been reeling it out; that the only replacement shoes are in size twelve ('It was like wearing landing barges. I used to haul myself around in the mud walking like Frankenstein's monster, my feet kept coming out of the bloody things, and I had to stand on one leg trying to tug the monster boot out of the mud').[122] Informed of these things, the reader must pause for a moment in disbelief; his or her reason, unable to assimilate the data in any meaningful sense, relinquishes it; there follows an inward or outward laughter response in the body. Spike Milligan, who reports all these incidents in his memoirs, laughs too, and provides summative commentary: 'bloody mad', 'terrible, unexplained lunacy', 'absurd'.[123]

It is notable that in Kant's explanation, laughter functions as an announcement that a period of hesitation is over and a conclusion has been arrived at.[124] As Mark Weeks perceptively points out, in Kant's termination of the period of heightened expectation by the collapse into laughter 'we can see that what is being posited is what under the current cultural regime is unthinkable: the subversion not by, but *of*, desire'; moreover this interruption of ongoing desire constitutes a temporal subversion that could be countered only by a 'futuristic', Nietzschean laughter 'that would defy the collapse of time in everyday laughter and thereby launch a joyfully unstoppable temporal momentum'.[125] Matching its synchronic temporality (discussed in Chapter 4), the laughter of the war zone is tmetic rather

---

[121] *Ibid.*, 209.   [122] Milligan, *Milligan's War*, 34, 104, 185, 186, 200.   [123] *Ibid.*, 34, 185, 295.

[124] There are affinities with Todorov's theory that the fantastic consists of the hesitation in deciding whether an apparently supernatural event is an illusion of the senses (the uncanny) or an integral part of reality (the marvellous) (Tsvetan Todorov, *The Fantastic: A Structural Approach to a Literary Genre* (Ithaca: Cornell University Press, 1975), 25, 31).

[125] Weeks, 'Beyond a Joke', 3, 13.

than futuristic: a disruption that is also – as Milligan's summary comments reveal – a judgement.

So the hyperlogic of the war zone, impervious to imagination and reason, is rejected by the mind and makes the body laugh. Waters's (almost) laughter in the death camp is a laughter that is wordless, without mirth and laughed alone. Such laughter is the best available response to the machinic god of conflict. As a mode of war representation, writing has extraordinary power both to depict and to evoke this laughter and hence to make the reader *feel* the truth that war, or at least some aspects of it, is beyond rational comprehension. Baudelaire, recognising this 'true and violent laughter', called it 'profound, primitive and axiomatic'.[126]

---

[126] Charles Baudelaire, 'On the Essence of Laughter' ('De L'essence du rire'), *The Mirror of Art*, trans. and ed. Jonathan Mayne (London: Phaidon, 1955), 144.

Conclusion
To perpetual peace

> But this too is true: stories can save us.
> Tim O'Brien, *The Things They Carried*

This book has set out some of the principal challenges involved in representing war and explored how writers have responded to them: with difficulty
and with success, with a range of formal devices, exploiting linguistic and
literary resources to their maxima. It has argued that the necessary task
of conveying conflict is accomplished by such means as enhancing credibility through the tropes of singularity and autopsy; using the Vietnam
Wall approach (taliation nominatim) and the Unknown Warrior approach
(synecdoche) to frame the scale of conflict for human comprehension;
deploying the techniques of pastoral to communicate the peculiar psycho-
physiologico-physical experience that is the war zone; maintaining superpositions to convey the synchronous, open-ended temporality of wartime;
mobilising diversionary tactics to set in motion the functioning of the
sublime; and invoking and depicting laughter to recreate the sense that the
turbulent flow of war is often inimical and incomprehensible to the individual caught up within it. The ability to cause and represent (mirthless)
laughter, in particular, has been characterised as one of war writing's great
achievements: a phenomenon beyond both words and silence; the product
of reason (at least, reason's decision to concede defeat) but felt in the body;
subversive but un-interpretable; shocking and imperative. By this means
and others, the challenges, to a great extent, have been met.

To what end?

The Introduction listed some of the reasons why war must be represented: to warn; to keep the record, for others and the self; to memorialise;
to carry information across the combatant/non-combatant divide and so
to facilitate the re-entry of the veteran into peacetime society; to impose
discursive order on the chaos and hence render it more manageable; and
to function as catharsis. A further reason was also suggested: to promote

peace. Can war literature stop war? In his still influential essay, 'To Perpetual Peace' ('Zum Ewigen Frieden. Ein Philosophischer Entwurf') (1795),
from which the title of this Conclusion is taken, Kant argues that peace
is not a natural state but must be *'established'*.[1] He gives three 'definitive
articles' for perpetuating peace among states: that the civil constitution of
every state should be republican, that the right of nations should be based
on a federalism of free states and that cosmopolitan right should be limited
to conditions of universal hospitality.[2] To these three articles might there
be added a fourth – that what war does should be brought home to people,
but by means of representation rather than by war itself?

To ask this question is to raise further queries about literature's extra-
textual impact. 'Make lit, not war' might be effective in two ways. The first
might be through forensic argument: James Dawes's 'emancipatory' model
of the relationship between language and violence[3] in which words are used
to dissuade from, or take the place of, force. The second might be through
mimesis: showing, rather than telling, the cost of armed conflict. Both
means might give rise to what J. Hillis Miller calls the 'necessary ethical
moment in the act of reading', a moment that both involves 'a response
to something, responsible to it, responsive to it, respectful of it … an
imperative, some "I must"' and also 'leads to an act', an entry 'into the
social, institutional, political realms'.[4] Hillis Miller's model resembles New
Historicism in its two-way porosity: text and world are mutually affective.
In his words, '[t]here must be an influx of performative power from the
linguistic transactions involved in the act of reading into the realms of
knowledge, politics, and history. Literature must be in some way a cause
and not merely an effect.'[5] On an appropriately grand scale, the ethical
moment might result in social and political action: protesting, voting,
lobbying, consulting, decision-making. The stakes are high; accordingly,
war literature demands careful reading. One of the aims of this book has
been to uncover the rhetorical tricks involved in writing about conflict,
to reveal how certain effects are achieved and so to assist the reader in
dismantling distortions and deceptions. Such informed reading is nothing
less than an act of good citizenship. But this is not the same as the actual
prevention of future armed conflict.

---

[1] Immanuel Kant, *Practical Philosophy*, trans. and ed. Mary J. Gregor (Cambridge: Cambridge
University Press, 1999), 322.
[2] *Ibid.*, 322, 325, 328.   [3] Dawes, *The Language of War*, 1.
[4] J. Hillis Miller, *The Ethics of Reading: Kant, De Man, Eliot, Trollope, James, and Benjamin* (New York:
Columbia University Press, 1987), 1, 4.
[5] *Ibid.*, 5.

If a war literature existed that had any hope of stopping war, it would be clear-eyed and purposeful. It would probably be messy. It would disconcert. It would do its best to convey the horror and the misery of conflict by whatever techniques it could find, and it would also discover a way to suggest how the horror and the misery might be avoided. It would have a tone of sorrow and of bravery. It might have to sugar the pill, even as it shocked. It would refrain from suggesting that there was redemption in the deaths. It would lament its own ineffectuality. It would find its task difficult and would go off the point (consider the examples of Tolstoy, Wharton, O'Brien and Ninh quoted in the Introduction). It would be very like the texts encountered in the course of this book.

It still wouldn't succeed. Even in Kant's essay, the original 'perpetual peace' is a 'satirical inscription on a Dutch innkeeper's sign upon which a burial ground [is] painted':[6] scant hope, in other words, in anyone's lifetime. Peace, whether perpetual or not, is elusive: ours is an age in which, as Nick Mansfield writes, the question 'why did we choose war instead of peace?' has been forever supplanted by 'what configuration of the peace-war complex embroils us now?'[7] Writers might as well attempt to move mountains. 'You know what I say to people when I hear they're writing anti-war books?' the movie-maker Harrison Starr asks Billy Pilgrim in *Slaughterhouse-Five*. 'I say, "Why don't you write an anti-*glacier* book instead?"'[8] But anti – or pro-glacier books do not cause glaciers, while a war book might contribute to the outbreak of war – as Yeats contemplated in his anguished self-questioning in 'Man and the Echo' (1938): 'Did that play of mine send out / Certain men the English shot?'[9] Moreover, war representation can also occasion delight in violence: a harmless-enough outlet for such delight it might be thought, though the thought is accompanied by uneasiness.

But some more positive claims can be made for war writing. To an extent, it is healing. 'Art, when successful,' writes Gene Ray, 'can function as an opening for the processing of traumatic history: for testimony and reflection, for the work and play of mourning, for "acting-out" and "working-through"'.[10] In the United States, since 2004, the Operation Homecoming programme, supported by the National Endowment for the Arts, The Boeing Company and writers including Richard Bausch, Tom

---

[6] Kant, *Practical Philosophy*, 317.   [7] Mansfield, 'War and its Other', unpaginated.
[8] Vonnegut, *Slaughterhouse-Five*, 3.
[9] W. B. Yeats, *The Poems Revised*, ed. Richard J. Finneran, *The Collected Works of W. B. Yeats*, 2nd edn, 12 vols. (Basingstoke: Macmillan, 1991), vol. I, 345.
[10] Ray, 'Reading the Lisbon Earthquake', 204.

Clancy, Mark Bowden, Bobbie Ann Mason, Tobias Wolff, Jeff Shaara and Marilyn Nelson, has run writing workshops for returning veterans. There is evidence that 'discomfort diminishes' during the writing process.[11] Similar claims have yet to be made for a 'reading cure', but the possibility deserves investigation.

Beyond this is a further claim: that war literature reveals and recommends love. In amongst the killing, pain and loss can be glimpsed acts of mercy, selfless bravery in rescuing, saving and protecting other human beings, sacrifices on the part of those waiting and those fighting for them. Describing what he took away from war, the *Herald Tribune* correspondent Roger Cohen listed 'the stubbornness of love', 'the fierceness of moral clarity', 'the quietness of courage', 'the indivisibility of integrity and the importance of a single dissenting voice'.[12] 'The head is useless without the heart. War teaches that', he concluded. The psychiatrist Jonathan Shay notes that 'combat calls forth a passion of care among men who fight beside each other'; comrades show each other 'special gentleness and compassion'.[13] Shay identifies such comradely love as 'philia': 'a love that is rich and passionate but not necessarily sexual'.[14] Alongside and resembling it, there is the love of and for waiting families and there is the authorial love which manifests itself in the taking of pains to keep the record and honour the dead.

And then there is love for the enemy. Emmanuel Lévinas, himself a Second World War veteran and concentration camp inmate, was unconvinced by Kant's arguments that reason can bring about, let alone perpetuate, peace. In *Totality and Infinity* (*Totalité et infini* (1961)), Lévinas assembled the arguments in support of his own conviction that love must precede reason – a love in which the sight of another's face is crucial. According to Lévinas, 'the concept of totality, which dominates Western philosophy,' must be breached.[15] War makes possible 'the breach of totality' through its combination of violence and unpredictability: 'no logistics guarantees victory' and so the individual warrior departs from the totality, resorting to tactics such as (Certeauesque) 'ruse and ambush' which are 'inscribed in the very existence of the body'.[16] Lévinas writes:

---

[11] Bill Asenjo, 'Writing Wrongs – Putting Pain on Paper', *Social Work Today* 7.3 (May/June 2007), 42.
[12] Roger Cohen, 'Karadzic and War's Lessons', *International Herald Tribune* 24 July 2008, 6.
[13] Shay, *Achilles in Vietnam*, 39, 47.   [14] *Ibid.*, 40, 43.
[15] Emmanuel Lévinas, *Totality and Infinity: An Essay on Exteriority*, trans. Alphonso Lingis (Pittsburgh: Duquesne University Press, 1969), 21, 35–40.
[16] *Ibid.*, 222, 223, 225, 225.

In war beings refuse to belong to a totality, refuse community, refuse law; no frontier stops one being by another, nor defines them. They affirm themselves as transcending the totality, each identifying itself not by its place in the whole, but by its *self*.[17]

But this is not the only means by which war produces the conditions for transcendence. The other means is the Other's face, which 'expresses my moral impossibility of annihilating'.[18] Moreover:

[The Other] can oppose to me a struggle, that is, oppose to the force that strikes him not a force of resistance, but the very *unforeseeableness* of his reaction. He thus opposes to me not a greater force, an energy assessable and consequently presenting itself as though it were part of a whole, but the very transcendence of his being by relation to that whole; not some superlative of power, but precisely the infinity of his transcendence. This infinity, stronger than murder, already resists us in his face, is his face, is the primordial *expression*, is the first word: 'you shall not commit murder.' ... The epiphany of the face brings forth the possibility of gauging the infinity of the temptation to murder, not only as a temptation to total destruction, but also as the purely ethical impossibility of this temptation and attempt.[19]

Perceiving and embracing the alterity of the Other is the beginning of not killing, of acceptance, of non-totality, of pluralism.

But armed conflict, as noted in the Introduction, is less and less a matter of face-to-face encounters. It is left to texts of war to stage Lévinasian meetings and thereby reveal the Other's countenance. Wilfred Owen's 'Strange Meeting' (1918) is such a staging.[20] The poem opens with a fugue from totality: 'It seemed that out of battle I escaped'.[21] There follows a Lévinasian epiphany of the face – a specifically described face, 'grained' '[w]ith a thousand pains': 'one sprang up, and stared / With piteous recognition in fixed eyes'. Though it is now too late to resile from killing, the speaker both learns the importance of transcendence ('None will break ranks, though nations trek from progress') and, belatedly, makes a tacit exchange: for having caused his death, he will publicise this 'Strange friend's' insights. Haunted by Wilde's line 'Yet each man kills the thing he loves',[22] the

---

[17] *Ibid.*, 222.   [18] *Ibid.*, 232.   [19] *Ibid.*, 199.

[20] Note, too, that in his dedication to *In Parenthesis*, David Jones lists, first his friends and comrades, and finally 'the enemy front-fighters who shared our pains against who we found ourselves by misadventure' (*In Parenthesis*, preliminary pages). It may be that he saw the faces of those fighting opposite, at the front.

[21] Owen, *The Complete Poems and Fragments*, vol. I, 148.

[22] 'I am the enemy you killed, my friend' (*ibid.*, 149). Wilde's line 'Yet each man kills the thing he loves' (*The Ballad of Reading Gaol*, line 37 (*ibid.*, 148n)) is misquoted in Owen's fragment 'With

poem, more sorrowing than bitter, stages the basic Lévinasian requirement for love and peace: the embracing of alterity. In affording glimpses of the face of the Other, texts of war can facilitate similar embracings.

'By my glee might many men have laughed, / And of my weeping something had been left': the tone of 'Strange Meeting' is yearningly hypothetical. 'What might have been' is the mode of much war writing, which mourns both the human cost of its subject and its own impotence. There is love, too, in the 'if only' – longing, best-intentioned, helpless love. Grander achievements impossible, it is a love well worth having. Hear it sound in the last lines of 'Last Post' (2009), Carol-Ann Duffy's elegy on the deaths of the last British veterans of the First World War, which wistfully imagines a poetry that could reverse history:

> There's coffee in the square,
> warm French bread
> and all those thousands dead
> are shaking dried mud from their hair
> and queuing up for home. Freshly alive,
> a lad plays Tipperary to the crowd, released
> from History; the glistening, healthy horses fit for heroes, kings.
> You lean against a wall,
> your several million lives still possible
> and crammed with love, work, children, talent, English beer, good food.
> You see the poet tuck away his pocket-book and smile.
> If poetry could truly tell it backwards,
> then it would.

Those That Are Become': 'For each man slays the one he loves' (Owen, *The Complete Poems and Fragments*, vol. II, 492). This might seem to refute Lévinas, except for the fact that 'Strange Meeting' cites a personal encounter as an apparent reversal of the impetus to kill.

Bibliography

'A Soldier of the Seventy-First', in *The Journal of a Soldier in the Peninsular War*, ed. Christopher Hibbert, Moreton-in-Marsh: The Windrush Press, 1997.

Abbott, W. H., *The Unknown Warrior and Other Poems*, London: Erskine Macdonald, 1929.

Addison, Joseph, *The Miscellaneous Works of Joseph Addison*, ed. A. C. Guthkelch, 2 vols., London: G. Bell, 1914.

'From *The Spectator*', in *The Sublime: A Reader in British Eighteenth-Century Aesthetic Theory*, ed. Andrew Ashfield and Peter de Bolla, Cambridge: Cambridge University Press, 1996, 62–9.

Adorno, Theodor, *Negative Dialectics*, trans. E. B. Ashton, London: Routledge & Kegan Paul, 1973.

'Commitment', in *Aesthetics and Politics*, ed. Ernest Bloch, Georg Lukács, Bertold Brecht, Walter Benjamin and Theodor Adorno, London: NLB, 1977, 177–95.

Prisms, ed. Samuel Weber and Shierry Weber, Cambridge, MA: MIT Press, 1981.

Aesthetic Theory, trans. C. Lenhardt, ed. Gretel Adorno and Rolf Tiedemann, London: Routledge & Kegan Paul, 1984.

Alcott, Louisa May, *Hospital Sketches*, ed. Bessie Z. Jones, Cambridge: The Belknap Press of Harvard University Press, 1960.

Aldington, Richard, *Death of a Hero*, London: Penguin, 1929.

Allan, Stuart, and Barbie Zelizer, 'Rules of Engagement: Journalism and War', *Reporting War: Journalism in Wartime*, ed. Stuart Allan and Barbie Zelizer, London and New York: Routledge, 2004, 3–21.

Alpers, Paul, 'What is Pastoral?', *Critical Inquiry* 8.3 (Spring 1982), 437–60.

Amis, Martin, *Visiting Mrs Nabokov and Other Excursions* (1987), London: Jonathan Cape, 1993.

Aneirin, 'From "The Goddodin"', trans. Joseph P. Clancy, in *The Oxford Book of War Poetry*, ed. Jon Stallworthy, Oxford: Oxford University Press, 1984, 15–17.

Anzieu, Didier, *The Skin Ego*, trans. Chris Turner, New Haven: Yale University Press, 1989.

Appleton, Jay, *The Experience of Landscape*, Chichester: John Wiley, 1996.

Aristotle, *The Physics*, trans. Philip H. Wicksteed and Francis M. Cornford, Loeb Classical Library, London and New York: William Heinemann / G. P. Putnam, 1929.

Parts of Animals. Movement of Animals. Progression of Animals, trans. A. L. Peck, Loeb Classical Library, London and Cambridge, MA: William Heinemann / Harvard University Press, 1937.

'Poetics', trans. Stephen Halliwell, *Aristotle, Poetics; Longinus, On the Sublime; Demetrius, On Style*, Loeb Classical Library, Cambridge, MA: Harvard University Press, 1995.

Asenjo, Bill, 'Writing Wrongs – Putting Pain on Paper', *Social Work Today* 7.3 (May/June 2007), 42.

Auden, W. H., *Collected Poems*, ed. Edward Mendelson, London: Faber, 1994.

Auden, W. H., and Christopher Isherwood, *Journey to a War*, London: Faber, 1973.

Augé, Marc, *Non-Places: Introduction to an Anthropology of Supermodernity*, trans. John Howe, London: Verso, 1995.

Austen, Gillian, 'The Literary Career of George Gascoigne: Studies in Self-Presentation', unpublished D.Phil. thesis, University of Oxford, 1997.

Bain, Donald, 'War Poet', in *The Terrible Rain: The War Poets 1939–1945*, ed. Brian Gardner, London: Methuen, 1966, 159.

Bakhtin, Mikhail, *The Dialogic Imagination: Four Essays*, trans. and ed. Michael Holquist, Austin: University of Texas Press, 1981, 84–258.

Rabelais and His World, trans. Hélène Iswolsky, Bloomington: Indiana University Press, 1984.

Barbusse, Henri, *Under Fire: The Story of a Squad*, trans. Fitzwater Wray, London: J. M. Dent, 1926.

Le Feu: journal d'une escouade, Paris: Gallimard, 2007.

Barthes, Roland, *Image, Music, Text*, trans. Stephen Heath, London: Fontana, 1977.

'The Photographic Message', in *A Barthes Reader*, ed. Susan Sontag, London: Jonathan Cape, 1982, 194–210.

Camera Lucida, trans. Richard Howard, London: Fontana, 1984.

Battenhouse, Roy, 'Falstaff as Parodist and Perhaps Holy Fool', *PMLA* 90.1 (January 1975), 32–52.

Baudelaire, Charles, 'On the Essence of Laughter' ('De L'essence du rire'), *The Mirror of Art: Critical Studies*, trans. and ed. Jonathan Mayne, London: Phaidon, 1955, 133–53.

Baudrillard, Jean, *The Gulf War Did Not Take Place*, trans. Paul Patton, London: Power Publications, 1994.

Bell, Robert H., 'Homer's Humor: Laughter in *The Iliad*', *Humanitas* 20.1/2 (2007), 96–116.

Bender, John, and David E. Wellbery. 'Rhetoricality: On the Modernist Return to Rhetoric', in *The Ends of Rhetoric: History, Theory, Practice*, eds. John Bender and David E. Wellbery, Stanford: Stanford University Press, 1990, 3–39.

Benjamin, Walter, *Charles Baudelaire: A Lyric Poet in the Era of High Capitalism*, trans. Harry Zohn, London: NLB, 1973.

Benthien, Claudia, *Skin: On the Cultural Border Between Self and the World*, trans. Thomas Dunlap, New York: Columbia University Press, 2002.

Bergson, Henri, *Matter and Memory*, trans. Nancy Margaret Paul and W. Scott Palmer, London: Allen & Unwin, 1919.

Laughter: An Essay on the Meaning of the Comic, trans. Cloudesley Brereton and Fred Rothwell, London: Macmillan, 1935.

Bernard-Donals, Michael, and Richard Glejzer, *Between Witness and Testimony: The Holocaust and the Limits of Representation*, Albany: State University of New York Press, 2001.

Bernstein, Michael André, *Foregone Conclusions: Against Apocalyptic History*, Berkeley: University of California Press, 1994.

Bevan, Robert, *The Destruction of Memory: Architecture at War*, London: Reaktion Books, 2006.

Bierce, Ambrose, *A Sole Survivor: Bits of Autobiography*, ed. S. T. Joshi and David E. Schultz, Knoxville: University of Tennessee Press, 1998.

Black, Donald W., 'Pathological Laughter: A Review of the Literature', *The Journal of Nervous and Mental Disease* 170.2 (February 1982), 67–71.

Blair, Sara, 'Cultural Geography and the Place of the Literary', *American Literary History* 10.3 (Autumn 1998), 544–67.

Blanchot, Maurice, *The Writing of the Disaster*, trans. Anne Smock, Lincoln: University of Nebraska Press, 1986.

Bloom, Harold, 'Introduction', in *Poets of Sensibility and the Sublime*, ed. Harold Bloom, New York: Chelsea House, 1986, 1–9.

The Anxiety of Influence, Oxford: Oxford University Press, 1997.

Blunden, Edmund, *The Poems of Edmund Blunden*, London: Cobden-Sanderson, 1930.

Undertones of War, Harmondsworth: Penguin, 1982.

Blundeville, Thomas, *The True Order and Methods of Wryting and Reading Hysteries*, London: William Seres, 1574.

Bonham Carter, Violet, in *Champion Redoubtable: The Diaries and Letters of Violet Bonham Carter 1914–1945*, ed. Mark Pottle, London: Phoenix, 1999.

Boorstin, Daniel J., *The Image*, London: Weidenfeld and Nicholson, 1961.

Booth, Wayne C., *The Rhetoric of Rhetoric*, Oxford: Blackwell, 2004.

Borg, Alan, *War Memorials: From Antiquity to the Present*, London: Leo Cooper, 1991.

Bourke, Joanna, *An Intimate History of Killing: Face-to-Face Killing in Twentieth-Century Warfare*, London: Granta, 1999.

Bowen, Elizabeth, *The Mulberry Tree*, ed. Hermione Lee, London: Vintage, 1999.

Boyd-Barrett, Oliver, 'Understanding: The Second Casualty', in *Reporting War: Journalism in Wartime*, ed. Stuart Allan and Barbie Zelizer, London and New York: Routledge, 2004, 25–42.

Braiterman, Zachary, 'Against Holocaust-Sublime: Naive Reference and the Generation of Memory', *History and Memory* 12.2 (Fall 2000), 7–28.

Braudy, Leo, *The Frenzy of Renown: Fame and Its History*, Oxford: Oxford University Press, 1986.

Brecht, Bertold, *Schweyk in the Second World War*, trans. William Rowlinson, ed. John Willett and Ralph Manheim, London: Eyre Methuen, 1976.

Brittain, Vera, *Testament of Youth*, London: Weidenfeld and Nicolson, 2009.

Bromwich, David, *Skeptical Music: Essays on Modern Poetry*, Chicago: University of Chicago Press, 2001.

Brooke, Nicholas, *Horrid Laughter in Jacobean Tragedy*, London: Open Books, 1979.

Brooke, Rupert, *The Poetical Works*, ed. Geoffrey Keynes, London: Faber, 1970.

Brooks, Peter, *Reading for the Plot: Design and Intention in Narrative*, Cambridge, MA: Harvard University Press, 1996.

Browning, Robert, *The Poems*, ed. John Pettigrew, 2 vols., New Haven: Yale University Press, 1981.

Buell, Lawrence, *The Environmental Imagination: Thoreau, Nature Writing, and the Formation of American Culture*, Cambridge, MA: Harvard University Press, 1995.

Burgass, Catherine, 'A Brief Story of Postmodern Plot', *The Yearbook of English Studies* 30 (2000), 177–86.

Burke, Gregory, *Black Watch*, London: Faber and Faber, 2007.

Burke, Edmund, *A Philosophical Enquiry into the Origin of Our Ideas of the Sublime and the Beautiful*, ed. Adam Phillips, Oxford: Oxford University Press, 1990.

Bushaway, Bob, 'Name Upon Name: The Great War and Remembrance', in *Myths of the English*, ed. Roy Porter, Cambridge: Polity Press, 1992, 136–67.

Butor, Michel, 'Travel and Writing', *Mosaic* 8.1 (Fall 1974), 1–16.

Byron, Lord, *The Works of Lord Byron: Letters and Journals*, ed. Rowland E. Prothero, vol. IV (6 vols.), London, 1898–1901.

   Don Juan, ed. T. G. Steffan, E. Steffan and W.W. Pratt, London: Penguin, 2004.

Campbell, James, 'Combat Gnosticism: The Ideology of First World War Criticism', *New Literary History* 30 (1999), 203–15.

Camus, Albert, 'Le Mythe de Sisyphe', *Essais*, ed. Roger Quilliot and Louis Faucon, Paris: Gallimard & Calman-Lévy, 1965.

Cannadine, David, 'War and Death, Grief and Mourning in Modern Britain', in *Mirrors of Mortality: Studies in the Social History of Death*, ed. Joachim Whaley, London: Europa, 1981, 187–242.

Canter, H. V., 'The Figure Adunaton in Greek and Latin Poetry', *American Journal of Philology* 51.1 (1930), 32–41.

Carrier, E. H., *The Unknown Warrior and Other Poems*, London, 1926.

Carson, Anne, 'Variations on the Right to Remain Silent', *A Public Space* 7 (2008), 179–87.

Caruth, Cathy, *Unclaimed Experience: Trauma, Narrative, and History*, Baltimore: The Johns Hopkins University Press, 1996.

Cashman, Greg, and Leonard C. Robinson, *An Introduction to the Causes of War: Patterns of Interstate Conflict from World War I to Iraq*, Lanham: Rowman & Littlefield, 2007.

'Chapter XXIII', *Edinburgh Annual Register* 1 (1 January 1808), 458–9.

Chatman, Seymour, *Story and Discourse: Narrative Structure in Fiction and Film*, Ithaca: Cornell University Press, 1978.

Clarke, Joseph, *Commemorating the Dead in Revolutionary France: Revolution and Remembrance 1789–1799*, Cambridge: Cambridge University Press, 2007.

Clausewitz, Carl von, *On War*, trans. Michael Howard and Peter Paret, Princeton: Princeton University Press, 1976.

Clodfelter, Micheal, *Warfare and Armed Conflicts: A Statistical Reference to Casualty and Other Figures, 1500–2000*, Jefferson: McFarland, 2002.

Cohen, Roger, 'Karadzic and War's Lessons', *International Herald Tribune* (24 July 2008), 6.

Cooper, Helen, *Pastoral: Mediaeval into Renaissance*, Ipswich: D. S. Brewer, 1977.

Crary, Jonathan, *Suspensions of Perception: Attention, Spectacle, and Modern Culture*, Cambridge, MA: MIT Press, 1999.

Crystal, David, 'Talking About Time', in *Time*, ed. Katinka Ridderbos, Cambridge: Cambridge University Press, 2002, 105–25.

Cunliffe, John W., 'Browning and the Marathon Race', *PMLA* 24.1 (1909), 154–63.

Currey, R. N., *Collected Poems*, Oxford and Cape Town: James Currey and David Philip Publishers, 2001.

Currie, Mark, 'Introduction', in *Metafiction*, ed. Mark Currie, London and New York: Longman, 1995, 1–18.

Postmodern Narrative Theory, Basingstoke: Macmillan, 1998.

About Time: Narrative, Fiction and the Philosophy of Time, Edinburgh: Edinburgh University Press, 2007.

Curtius, Ernst Robert, *European Literature and the Latin Middle Ages*, trans. Willard R. Trask, London: Routledge & Kegan Paul, 1953.

Dakers, Caroline, *The Countryside at War 1914–1918*, London: Constable, 1987.

Das, Santanu, *Touch and Intimacy in First World War Literature*, Cambridge: Cambridge University Press, 2005.

Davies, D. R., and R. Parasuraman, *The Psychology of Vigilance*, London and New York: Academic Press, 1981.

Davies, Stevie, *Henry Vaughan*, Bridgend: Seren, 1995.

Davis, Richard Harding, *Notes of a War Correspondent*, New York: Scribner's, 1911.

Dawes, James, *The Language of War: Literature and Culture in the U.S. from the Civil War through World War II*, Cambridge, MA: Harvard University Press, 2002.

Dawson, Coningsby, *The Unknown Soldier*, London: Hutchinson, 1930.

Day Lewis, Cecil, *The Complete Poems*, London: Sinclair-Stevenson, 1992.

Day-Lewis, Tamasin, ed., *Last Letters Home*, Macmillan, 1995.

de Certeau, Michel, *The Practice of Everyday Life*, trans. Steven Rendall, Berkeley: University of California, 1984.

De Jong, Irene J. F., *Narrative in Drama: The Art of the Euripidean Messenger-Speech*, Leiden: Brill, 1991.

de Man, Paul, 'Phenomenality and Materiality in Kant', in *The Textual Sublime: Deconstruction and Its Differences*, ed. Hugh J. Silverman and Gary E. Aylesworth, New York: State University of New York Press, 1990, 87–108.

de Montaigne, Michel, *The Complete Essays*, trans. and ed. M. A. Screech, London: Penguin, 1987.

de Quincey, Thomas, *The Works of Thomas De Quincey*, ed. Robert Morrison, vol. XVI (21 vols.), London: Pickering and Chatto, 2003.

de Saint-Exupéry, Antoine, *Pilote de guerre*, New York: Éditions de la Maison Française, 1942.

  Flight to Arras, trans. Lewis Galantière, Harmondsworth: Penguin, 1961.

de Saussure, Ferdinand, *Course in General Linguistics*, trans. Wade Baskin, ed. Charles Bally and Albert Sechehaye, New York: McGraw-Hill, 1966.

de Somogyi, Nick, *Shakespeare's Theatre of War*, Aldershot: Ashgate, 1998.

Dee, E. C., *The Unknown Warrior and Other Poems*, London: Arthur H. Stockwell, 1926.

Defoe, Daniel, *Memoirs of a Cavalier, or A Military Journal of the Wars in Germany and the Wars in England from the Year 1632, to the Year 1648*, Oxford: Blackwell, 1974.

Deleuze, Gilles, and Félix Guattari, *A Thousand Plateaus: Capitalism and Schizophrenia*, trans. Brian Massumi, London and New York: Continuum, 2004.

Delupis, Ingrid Detter, *The Law of War*, 2nd edn, Cambridge: Cambridge University Press, 2000.

Dennis, John, 'From *the Grounds of Criticism in Poetry*', in *The Sublime: A Reader in British Eighteenth-Century Aesthetic Theory*, ed. Andrew Ashfield and Peter de Bolla, Cambridge: Cambridge University Press, 1996, 35–9.

Derrida, Jacques, *Speech and Phenomena and Other Essays on Husserl's Theory of Signs*, trans. David B. Allison, Evanston: Northwestern University Press, 1973.

  The Truth in Painting, trans. Geoff Bennington and Ian McLeod, Chicago: University of Chicago Press, 1987.

  'The Law of Genre', in *Acts of Literature*, ed. Derek Attridge, London and New York: Routledge, 1992, 221–52.

Des Pres, Terrence, 'Holocaust Laughter?' in *Writing and the Holocaust*, ed. Berel Lang, New York: Holmes & Meier, 1988, 216–33.

Dickens, Charles, *The Pickwick Papers*, ed. James Kinsley, Oxford: Clarendon, 1986.

Dickey, James, *Poems 1957–1967*, London: Rapp & Carroll, 1967.

Dickinson, Emily, *The Complete Poems of Emily Dickinson*, ed. Thomas H. Johnson, Boston: Little, Brown, 1960, 316.

Dos Passos, John, *U.S.A.*, Boston: Houghton Mifflin, 1946.

Douglas, Keith, *Alamein to Zem-Zem*, ed. Desmond Graham, London: Faber, 1992.

The Complete Poems, ed. Desmond Graham, Oxford: Oxford University Press, 1998.

Duffy, Carol-Anne, 'Last Post', *The Guardian* (31 July 2009), sec. News, 7.

Dundes, Alan, and Thomas Hauschild, 'Auschwitz Jokes', *Western Folklore* 42.4 (October 1983), 249–60.

Dutoit, Thomas, 'Translating the Name?', in Jacques Derrida, *On the Name*, ed. Thomas Dutoit, Stanford: Stanford University Press, 1995, ix–xvi.

Dyer, Geoff, *The Missing of the Somme*, London: Hamish Hamilton, 1994.

Eagleton, Terry, *Against the Grain: Essays 1975–1985*, London and New York: Verso, 1986.

The English Novel, Oxford: Blackwell, 2005.

Eberhart, Richard, 'Preface: Attitudes to War', in *War and the Poet. An Anthology of Poetry Expressing Man's Attitudes to War from Ancient Times to the Present*, ed. Richard Eberhart and Selden Rodman, Westport: Greenwood Press, 1945, v–xv.

Eliot, T. S., *The Complete Poems and Plays*, London: Faber, 1969.

The Sacred Wood. London: Faber, 1997.

Emcke, Carolin, *Echoes of Violence: Letters from a War Reporter*, Princeton: Princeton University Press, 2007.

Emerson, Ralph Waldo, *Collected Poems and Translations*, ed. Harold Bloom and Paul Kane, New York: Library of America, 1994.

Empson, William, *Some Versions of Pastoral*, London: Chatto and Windus, 1950.

'Dylan Thomas', *Essays in Criticism* 13.2 (1963), 205–7.

Esdaile, Charles, *The Peninsular War: A New History*, London: Penguin, 2003.

Esslin, Martin, *The Theatre of the Absurd*, London: Eyre & Spottiswoode, 1962.

Evans, Martin, 'Opening Up the Battlefield: War Studies and the Cultural Turn', *Journal of War and Culture Studies* 1.1 (2008), 47–51.

Ewart, Gavin, 'War Dead', in *The Terrible Rain. The War Poets 1939–1945*, ed. Brian Gardner, London: Methuen, 1977, 178.

Favret, Mary A., *War at a Distance: Romanticism and the Making of Modern Wartime*, Princeton: Princeton University Press, 2009.

Feinstein, Elaine, *Selected Poems*, Manchester: Carcanet, 1994.

Felman, Shoshana, and Dori Laub, *Testimony: Crises of Witnessing in Literature, Psychoanalysis, and History*, New York and London: Routledge, 1992.

Felstiner, John, 'Translating Paul Celan's 'Todesfuge': Rhythm and Repetition as Metaphor', in *Probing the Limits of Representation: Nazism and the 'Final Solution'*, ed. Saul Friedlander, Cambridge, MA: Harvard University Press, 1992, 240–58.

Fenton, James, *The Memory of War and Children in Exile: Poems 1968–1983*, London: Penguin, 1983.

Ferguson, Harvie, 'The Sublime and the Subliminal: Modern Identities and the Aesthetics of Combat', *Theory, Culture and Society* 21.3 (2004), 1–33.

Ferris, Paul, *Dylan Thomas*, London: Hodder & Stoughton, 1977.

Figley, Charles R., and William P. Nash, 'Introduction: For Those Who Bear the Battle', in *Combat Stress Injury. Theory, Research, and Management*,

ed. Charles R. Figley and William P. Nash, New York and London: Routledge, 2007, 1–8.

Fischer, David Hackett, *Paul Revere's Ride*, Oxford: Oxford University Press, 1994.

Foucault, Michel, *Fearless Speech*, ed. Joseph Pearson, Los Angeles: Semiotext(e), 2001.

Freud, Sigmund, *Wit and Its Relation to the Unconscious*, trans. A. A. Brill, London: Kegan Paul, Trench, Trübner, 1922.

   Beyond the Pleasure Principle, trans. C. J. M. Hubback, *Collected Papers*, ed. Ernest Jones, London: The Hogarth Press / The Institute for Psycho-Analysis, 1942.

   'Thoughts for the Times on War and Death', trans. under the supervision of Joan Rivière, *Collected Papers*, ed. Ernest Jones, London: The Hogarth Press / The Institute for Psycho-Analysis, 1950, 288–317.

Friedlander, Saul, 'Introduction', in *Probing the Limits of Representation. Nazism and the 'Final Solution'*, ed. Saul Friedlander, Cambridge, MA: Harvard University Press, 1992, 1–21.

Frost, Robert, *The Poetry of Robert Frost*, ed. Edward Connery Lathem, London: Jonathan Cape, 1971.

Fry, Ron, *Improve Your Memory*, London: Kogan Page, 1997.

Furbank, P. N., and W. R. Owens, *A Critical Bibliography of Daniel Defoe*, London: Pickering and Chatto, 1998.

Fussell, Paul, *The Great War and Modern Memory*, Oxford: Oxford University Press, 1975.

   Wartime: Understanding and Behaviour in the Second World War, Oxford: Oxford University Press, 1989.

Gardiner, Juliet, *The Animals' War: Animals in Wartime from the First World War to the Present Day*, London: Portrait in association with the Imperial War Museum, 2006.

Garrard, Greg, *Ecocriticism*, London: Routledge, 2004.

Gascoigne, George, *The Complete Works of George Gascoigne*, ed. John W. Cunliffe, 2 vols., Cambridge: Cambridge University Press, 1907.

Gat, Azar, *War in Human Civilisation*, Oxford: Oxford University Press, 2006.

Gifford, Terry, *Pastoral*, London and New York: Routledge, 1999.

Gilbert, Martin, *Second World War*, London: Phoenix Press, 1989.

   First World War, London: HarperCollins, 1994.

Gilbert, Sandra, '"Rats' Alley": The Great War, Modernism, and the (Anti)pastoral Elegy', *New Literary History* 30 (1999), 179–201.

Gilbert, Sandra, and Susan Gubar, *The Madwoman in the Attic: The Woman Writer and the Nineteenth-Century Imagination*, New Haven: Yale Nota Bene Press, 2000.

Glasgow, R. D. V., *Madness, Masks, and Laughter: An Essay on Comedy*, London and Toronto: Associated University Presses, 1995.

Glenn, Philip, *Laughter in Interaction*, Cambridge: Cambridge University Press, 2003.

Goethe, Johann Wolfgang von, *Poetry and Truth from My Own Life*, trans. Minna Steele Smith, vol. I (2 vols.), London: George Bell, 1908.

Goldensohn, Lorrie, 'Preface', in *American War Poetry: An Anthology*, ed. Lorrie Goldensohn, New York: Columbia University Press, 2006, xxi–xiv.

Graham, Virginia, 'It's All Very Well Now', in *Chaos of the Night. Women's Poetry & Verse of the Second World War*, ed. Catherine Reilly, London: Virago, 1984, 51–2.

Graves, Robert, 'The Garlands Wither', *The Times Literary Supplement* (26 June 1930), 534.

Green, Leslie C., *The Contemporary Law of Armed Conflict*, 2nd edn, Manchester and New York: Manchester University Press / Juris Publishing, 2000.

Gregory, Adrian, *The Silence of Memory: Armistice Day 1919–1946*, Oxford and Providence: Berg, 1994.

Gribbin, John, *In Search of Schrödinger's Cat*, London: Wildwood House, 1984.

Griffiths, Trevor, *Comedians*, London: Faber, 1979.

Gurney, Ivor, *Collected Poems of Ivor Gurney*, ed. P. J. Kavanagh, Oxford: Oxford University Press, 1984.

Haidu, Peter, 'The Dialectics of Unspeakability: Language, Silence, and the Narratives of Desubjectification', in *Probing the Limits of Representation. Nazism and the 'Final Solution'*, ed. Saul Friedlander, Cambridge, MA: Harvard University Press, 1992, 277–99.

Hale, John, 'Shakespeare and Warfare', in *William Shakespeare: His World, His Work, His Influence*, ed. John F. Andrews, vol. I (3 vols.), New York: Scribner's, 1985, 85–98.

Hall, Jeffrey C., *The Stand of the U.S. Army at Gettysburg*, Bloomington: Indiana University Press, 2003.

Halliwell, Stephen, *Greek Laughter: A Study of Cultural Psychology from Homer to Early Christianity*, Cambridge: Cambridge University Press, 2008.

Hammond, J. R., *A Defoe Companion*, Basingstoke: Macmillan, 1993.

Hanrahan, Brian, and Robert Fox, *'I counted them all out and I counted them all back': The Battle for the Falklands*, London: BBC Books, 1982.

Hardy, Barbara, *Dylan Thomas: An Original Language*, Athens: University of Georgia Press, 2000.

Hardy, Thomas, *The Complete Poetical Works of Thomas Hardy*, ed. Samuel Hynes, vol. I (5 vols.), Oxford: Clarendon, 1982.

Harley, J. B., 'Maps, Knowledge, and Power', in *The Iconography of Landscape: Essays on the Symbolic Representation, Design and Use of Past Environments*, ed. Stephen Daniels and Denis Cosgrove, Cambridge: Cambridge University Press, 1988, 277–312.

Hartman, Geoffrey H., 'The Book of the Destruction', in *Probing the Limits of Representation: Nazism and the 'Final Solution'*, ed. Saul Friedlander, Cambridge, MA: Harvard University Press, 1992, 318–34.

Hašek, Jaroslav, *The Good Soldier Schweik*, trans. Paul Selver, Harmondsworth: Penguin, 1951.

Hazlitt, William, 'Preface', in *The Complete Poems of George Gascoigne*, ed. William Hazlitt, vol. I (2 vols.), London: The Roxburghe Library, 1869, v–xxx.

Healy, Tom, 'Remembering with Advantages: Nation and Ideology in *Henry V*', in *Shakespeare in the New Europe*, ed. Michael Hattaway, Boika Sokolova and Derek Roper, Sheffield: Sheffield Academic Press, 1994, 174–93.

Heaney, Seamus, *New Selected Poems 1966–1987*, London: Faber, 1990.

Heidegger, Martin, *Being and Time*, trans. John Macquarrie and Edward Robinson, Oxford: Blackwell, 1978.

Heiden, Bruce, 'Common People and Leaders in Iliad Book 2: The Invocation of the Muses and the Catalogue of Ships', *Transactions of the American Philological Association* 138.1 (Spring 2008), 127–54.

Heller, Joseph, *Catch-22*, London: Jonathan Cape, 1962.

Hemingway, Ernest, *Death in the Afternoon*, New York: Scribner's, 1932.
   Selected Letters 1917–1961, ed. Carlos Baker, London: Granada, 1981.
   The First Forty-Nine Stories, London: Arrow, 1993.
   A Farewell to Arms, London: Vintage, 1999.
   In Our Time, New York: Scribner's, 2003.

Herodotus, *Herodotus Books V–VII*, trans. A. D. Godley, Loeb Classical Library, vol. III (4 vols.), London and New York: William Heinemann, 1922.

Herrnstein Smith, Barbara, *Poetic Closure: A Study of How Poems End*, Chicago: University of Chicago Press, 1968.

Hibberd, Dominic, *Owen the Poet*, Basingstoke: Macmillan, 1986.

Hill, Geoffrey, *Collected Poems*, Harmondsworth: Penguin, 1985.

Hillary, Richard, *The Last Enemy*, London: Pimlico, 1997.

Hillis Miller, J., *The Ethics of Reading: Kant, De Man, Eliot, Trollope, James, and Benjamin*, New York: Columbia University Press, 1987.

Hobbes, Thomas, *Leviathan*, ed. Richard Tuck, Cambridge: Cambridge University Press, 1991.

Holt, Jim, *Stop Me If You've Heard This: A History and Philosophy of Jokes*, London: Profile Books, 2008.

Homer, *The Odyssey Books 1–12*, trans. A. T. Murray and George E. Dimock, Loeb Classical Library, Cambridge, MA: Harvard University Press, 1995.
   The Odyssey Books 13–24, trans. A. T. Murray and George E. Dimock, Loeb Classical Library, Cambridge, MA: Harvard University Press, 1995.
   The Iliad Books 1–12, trans. A. T. Murray and William F. Wyatt, Loeb Classical Library, Cambridge, MA: Harvard University Press, 1999.
   The Iliad Books 13–24, trans. A. T. Murray and William F. Wyatt, Loeb Classical Library, Cambridge, MA: Harvard University Press, 1999.

Hurley, Kelly, *The Gothic Body: Sexuality, Materialism, and Degeneration at the Fin de Siècle*, Cambridge: Cambridge University Press, 1996.

Hynes, Samuel, *A War Imagined: The First World War and English Culture*, London: Pimlico, 1992.
   The Soldiers' Tale: Bearing Witness to Modern War, London: Pimlico, 1998.

Ifrah, Geoffrey, *The Universal History of Numbers: From Prehistory to the Invention of the Computer*, trans. David Bellos, E. F. Harding, Sophie Wood and Ian Monk, London: Harvill, 1998.

'In the Abbey: The Warrior Laid to Rest', *Times* (12 November 1920), sec. Supplement, ii.

Jakobson, Roman, 'Two Aspects of Language and Two Types of Aphasic Disturbance', in *Fundamentals of Language*, ed. Roman Jakobson and Morris Halle, 'S-Gravenhage: Mouton, 1956, 53–82.

James, William, *Psychology: Briefer Course*, New York: Macmillan, 1962.

Jameson, Storm, *The Writer's Situation and Other Essays*, London: Macmillan, 1950.

Jeffers, Robinson, *The Collected Poetry of Robinson Jeffers*, ed. Tim Hunt, vol. III (3 vols.), Palo Alto: Stanford University Press, 1991.

Jenkins, Ron, *Subversive Laughter: The Liberating Power of Comedy*, New York: The Free Press, 1994.

John, Augustus, *Chiaroscuro: Fragments of Autobiography, First Series*, London: Jonathan Cape, 1952.

Johnson, Addie, and Robert W. Proctor, *Attention: Theory and Practice*, Thousand Oaks, London, New Delhi: Sage Publications, 2004.

Jones, David, *In Parenthesis: Seinnyessit E Gledyf Ym Penn Mameu*, London: Faber, 1963.

Jones, E. L., *Growth Recurring: Economic Change in World History*, Ann Arbor: University of Michigan Press, 2000.

Jünger, Ernst, *Storm of Steel*, trans. Michael Hofmann, London: Penguin, 2003.

Kant, Immanuel, 'Concerning the Ultimate Ground of the Differentiation of Directions in Space', *Theoretical Philosophy, 1755–1770*, trans. and ed. David Walford, Cambridge: Cambridge University Press, 1992, 361–72.

  Practical Philosophy, trans. and ed. Mary J. Gregor, Cambridge: Cambridge University Press, 1999.

  Critique of the Power of Judgment, trans. Paul Guyer and Eric Matthews, ed. Paul Guyer, Cambridge: Cambridge University Press, 2000.

Keeble, Richard, 'Information Warfare in an Age of Hyper-Militarism', in *Reporting War. Journalism in Wartime*, ed. Stuart Allan and Barbie Zelizer, London and New York: Routledge, 2004, 43–58.

Kelly, H. A., '*Occupatio* as Negative Narration: A Mistake for Occultatio/ Praeteritio', *Modern Philology* 74.3 (February 1977), 311–15.

Kendall, Tim, *Modern English War Poetry*, Oxford: Oxford University Press, 2006.

Kermode, Frank, *The Sense of an Ending: Studies in the Theory of Fiction*, Oxford: Oxford University Press, 1967.

Kerrigan, John, *Revenge Tragedy: Aeschylus to Armageddon*, Oxford: Oxford University Press, 1996.

Keyes, Sidney, *Collected Poems*, ed. Michael Meyer, Manchester: Carcanet, 2002.

Kipling, Rudyard, *Rudyard Kipling: Selected Poems*, ed. Peter Keating, London: Penguin, 2000.

Klinkowitz, Jerome, *Kurt Vonnegut*, London and New York: Methuen, 1982.

Kneale, J. Douglas, 'Romantic Aversions: Apostrophe Reconsidered', *English Literary History* 58 (Spring 1991): 141–65.

Knibb, James, 'Literary Strategies of War, Strategies of Literary War', in *Literature and War*, ed. David Bevan, Atlanta: Rodopi, 1990, 7–24.

Kracauer, Siegfried, *The Mass Ornament: Weimar Essays*, trans. and ed. Thomas Y. Levin, Cambridge: Harvard University Press, 1995.

Kristeva, Julia, 'Word, Dialogue and Novel', in *The Kristeva Reader*, ed. Toril Moi, Oxford: Blackwell, 1986, 35–61.

LaCapra, Dominick, *History and Memory After Auschwitz*, Ithaca: Cornell University Press, 1998.

Writing History, Writing Trauma, Baltimore: The Johns Hopkins University Press, 2003.

Lang, Berel, *Act and Idea in the Nazi Genocide*, Chicago: University of Chicago Press, 1990.

'The Representation of Limits', in *Probing the Limits of Representation. Nazism and the 'Final Solution'*, ed. Saul Friedlander, Cambridge, MA: Harvard University Press, 1992, 300–17.

Langer, Lawrence L., *The Holocaust and the Literary Imagination*, New Haven: Yale University Press, 1975.

Holocaust Testimonies: The Ruins of Memory, New Haven: Yale University Press, 1991.

Laqueur, Thomas, 'Memory and Naming in the Great War', in *Commemorations: The Politics of National Identity*, ed. John R. Gillis, Princeton: Princeton University Press, 1994, 150–67.

Ledford, Heidi, 'Psychiatry Manual Revisions', *Nature* 460 (23 July 2009), 445.

Leed, Eric J., *No Man's Land: Combat and Identity in World War I*, Cambridge: Cambridge University Press, 1979.

Lejeune, Philippe, *Le Pacte autobiographique*, Paris: Seuil, 1974.

Les Brouillons de soi, Paris: Seuil, 1998.

Leonard, John, *Naming in Paradise: Milton and the Language of Adam and Eve*, Cambridge: Cambridge University Press, 1990.

Lessing, Gotthold Ephraim, *Laocoön: An Essay upon the Limits of Painting and Poetry*, trans. Ellen Frothingham, Boston: Roberts Brothers, 1880.

Levertov, Denise, *Poems 1968–1972*, New York: New Directions, 1987.

Poems 1972–1982, New York: New Directions, 2001.

Lévinas, Emmanuel, *Totality and Infinity: An Essay on Exteriority*, trans. Alphonso Lingis, Pittsburgh: Duquesne University Press, 1969.

Existence and Existents, trans. Alphonso Lingis, Dordrecht: Kluwer Academic Publishers, 1988.

Lewis, C. S., *Surprised by Joy*, London: Geoffrey Bles, 1955.

Limon, John, *Writing After War: American War Fiction from Realism to Post-Modernism*, Oxford: Oxford University Press, 1994.

Lipman, Steve, *Laughter in Hell: The Use of Humor During the Holocaust*, Northvale and London: Jason Aronson, 1993.

Lippitt, John, 'Nietzsche, Zarathustra and the Status of Laughter', *British Journal of Aesthetics* 32.1 (January 1992), 39–49.

Litton Falkiner, C., 'Introductory Memoir', *The Burial of Sir John Moore and Other Poems by Charles Wolfe*, London: Sidgwick & Jackson, 1909.

Lodge, David, *The Modes of Modern Writing: Metaphor, Metonymy, and the Typology of Modern Literature*, London: Edward Arnold, 1977.

Longfellow, Henry Wadsworth, *Poems and Other Writings*, ed. J. D. McClatchy, New York: Library of America, 2000.

Longinus, Dionysus, *Dionysius Longinus on the Sublime: Translated from the Greek, with Notes and Observations; and some Account of the Life, Writings, and Character of the Author*, trans. William Smith, 5th edn, Dublin: William Sleater, 1792.

Longley, Edna, 'The Great War, History, and the English Lyric', in *The Cambridge Companion to the Literature of the First World War*, ed. Vincent Sherry, Cambridge: Cambridge University Press, 2005, 57–84.

Longley, Michael, *Poems 1963–1983*, Edinburgh and Dublin: Salamander Press / Gallery Press, 1985.

Lovell, Jr, Ernest J., ed., *Lady Blessington's Conversations of Lord Byron*, Princeton: Princeton University Press, 1969.

Lucian, *Lucian*, trans. K. Kilburn, vol. VI (8 vols.), Loeb Classical Library, London and Cambridge, MA: William Heinemann / Harvard University Press, 1959.

Lueck, Micah D., 'Anxiety Levels: Do They Influence the Perception of Time?' *UW-L Journal of Undergraduate Research* 10 (2007), 1–5.

Lyons, Judith A., 'The Returning Warrior: Advice for Family and Friends', in *Combat Stress Injury: Theory, Research, and Management*, eds. Charles R. Figley and William P. Nash, New York and London: Routledge, 2007, 311–24.

Lyotard, Jean-François, *The Differend: Phrases in Dispute*, trans. Georges Van Den Abbeele, Manchester: Manchester University Press, 1988.

Heidegger and "the jews", trans. Andreas Michel and Mark S. Roberts, Minneapolis: University of Minnesota Press, 1990.

Mackay, Dorothy, *Laughter in Khaki*, Edinburgh: Pentland Press, 1987.

Malpas, J. E., *Place and Experience: A Philosophical Topography*, Cambridge: Cambridge University Press, 1999.

Malvern, Sue, *Modern Art, Britain and the Great War: Witnessing, Testimony and Remembrance*, New Haven: Yale University Press, 2004.

Mansfield, Nick, 'War and Its Other: Between Bataille and Derrida', *Theory & Event* 9.4 (2006), unpaginated.

Theorizing War: From Hobbes to Badiou, Basingstoke: Palgrave Macmillan, 2008.

Martindale, Charles, *John Milton and the Transformation of Ancient Epic*, Bristol: Bristol Classical Press, 2002.

Matless, David, *Landscape and Englishness*, London: Reaktion, 1998.

McEwan, Ian, *Atonement*, London: Vintage, 2002.

McGann, Jerome J., *Don Juan in Context*, London: John Murray, 1976.

McKeon, Michael, *The Origins of the English Novel 1600–1740*, London: Radius, 1988.

McLoughlin, Kate, *Martha Gellhorn: The War Writer in the Field and in the Text*, Manchester: Manchester University Press, 2007.

McNally, Richard J., *Remembering Trauma*, Cambridge, MA: The Belknap Press of Harvard University Press, 2003.

Mikhail, Dunya, *The War Works Hard*, trans. Elizabeth Winslow, Manchester: Carcanet, 2006.

Miller, George A., 'The Magical Number Seven, Plus or Minus Two: Some Limits on our Capacity for Processing Information', in *Essential Sources in the Scientific Study of Consciousness*, ed. Bernard J. Baars, William P. Banks and James B. Newman, Boston: MIT Press, 2003, 357–72.

Milligan, Spike, *Milligan's War: The Selected War Memoirs of Spike Milligan*, ed. Jack Hobbs, London: Penguin, 1989.

Milton, John, *Paradise Lost*, ed. Alastair Fowler, London: Longman, 1998.

Mitchell, Silas Weir, 'The Case of George Dedlow', *Atlantic Monthly* 18.105 (July 1866), 1–11.

Mitchell, W. T. J., *Picture Theory: Essays on Verbal and Visual Representation*, Chicago: University of Chicago Press, 1994.

Moore, James Carrick, *A Narrative of the Campaign of the British Army in Spain: Commanded by His Excellency Sir John Moore . . . Authenticated by Official Papers and Original Letters*, London: J. Johnson, 1809.

Mulkay, Michael, *On Humour: Its Nature and Its Place in Modern Society*, Cambridge: Polity Press, 1988.

Mullan, John, 'Introduction', in Daniel Defoe, *Memoirs of a Cavalier, or A Military Journal of the Wars in Germany and the Wars in England from the Year 1632, to the Year 1648*, ed. James T. Boulton, Oxford: Oxford University Press, 1991, vii–xxvi.

Neiberg, Michael S., *Warfare in World History*, London: Routledge, 2001.

Nelson, Emily, and Matthew Rose, 'Media Reassess Risks to Reporters in Iraq', *The Wall Street Journal* 9 April 2003, sec. Marketplace, B1.

Nettlefold, W. T., 'Remembrance Day', *Left Review* 3 (December 1937), 661.

Nicolson, Harold, *Diaries and Letters 1939–45*, ed. Nigel Nicolson, vol. II (3 vols.), London: Collins, 1967.

Nietzsche, Friedrich, *Thus Spoke Zarathustra*, Harmondsworth: Penguin, 1969.

Ninh, Bao, *The Sorrow of War*, trans. Frank Palmos, London: Minerva, 1994.

Norris, Margot, *Writing War in the Twentieth Century*, Charlottesville: University Press of Virginia, 2000.

O'Brien, Tim, *Going After Cacciato*, London: Flamingo, 1988.

The Things They Carried, London: Flamingo, 1991.

O'Leary, Stephen D., *Arguing the Apocalypse: A Theory of Millennial Rhetoric*, Oxford: Oxford University Press, 1994.

Oakley, S. P., 'Single Combat in the Roman Republic', *The Classical Quarterly* 35.2 (1985), 392–410.

Orpen, William, *An Onlooker in France*, London: Williams and Norgate, 1921.

Orwell, George, *Homage to Catalonia*, in *The Complete Works of George Orwell*, ed. Peter Davison, vol. VI (20 vols.), London: Secker & Warburg, 1986–7.

'Looking Back on the Spanish War', in *All Propaganda is Lies 1941–1942, The Complete Works of George Orwell*, ed. Peter Davison, vol. XIII (20 vols.), London: Secker & Warburg, 1986–7, 497–511.

Owen, Wilfred, *Collected Letters*, ed. Harold Owen and John Bell, Oxford: Oxford University Press, 1967.

The Complete Poems and Fragments, vol. I: The Poems, ed. Jon Stallworthy, London: Chatto and Windus / The Hogarth Press / Oxford University Press, 1983.

The Complete Poems and Fragments, vol. II: The Manuscripts of the Poems and Fragments, ed. Jon Stallworthy, London: Chatto and Windus / The Hogarth Press / Oxford University Press, 1983.

Palmer, Jerry, *Taking Humour Seriously*, London: Routledge, 1994.

Panofsky, Erwin, *Meaning in the Visual Arts*, New York: Doubleday, 1955.

Parker, Patricia, 'Uncertain Unions: Welsh Leeks in *Henry V*', in *British Identities and English Renaissance Literature*, ed. David J. Baker and Willy Maley. Cambridge: Cambridge University Press, 2002, 81–100.

Partridge, Frances, *A Pacifist's War*, London: The Hogarth Press, 1978.

Parvizi, Josef, Steven W. Anderson, Coleman O. Martin, Hanna Damasio and Antonio R. Damasio, 'Pathological Laughing and Crying', *Brain* 124.9 (September 2001), 1708–19.

Patterson, Annabel, *Pastoral and Ideology: Virgil to Valéry*, Oxford: Clarendon, 1988.

Paulin, Tom, *The Invasion Handbook*, London: Faber, 2002.

Peirce, Charles S., 'From "On the Algebra of Logic: A Contribution to the Philosophy of Notation"', in *The Essential Peirce: Selected Philosophical Writings. Volume 1 (1867–1893)*, ed. Nathan Hauser and Christian Kloesel, Bloomington: Indiana University Press, 1992, 226–8.

Peterson, Kirtland C., Maurice F. Prout and Robert A. Schwarz, *Post-Traumatic Stress Disorder: A Clinician's Guide*, New York and London: Plenum Press, 1991.

Pfister, Manfred, 'Beckett, Barker, and Other Grim Laughers', in *A History of English Laughter: Laughter from Beowulf to Beckett and Beyond*, ed. Manfred Pfister, Amsterdam and New York: Rodopi, 2005, 175–89.

Pigman III, G. W., 'George Gascoigne', in *The Oxford Dictionary of National Biography*, ed. H. C. G. Matthew and Brian Harrison, vol. XXI (60 vols.), Oxford: Oxford University Press, 2004, 582–5.

Pitcher, L. V., 'Classical War Literature', in *The Cambridge Companion to War Writing*, ed. Kate McLoughlin, Cambridge: Cambridge University Press, 2009, 71–80.

Plato, *Cratylus, Parmenides, Greater Hippias, Lesser Hippias*, trans. H. N. Fowler, Loeb Classical Library, London and New York: William Heinemann / G. P. Putnam, 1926.

Timaeus. Critias. Cleitophon. Menexenus. Epistles, trans. R. G. Bury, Loeb Classical Library, London and Cambridge, MA: William Heinemann / Harvard University Press, 1959.

Plutarch, *Lives*, trans. Bernadotte Perrin, vol. VII (11 vols.), Loeb Classical Library, London and New York: William Heinemann / G. P. Putnam, 1919.

Moralia, trans. Frank Cole Babbitt, vol. IV (11 vols.), Loeb Classical Library, Cambridge, MA and London: Harvard University Press / William Heinemann, 1936.

Poggioli, Renato, *The Oaten Flute: Essays on Pastoral Poetry and the Pastoral Ideal*, Cambridge, MA: Harvard University Press, 1975.

Polkinghorne, J. C., *The Quantum World*, London: Penguin, 1984.

Pound, Ezra, *Selected Poems 1908–1959*, London: Faber, 1975.

Price, Ruth, *The Lives of Agnes Smedley*, Oxford: Oxford University Press, 2005.

Prince, Gerald, *Narratology: The Form and Functioning of Narrative*, Berlin, New York and Amsterdam: Mouton, 1982.

Proctor, Ida, 'The One', in *Chaos of the Night. Women's Poetry and Verse of the Second World War*, ed. Catherine Reilly, London: Virago, 1984, 102.

Prouty, C. T., *George Gascoigne: Elizabethan Courtier, Soldier and Poet*, New York: Columbia University Press, 1942.

Provine, Robert R., *Laughter: A Scientific Investigation*, London: Faber, 2000.

Puttenham, George, *The Arte of English Poesie*, ed. Gladys Dodge Willcock and Alice Walker, Cambridge: Cambridge University Press, 1936.

Quintilian, *Institutio Oratoria Books 6–8*, trans. and ed. Donald A. Russell, Loeb Classical Library, Cambridge, MA: Harvard University Press, 2001.

Quirk, Tom, 'Introduction', in *Ambrose Bierce. Tales of Soldiers and Civilians*, ed. Tom Quirk, Harmondsworth: Penguin, 2000, vii–xxvi.

Rae, Patricia, 'Proleptic Elegy and the End of Arcadianism in 1930s Britain', *Twentieth Century Literature* 49.2 (Summer 2003), 246–75.

Ramazani, Jahan, *Poetry of Mourning: The Modern Elegy from Hardy to Heaney*, Chicago: University of Chicago Press, 1994.

Randall, Bryony, *Modernism, Daily Time and Everyday Life*, Cambridge: Cambridge University Press, 2007.

Rawlinson, Mark, *British Writing of the Second World War*, Oxford: Clarendon, 2000.

Ray, Gene, 'Reading the Lisbon Earthquake: Adorno, Lyotard, and the Contemporary Sublime', *Yale Journal of Criticism* 17.1 (2004), 1–18.

Terror and the Sublime in Art and Critical Theory: From Auschwitz to Hiroshima to September 11, Basingstoke and New York: Palgrave Macmillan, 2005.

Read, Herbert, *Collected Poems*, London: Sinclair-Stevenson, 1966.

Reed, Henry, *Collected Poems*, ed. Jon Stallworthy, Oxford: Oxford University Press, 1991.

Reeves, Gareth, '"This is Plenty: This is More than Enough": Poetry and the Memory of the Second World War', in *The Oxford Handbook of British and Irish War Poetry*, ed. Tim Kendall, Oxford: Oxford University Press, 2007, 579–91.

Renehan, R., 'The Heldentod in Homer: One Heroic Ideal', *Classical Philology* 82.2 (April 1987), 99–116.

Revard, Stella Purce, *The War in Heaven: Paradise Lost and the Tradition of Satan's Rebellion*, Ithaca: Cornell University Press, 1980.

Reynolds, Michael, 'Hemingway's *In Our Time*: The Biography of a Book', in *Modern American Short Story Sequences: Composite Fictions and Fictive Communities*, ed. J. Gerald Kennedy, Cambridge: Cambridge University Press, 1995, 35–51.

Ricoeur, Paul, *Time and Narrative*, trans. Kathleen McLaughlin and David Pellauer, vol. I (3 vols.), Chicago: University of Chicago Press, 1984.

   Time and Narrative, trans. Kathleen McLaughlin and David Pellauer, vol. II (3 vols.), Chicago: University of Chicago Press, 1985.

Rieu, E. V., ed., *Virgil: The Pastoral Poems (The Eclogues)*, Harmondsworth: Penguin, 1954.

   'Introduction', in Homer, *The Iliad*, trans. E. V. Rieu, 1950. Harmondsworth: Penguin, 1983, vii–xxii.

Robinson, Jane, *Mary Seacole: The Charismatic Black Nurse Who Became a Heroine of the Crimea*, London: Constable & Robinson, 2005.

Rodaway, Paul, *Sensuous Geographies: Body, Sense and Place*, London and New York: Routledge, 1994.

Rosenberg, Isaac, *The Poems and Plays of Isaac Rosenberg*, ed. Vivien Noakes, Oxford: Oxford University Press, 2004.

Rothberg, Michael, *Traumatic Realism: The Demands of Holocaust Representation*, Minneapolis: University of Minnesota Press, 2000.

Rowland, Antony, *Holocaust Poetry: Awkward Poetics in the Work of Sylvia Plath, Geoffrey Hill, Tony Harrison and Ted Hughes*, Edinburgh: Edinburgh University Press, 2005.

Rudrum, Alan, 'Henry Vaughan's Poems of Mourning', in *Of Paradise and Light: Essays on Henry Vaughan and John Milton in Honor of Alan Rudrum*, ed. Donald R. Dickson and Holly Faith Nelson, Newark: University of Delaware Press, 2004, 309–28.

Rutherford, Andrew, *The Literature of War: Five Studies in Heroic Virtue*, London and Basingstoke: Macmillan, 1978.

Santner, Eric, 'History Beyond the Pleasure Principle: Some Thoughts on the Representation of Trauma', in *Probing the Limits of Representation. Nazism and the 'Final Solution'*, ed. Saul Friedlander, Cambridge, MA: Harvard University Press, 1992, 143–54.

Sassoon, Siegfried, *Collected Poems 1908–1956*, London: Faber, 1961.

   The Complete Memoirs of George Sherston, London: Faber, 1972.

Scarry, Elaine, *The Body in Pain: The Making and Unmaking of the World*, Oxford: Oxford University Press, 1985.

Schama, Simon, *Landscape and Memory*, London: Fontana, 1996.

Schimanski, Stefan, and Henry Treece, eds., *Leaves in the Storm: A Book of Diaries*, London: Lindsay Drummond, 1947.

Schopenhauer, Arthur, *The World as Will and Idea*, trans. R. B. Haldane and J. Kemp, 3rd edn, vol. I (3 vols.), London: Kegan Paul, Trench, Trübner, 1891.

Schrödinger, Erwin, 'Die Gegenwärtige Situation in der Quantenmechanik', *Naturwissenschaften* 23 (November 1935), 807–12, 823, 844–9.

Schweik, Susan, 'Writing War Poetry Like a Woman', *Critical Inquiry* 13.3 (1987), 532–56.

Scruggs, Jan C., and Joel L. Swerdlow, *To Heal a Nation: The Vietnam Veterans' Memorial*, New York: Harper & Row, 1985.

Seacole, Mary, *Wonderful Adventures of Mrs Seacole in Many Lands*, ed. Sara Salih, London: Penguin, 2005.

Seaton, Jean, *Carnage and the Media: The Making and Breaking of News About Violence*, London: Allen Lane, 2005.

Sebald, W. G., *The Rings of Saturn*, trans. Michael Hulse, London: Harvill, 1999.

Semprun, Jorge, *Literature or Life*, trans. Linda Coverdale, New York: Viking, 1997.

Shakespeare, William, *The Alexander Text of William Shakespeare: The Complete Works*, ed. Peter Alexander, London and Glasgow: Collins, 1992.

    Henry V, The Arden Shakespeare (3rd Series), ed. T. W. Craik, London and New York: Routledge, 1995.

Shapiro, Karl, *Selected Poems*, New York: Random House, 1968.

Shay, Jonathan, *Achilles in Vietnam: Combat Trauma and the Undoing of Character*, New York and London: Simon & Schuster Touchstone, 1995.

Sheppard, Philippa, 'Tongues of War: Studies in the Military Rhetoric of Shakespeare's History Plays', unpublished D.Phil. thesis, University of Oxford, 1994.

Sherry, Vincent, *The Great War and the Language of Modernism*, Oxford: Oxford University Press, 2003.

Silkin, Jon, 'Introduction', in *The Penguin Book of First World War Poetry*, ed. Jon Silkin, 2nd edn, London: Penguin, 1981, 15–77.

Sime, Jonathan D., 'Creating Places or Designing Spaces?' *Journal of Environmental Psychology* 6.1 (1986), 49–63.

Simpson, Louis, *Selected Poems*, Oxford: Oxford University Press, 1966.

Small, Harold A., *The Field of his Fame: A Ramble in the Curious History of Charles Wolfe's Poem 'The Burial of Sir John Moore'*, Berkeley: University of California Press, 1953.

Smedley, Agnes, *China Fights Back: An American Woman with the Eighth Route Army*, London: Victor Gollancz, 1938.

    China Correspondent, London: Pandora Press, 1984.

Soja, Edward W., *Thirdspace. Journeys to Los Angeles and Other Real-and-Imagined Places*, Oxford: Blackwell, 1996.

Sorley, Charles Hamilton, *The Collected Poems of Charles Hamilton Sorley*, ed. Jean Moorcroft Wilson, London: Cecil Woolf, 1985.

Southey, Robert, *History of The Peninsular War*, vol. I (3 vols.), London: J. Murray, 1823.

Poems of Robert Southey, ed. Maurice H. Fitzgerald, Oxford: Oxford University Press, 1909.

New Letters of Robert Southey, ed. Kenneth Curry, vol. I (2 vols.), Cambridge: Cambridge University Press, 1965.

Southwell, Robert, 'New Heaven, New War', in *Chapters into Verse*, ed. Robert Atwan and Laurance Wieder, vol. II (2 vols.), Oxford: Oxford University Press, 1993, 31–2.

Speck, W. A., *Robert Southey: Entire Man of Letters*, New Haven and London: Yale University Press, 2006.

Spender, Stephen, *New Collected Poems*, ed. Michael Brett, London: Faber, 2004.

Stabler, Jane, *Byron, Poetics and History*, Cambridge: Cambridge University Press, 2002.

Stallworthy, Jon, *Wilfred Owen*, London: Oxford University Press / Chatto and Windus, 1974.

Survivors' Songs: From Maldon to the Somme, Cambridge: Cambridge University Press, 2008.

Stein, Gertrude, *Wars I Have Seen*, London: Brilliance Books, 1984.

Steiner, George, *Language and Silence*, Harmondsworth: Penguin, 1969.

Stern, J. P., 'War and the Comic Muse: *The Good Soldier Schweik* and *Catch-22*', *Comparative Literature* 20.3 (Summer 1968), 193–216.

Sterne, Laurence, *The Life and Opinions of Tristram Shandy*, London: Penguin, 1967.

Stewart, Matthew, '"It Was All A Pleasant Business": The Historical Context of "On the Quai at Smyrna"', *The Hemingway Review* 23.1 (Fall 2003), 58–70.

Strachan, Hew, 'The Idea of War', in *The Cambridge Companion to War Writing*, ed. Kate McLoughlin, Cambridge: Cambridge University Press, 2009, 7–14.

Sweetman, John, 'Moore, Sir John (1761–1809)', in *The Oxford Dictionary of National Biography*, ed. H. C. G. Matthew and Brian Harrison, vol. XXXVIII (60 vols.), Oxford: Oxford University Press, 2004, 975–80.

Tate, Allen, *Collected Poems 1919–1976*, New York: Farrar Straus Giroux, 1977.

Tate, Trudi, *Modernism, History and the First World War*, Manchester: Manchester University Press, 1998.

Taylor, Irene, and Alan Taylor, eds., *The Secret Annexe: An Anthology of the World's Greatest War Diarists*, Edinburgh: Canongate, 2004.

Taylor, John, *Body Horror: Photojournalism, Catastrophe and War*, Manchester: Manchester University Press, 1998.

Tennyson, Alfred Lord, *The Poems of Tennyson*, ed. Christopher Ricks, vol. II (3 vols.), London: Longman, 1969.

Terr, Lenore C., 'Time Sense Following Psychic Trauma: A Clinical Study of Ten Adults and Twenty Children', *American Journal of Orthopsychiatry* 53.2 (April 1983), 244–61.

'Time and Trauma', *Psychoanalytic Study of the Child* 39 (1984), 633–65.

'The Burial of the Unknown Warrior', *The Times* (12 November 1920), sec. Supplement, i.

'The Quick and the Dead', *The Times* (12 November 1919), 13.

Thomas, Dylan, *Collected Poems 1934–1952*, London: J. M. Dent, 1952.

Thomas, Edward, *Selected Poems and Prose*, ed. David Wright, Harmondsworth: Penguin, 1981.

Thucydides, *History of the Peloponnesian War*, trans. Charles Forster Smith, vol. II (4 vols.), Loeb Classical Library, Cambridge, MA and London: Harvard University Press / William Heinemann, 1953.

Tillyard, Aelfrida, 'A Letter from Ealing Broadway Station (*From E. M. W. T.*)', in *Scars Upon My Heart: Women's Poetry and Verse of the First World War*, ed. Catherine Reilly, London: Virago, 1981, 113–14.

To My 'Unknown' Warrior, London, New York, Toronto: Hodder & Stoughton, 1920.

Todorov, Tzvetan, *The Fantastic: A Structural Approach to a Literary Genre*, Ithaca: Cornell University Press, 1975.

'The Journey and its Narratives', trans. Alyson Waters, in *Transports: Travel, Pleasure, and Imaginative Geography, 1600–1830*, ed. Chloe Chard and Helen Langdon, New Haven: Yale University Press, 1996, 287–96.

Tolstoy, L. N., *War and Peace*, trans. Rosemary Edmonds, London: Penguin, 1957, 1982.

Voina i mir [*War and Peace*], Moscow: Zakharov, 2000.

Treharne, Elaine, ed., *Old and Middle English c.890–c.1400: An Anthology*, 2nd edn, Oxford: Blackwell, 2004.

Trezise, Thomas, 'Unspeakable', *The Yale Journal of Criticism* 14.1 (2001), 39–66.

Trimmer, John D., 'The Present Situation in Quantum Mechanics: A Translation of Schrödinger's "Cat Paradox" Paper', *Proceedings of the American Philosophical Society* 124.5 (1980), 323–38.

Tritle, Lawrence A., *From Melos to My Lai: War and Survival*, London, New York: Routledge, 2000.

Trumbo, Dalton, *Johnny Got His Gun*, New York: Citadel, 2007.

van Wees, Hans, 'Kings in Combat: Battles and Heroes in the Iliad', *The Classical Quarterly* 38.1 (1988), 1–24.

Vaughan, Henry, *The Complete Poems*, ed. Alan Rudrum, New Haven: Yale University Press, 1976.

Vickers, Brian, *In Defence of Rhetoric*, Oxford: Oxford University Press, 1988.

Virgil, *Eclogues, Georgics, Aeneid I–VI*, trans. H. Rushton Fairclough and G. P. Goold, Loeb Classical Library, Cambridge, MA: Harvard University Press, 1999.

Aeneid VII–XII, trans. H. Rushton Fairclough, Loeb Classical Library, Cambridge, MA: Harvard University Press, 2000.

Virilio, Paul, *War and Cinema: The Logistics of Perception*, trans. Patrick Camiller, London: Verso, 1989.

Vismann, Cornelia, 'Starting from Scratch: Concepts of Order in No Man's Land', in *War, Violence and the Modern Condition*, ed. Bernd Hüppauf, Berlin and New York: Walter de Gruyter, 1997, 46–64.

Vonnegut, Kurt, *Slaughterhouse-Five*, London: Vintage, 2000.

A Man Without A Country, ed. Daniel Simon, London: Bloomsbury, 2006.

Wallace, Edgar, 'War', in *The Oxford Book of War Poetry*, ed. Jon Stallworthy, Oxford: Oxford University Press, 1984, 155–6.

Walter, Eugene Victor, *Placeways: A Theory of the Human Environment*, Chapel Hill: University of North Carolina Press, 1988.

Waugh, Evelyn, *Scoop: A Novel About Journalists*, London: Chapman and Hall, 1948.

Waugh, Patricia, *Metafiction: The Theory and Practice of Self-Conscious Fiction*, London: Routledge, 2003.

Webb, Beatrice, *The Diaries of Beatrice Webb*, ed. Norman MacKenzie and Jeanne MacKenzie, London: Virago in association with the London School of Economics and Political Science, 2000.

Weber, Ronald, *Hemingway's Art of Non-Fiction*, Basingstoke: Macmillan, 1990.

Weber, Samuel, 'Laughing in the Meanwhile', *Modern Language Notes* 102.4 (September 1987), 691–706.

Weeks, Mark, 'Beyond a Joke: Nietzsche and the Birth of "Super-Laughter"', *Journal of Nietzsche Studies* 27 (Spring 2004), 1–17.

Weil, Simone, *War and the Iliad*, trans. Mary McCarthy, New York: New York Review Books, 2005.

Weinstein, Philip, *Unknowing: The Work of Modernist Fiction*, Ithaca: Cornell University Press, 2005.

Weir, Becca, '"Degrees in Nothingness": Battlefield Topography in the First World War', *Critical Quarterly* 49.4 (2007), 40–55.

West, Philip, *Henry Vaughan's Silex Scintillans: Scripture Uses*, Oxford: Oxford University Press, 2001.

West, William N., 'Less Well-Wrought Urns: Henry Vaughan and the Decay of the Poetic Monument', *English Literary History* 75.1 (Spring 2008), 197–217.

Wharton, Edith, *Collected Stories 1911–1937*, sel. Maureen Howard, New York: Library of America, 2001.

Whitman, Walt, *Complete Poetry and Selected Prose*, sel. Justin Kaplan, New York: Library of America, 1982.

Wild, Barbara, Frank A. Rodden, Wolfgang Grodd and Willibald Ruch, 'Neural Correlates of Laughter and Humour', *Brain* 126.10 (October 2003), 2121–38.

Wilkinson, L. P., *The Georgics of Virgil: A Critical Survey*, Cambridge: Cambridge University Press, 1969.

Winter, Jay, *Sites of Memory, Sites of Mourning: The Great War in European Culture*, Cambridge: Cambridge University Press, 1995.

Wolfe, Charles, 'The Burial of Sir John Moore After Corunna', in *The Oxford Book of War Poetry*, ed. Jon Stallworthy, Oxford: Oxford University Press, 1984, 83–4.

Wordsworth, William, *The Fourteen-Book Prelude*, in *The Cornell Wordsworth*, ed. W. J. B. Owen, vol. XIV (21 vols.), Ithaca: Cornell University Press, 1985.

Wormald, Jenny, 'Scotland: Reformation and Inflation', in *The Cambridge Historical Encyclopaedia of Great Britain and Ireland*, ed. Christopher Haigh, Cambridge: Cambridge University Press, 1990, 164–7.

Yaeger, Patricia, 'Introduction: Narrating Space', in *The Geography of Identity*, ed. Patricia Yaeger, Ann Arbor: The University of Michigan Press, 1996, 1–38.

Yeats, W. B., 'Introduction', in *The Oxford Book of Modern Verse, 1892–1935*, ed. W. B. Yeats, Oxford: Clarendon, 1936, i–ix.

The Poems Revised, ed. Richard J. Finneran, in *The Collected Works of W. B. Yeats*, 2nd edn, vol. I (12 vols.), Basingstoke: Macmillan, 1991.

Young, James E., *The Texture of Memory: Holocaust Memorials and Meaning*, New Haven: Yale University Press, 1993.

Yule, William, Ruth Williams and Stephen Joseph, 'Post-Traumatic Stress Disorder in Adults', in *Post-Traumatic Stress Disorders, Concepts and Therapy*, ed. William Yule, Chichester: John Wiley, 1999, 1–24.

Index